E. FRANCIS BALDWIN, ARCHITECT

E. FRANCIS BALDWIN, ARCHITECT

The B&O, Baltimore, and Beyond

CARLOS P. AVERY

Foreword by Herbert H. Harwood, Jr.
Introduction by Michael J. Lewis

Baltimore Architecture Foundation
Baltimore, Maryland
Published in Association with the B&O Railroad Museum

Baltimore Architecture Foundation
1016 Morton Street
Baltimore, MD 21201

Library of Congress Cataloging-in-Publication Data

Avery, Carlos P., 1938–
    E. Francis Baldwin, architect: the B&O, Baltimore,
and beyond / Carlos P. Avery; foreword by Herbert
H. Harwood; introduction by Michael J. Lewis.
      p. cm.
    Includes bibliographical references and index.
    ISBN 0-9729743-0-X (alk. paper)
    1. Baldwin, Ephraim Francis, 1837–1916. 2.
Eclecticism in architecture—Maryland. I. Baldwin,
Ephraim Francis, 1837–1916. II. Title.

NA737.B24A84 2003
720'.92—dc21
                           2003052104

Frontispiece: Ephraim Francis Baldwin (1837–1916),
circa 1910. Courtesy of Eugene F. Baldwin

Contents

Contents

Color plates follow page 78

Preface

I did not set out—or even imagine attempting—in late 1977 to write a book. I had merely become curious about the local Baltimore & Ohio Railroad station in Rockville, Maryland. One thing just led to another until finally, after much luck, many hours of research, and miles and miles of local (and much not-so-local) travel, I was compelled to attempt to document my findings on the life and work of a prolific nineteenth-century Baltimore architect.

What I've come to recognize and appreciate is the significant role that Ephraim Francis Baldwin played in the architectural development, history, and heritage of the city of Baltimore, the State of Maryland, the B&O Railroad, and the Catholic Church. In the heart of Baltimore near the harbor, it seems fair to say that by the time of Baldwin's death in 1916 one could have walked on Charles Street from Baltimore Street to Franklin Street and often been within a few yards of one of his buildings and almost never out of sight of one. Baldwin and his partners, Bruce Price and Josias Pennington, made significant contributions to the ambience and architecture of Baltimore and Maryland, much of which is still evident, even after all of the tragic losses from neglect, fires, and redevelopment.

The body of Baldwin's known work consists of more than five hundred buildings or projects, located from New York to Chicago to Savannah. Fully one-fifth were railroad stations—built for the B&O, the Western Maryland, and the beloved Ma & Pa. His work also included dozens of churches and ecclesiastical buildings, public buildings, college buildings, banks, stores, industrial buildings, warehouses, clubs, and private residences.

Outside of Maryland, E. Francis Baldwin is not well known. Even in Baltimore, where much of his work was done and still stands, that work is not fully recognized or appreciated. In spite of his accomplishments, Baldwin is conspicuously absent from many of the usual books and references on architects of his era. He is not listed, for example, in *American Architects from the Civil War to WWII,* though his one-time partner Bruce Price and his arch-rival George Frederick are. In the write-up on Bruce Price, moreover, Price's early association with Baldwin in Baltimore is not even mentioned.

Baldwin did not, in my opinion, create a unique style. Few architects do. But he was quite adept at adopting the popular architectural styles of others, such as Henry Hobson Richardson or Frank Furness, and applying them successfully to his projects. Baldwin showed skill in his application of a variety of styles, including Victorian Gothic, Italianate, Richardsonian Romanesque, Stick, Queen Anne, and Eastlake. And he worked on a large number of projects for a wide-ranging clientele—secular and ecclesiastical, public and private, commercial and social. My opinion of Baldwin and his work is obviously favorably biased; more balanced or objective assessments are likelier to come from professional architects or experts in the relevant local or architectural history. The breadth and extent of Baldwin's work provides a record that speaks for itself. More than two dozen buildings that were designed wholly or in part by Baldwin himself or by his firms are on the National Register of Historic Places. (Baldwin has fared better than his more famous partner Bruce Price, who has only a half-dozen Register buildings to his credit. Baldwin's nemesis, George A. Frederick, has even fewer.)

This volume contains the most complete accounting of the work of Baldwin ever assembled. I consider it a "cross-cutting" reference work, intended to intersect with published works of local, railroad, or architectural history. It should be of interest to architectural historians, students of local history of Maryland and Baltimore, railroad enthusiasts, and industrial archeologists.

The contributions and involvement of the builders and contractors who transformed the architect's two-dimensional plans and drawings into three-dimensional reality have often been ignored by students and architectural historians. Given the nature and richness of the data base, I tried to identify and report on the builders and contractors with whom Baldwin worked. The competition between these individuals and the connections and associations among them and the architects remains a subject for others to pursue in greater detail.

Although I have mentioned every identified building and project of Baldwin's, the coverage and the detail allocated to each of them is uneven, for a variety of reasons. The amount of information available on a given work is itself a major variable. For some buildings, no records or data exist save some fragmentary or cryptic notes or a brief mention in a newspaper. Some buildings are no longer standing, long gone, and faintly remembered; other buildings still stand, are well known, and may even have been fully researched and documented by others in the course of their nomination to the National Register of Historic Places.

The attention I've given to Baldwin's work for the railroads reflects my own lifelong fascination with railroads, particularly in the era of the steam engine, but it also highlights the fact that during Baldwin's early professional years railroad projects were an important bread-and-butter account for him. Older, pre-1900 buildings are more interesting to me than those built later on. Some of the buildings or projects had a more complex history than others. I tended to dig deepest into some of the lesser-known or long-forgotten buildings—and I chose not to explore some buildings or projects deeply simply because I wasn't drawn to them.

During my research I came to appreciate the tragic rate at which old buildings disappear. In the relatively short time that I have been investigating Baldwin's work, many of his buildings have been destroyed through "demolition by neglect," urban renewal, or arson. Some of the buildings that I visited and photographed early in my work have since been lost. In some instances, a building of interest was not identified until it was too late to see it firsthand. Considering the rate at which buildings have been lost, I regret not having started this work even five or ten years sooner.

The record is undoubtedly incomplete. Local residents and researchers who are focused on a building near and dear to them will be able to unearth more information than I ever could. Considering the extremely large number of Baldwin's works, I was not able to treat them all as thoroughly as could one whose sights are set on only one or two projects of interest. For me, this work had to have some bounds. While there are undoubtedly still gaps and some inaccuracies in my account, the sheer breadth and magnitude of Baldwin's accomplishments are surely not diminished by such failings.

Sources

The singularly most important sources of information used in my research were the journals, ledgers, and personal notebooks of E. Francis Baldwin. The *Baltimore Sun* newspapers constituted the next most important source of data. The *Annual Reports* of the Baltimore & Ohio Railroad from 1870 to 1900 were useful, as were the various architecture journals, particularly the *American Architect and Building News.* Insurance maps and city directories of Baltimore were used to locate and identify buildings and their addresses. Finally, the published works of other researchers, on-site visits to take photos and measure buildings, and correspondence with scores of individuals rounded out my data base.

Baldwin's surviving professional records consist of a half-dozen ledger-journals and a larger number of small pocket-sized notebooks. The oldest journal, which is labeled "A. A. White," has entries from 1869 to 1882; the second is the "Baldwin & Price Journal" and covers the period 1871 to the late 1890s; the third, in which most of the projects for the Baltimore & Ohio Railroad appear, covers the years 1884 to 1897; the fourth journal begins in 1888 and runs to 1912; and the fifth is a larger-format legal-sized ledger entitled "Baldwin & Pennington," which covers the years 1897–1912. Another ledger contains mostly Baldwin's personal financial matters. The ledgers are not strictly consecutive and they overlap time periods. Considering the significant number of known works that do not appear in these journals or ledgers, it is likely that some have been lost. At least one ledger should have existed to cover some of the years before the turn of the century, especially the 1880s, and another one or two for the post-1900 years. Excerpts from these records that are included in the text and the appendixes have been transcribed for legibility, with only minor corrections in punctuation and spelling.

My search of the *Sun* newspapers from 1865 to 1917 was a tedious and time-consuming task, which took two years of part-time effort. Scanning more than two hundred rolls of sometimes dim and often hard-to-read microfilm, page by page, was not pleasant. Though these searches were admittedly superficial, I found many dozens of buildings by Baldwin in the accounts. Of these, some were already well known and the paper merely provided some additional details; for others, dates of construction or locations were identified, corroborated, or corrected. A real thrill was the discovery of previously unknown Baldwin projects or the identification of a work described incompletely elsewhere.

The value of scanning local newspapers cannot be overstated. Though sometimes garbled, confusing, or even self-contradictory, these accounts—when combined with other records and sources and cross-checked against the city directories and maps—provided insights into Baldwin's work that otherwise would have been overlooked. Sanborn fire insurance maps of Baltimore were particularly valuable in making these correlations.

Another useful body of source materials, particularly for their photographs and advertisements, are the commemorative publications of church and newspaper organizations. Good examples are the *Catholic Red Book of Baltimore-Washington and Environs* (1908), the *Catholic Red Book* (1902), the 1922 *Yearbook of the Archdiocese of Baltimore,* and the Baltimore American books *The Monumental City* (1894) and *A History of the City of Baltimore: Its Men and Institutions* (1902). The annual almanacs published by the *Sun* were also helpful for advertisements, important events, items on building construction, fires, and the necrology lists.

Acknowledgments

Dozens of individuals and many organizations provided help and information for my research; without their cooperation and support it could never have gotten this far. I especially thank the Baltimore & Ohio Railroad Museum, the Baltimore Architecture Foundation, and the Baldwin family members whose financial support made this publication possible.

I am most grateful to the Baldwin family members who gave me unlimited access to their grandfather's notebooks, ledgers, and family photographs. I particularly thank Eugene Francis Baldwin and his family, of Catonsville, Maryland, for their unstinting help and cooperation. (Gene also provided valuable professional editorial advice and assistance.) I also thank Gene's sister Elizabeth Baldwin, of Towson, and his cousin Laurence V. Baldwin, of Miami Beach, Florida, for information and photographs. Their interest and encouragement—and patience with what has become a very long-term project—was vital to this undertaking.

James T. Wollon and James D. Dilts—my fellow participants in the informal research and study group of the Baltimore Architecture Foundation, which we call the "Dead Architects' Society"—were stalwart supporters and contributors to my efforts and provided valuable technical and substantive reviews of and corrections to earlier drafts of my manuscript. Needless to say, any remaining errors and omissions are my sole responsibility.

Herbert H. Harwood Jr. provided early encouragement and leads on Baldwin works, particularly those on the B&O Railroad. Randolph Chalfant, a Baltimore architect, provided information from his own research on Baldwin's mentor, John R. Niernsee. Robert Vogel, a curator at the Smithsonian Institution, and John Hankey, a curator of the B&O Museum in Baltimore, supplied valuable information and photographs.

Other individuals to whom I owe a special debt of gratitude include Rev. John W. Bowen, S.S., Sulpician Archives, Catonsville, Maryland; Robert B. Davis, Silver Spring, Maryland; W. Raymond Hicks, Westminster, Maryland; Michael J. Lewis, Williams College, Williamstown, Massachusetts; Eileen McGuckian, Peerless Rockville, Rockville, Maryland; John McLeod, library of the Association of American Railroads, Washington, D.C.; Walter Schamu, F.A.I.A., Baltimore; and Edward Weber, Ashland, Kentucky. I also thank dozens of friends and individuals, too numerous to list here by name, who provided information, photographs, and suggestions.

A few institutions and organizations from which I obtained data and information deserve special mention: the McKeldin Library of the University of Maryland at College Park; the Enoch Pratt Free Library, Baltimore; the American Institute of Architects, Washington; AAR library, Washington, D.C.; the Montgomery County Historical Society, Rockville; the Maryland Historical Society, Baltimore; the National Register of Historic Places of the National Park Service; the Maryland Historical Trust, Annapolis; the Smithsonian Institution, Washington; the Baltimore & Ohio Railroad Museum, Baltimore; and the Sulpician Archives, Baltimore.

I wish to thank a number of anonymous individuals, residents, post-office clerks, and passers-by who gave me much-needed directions to buildings when I visited their localities in search of "ground-truth"—and a Baltimore police officer who got me out of a jam when I locked my keys in my car on a very cold January Sunday morning photo-expedition. (Photo credits are given in the legends. Photos with no attribution were taken by the author.)

Finally, I thank my family for putting up with me and this hobby-obsession of mine for nearly twenty-five years. I apologize for my absences on weekends while out on one of my "expeditions" to Baltimore and beyond, and for sometimes dragging them off on a "side trip" while on a family vacation to "check out" an old building or railroad station. Sometimes they didn't understand what I would see in a vacant lot—or why I was so disappointed that it was just that.

Foreword

E. Francis Baldwin and the Railroad Era

HERBERT H. HARWOOD, JR.

E. Francis Baldwin and Baltimore's railroads had their greatest years together—the railroads as they underwent a spectacular growth spurt and Baldwin as he put a memorable face on it. The end of the Civil War had signaled the beginning of almost four decades of headlong railroad building and upgrading. Between 1870 and 1890 alone, U.S. railroad miles more than tripled. Every community had to have a railroad, traffic grew spectacularly, and in the process the railroads changed the entire nature of travel and shipping—not to mention making modern mass production and nationwide marketing possible. And as they grew, they also began to combine into large, sometimes bitterly competitive systems. In short, it was an expansive, exhilarating era, and, flush with investment money (if not always real profits), the railroads were not reluctant to show off their status and power.

Baldwin happened to be in the right spot, too. His adopted city of Baltimore had become one of the country's major railroad centers, the home base of the Baltimore & Ohio Railroad—one of the East's largest trunk-line systems—along with several lesser lines. And it was more than just that: The city could truthfully claim to be the mother of American railroading. Baltimore's merchants and bankers had created the B&O in 1827 as a bold and risky way of linking their city with the Ohio River, more than three hundred miles away, inventing and adapting the technology as they went. Inevitably, the early years were a struggle, and it took twenty-five years to reach the Ohio, but only four years afterward the B&O had established a through route between Baltimore, Cincinnati, and St. Louis. Along the way, it helped to prove the superiority of rail transportation.

Since 1858 the company had been ruled by John Work Garrett, an ambitious Baltimore investment banker turned railroad president. For better or worse—and it was both—the autocratic Garrett dominated the railroad until his death in 1884. Through sometimes heroic effort, he brought his badly battered B&O through the Civil War and by the early 1870s had launched an ambitious rebuilding and expansion program aimed at building his railroad into a major power in the East, Midwest, and even the Deep South. Challenging him were large and growing rival systems—Vanderbilt's New York Central lines and, more particularly, the powerful and aggressive Pennsylvania Railroad.

On the positive side Garrett partially achieved his aims, creating or maintaining a B&O presence as far west as Chicago and St. Louis. At home he was establishing the port of Baltimore as a major competitor in international trade, served by the B&O's fine new pier and storage facilities. Unhappily, though, his accounting, financial, and rate-making policies were less exalted; they concealed and contributed to financial weaknesses that finally resulted in an 1896 receivership. Baldwin's career was to be tied to both sides of John Work Garrett.

But whatever Garrett's failings, and whatever the B&O's true financial position, the railroad was making a place for itself in an ever-growing and ever more competitive world. Garrett was determined that it would have a public image that communicated solidity and prosperity. That became Baldwin's job.

Thus, in the early 1870s, Baldwin embarked on what became a close quarter-century relationship with the B&O, which extended beyond Garrett's death and ended about the time of the B&O's financial collapse in the late 1890s. (Soon after, the railroad underwent a significant management change and, to Baltimore's dismay, policy power shifted away from the city that gave it birth.)

During this association, Baldwin gave the railroad its own distinctive image—less truly original than, say, that of Henry Hobson Richardson or Philadelphia's Frank Furness, but always inspired and always recognizably "B&O." This was especially true during the exceptionally creative and productive period of the 1870s and 1880s, when Baldwin was essentially the company's in-house architect and apparently allowed generous budgets for attractive masonry structures. And while many railroads hired ranking architects only for their most publicly visible buildings—meaning mostly their passenger stations—Baldwin designed virtually everything.

And almost everything was needed. During the Baldwin years B&O's revenues and mileage both doubled. New facilities to shelter and handle the burgeoning passenger business and replace old or nonexistent stations were essential. Then there were newly built lines and extensions to be fully equipped, such as the Metropolitan Branch, linking Washington with the West, or Garrett's doomed foray into the Deep South via the Shenandoah Valley.

Expanding fleets of locomotives and cars also demanded larger and more efficient shops to build and repair them. Trainloads of merchandise and bulk products for export had to be stored, particularly grain and tobacco. And then there was the halcyon side of the B&O—its fashionable summer resorts in the western Maryland mountains, with their rambling hotels, cottages, and ancillary buildings. With a versatility that borders on astonishing, Baldwin designed them all, even accessorial buildings like signal towers.

Indeed, several of these "other" structures were his most notable. At the top of the list is his spectacular "roundhouse" at the railroad's Mount Clare Shops in West Baltimore (fig. 38), originally built as a shop to build and repair passenger cars and still revered as both a local and a national industrial landmark. (Strictly speaking, it is a twenty-two-sided polygon, which industrial archeologists prefer to call the Passenger Car Shop.) Its soaring, 123-foot-high multitiered design is more than mere monumentality, however. The high ground-level windows and ascending windowed tiers provided maximum natural light in an era when the artificial kind was questionable, and the lofty ceiling also allowed ventilation during Baltimore's semitropical summers.

Far less noticed and completely uncelebrated—but a landmark in railroad history—was Baldwin's so-called Baltimore Belt Railroad power house (fig. 39), completed in 1895. During the early and mid-1890s the B&O built a difficult and highly expensive

new main line through the center of Baltimore, including a 1.4-mile tunnel on an upgrade beneath Howard Street. Using steam locomotives in the long tunnel was dangerous, impractical, and illegal. Working with the new General Electric Company, the B&O pioneered again by installing the world's first main-line electrification—and Baldwin's powerhouse housed the generators that produced its current.

Leaner times for the B&O arrived in the early 1890s, as some of Garrett's financial and strategic sins finally caught up. Improvements continued as best the railroad could afford them, but much of Baldwin's work now consisted of more austere frame buildings, many of which were built to standardized designs, duplicated with variations only in size. Even so, Baldwin managed some modest charm in their details. Ironically, Baldwin's last B&O station was surely his grandest—the imposing Romanesque Revival Mount Royal Station in north Baltimore (fig. 26), designed with the area's carriage trade in mind. An extravagance the railroad could hardly afford by then, it was the necessary capstone of the long and expensive Baltimore Belt Railroad project.

Although the B&O was by far Baldwin's largest and most important client, two other railroads also were headquartered in Baltimore, and to the extent they could afford it, they too used him. One, the Western Maryland Railway, had started as a local farmer's road serving Carroll and Frederick Counties, but in the late nineteenth century was being extended, rebuilt, and reborn as an important regional carrier by the dynamic John Mifflin Hood. In 1892, as the Hood era was reaching its peak, Baldwin was commissioned to design at least four way stations for the railroad, including at least three elaborate masonry structures, which echoed his B&O work. While only one survived in 2002, all were the most distinctive and attractive on the line.

Last and definitely least of Baltimore's railroads was a rural narrow-gauge line that underwent regular reorganizations and name changes, finally emerging in the early twentieth century as the standard-gauge Maryland & Pennsylvania Railway—universally known as the Ma & Pa to generations of Marylanders. This line climbed and twisted its uncertain way northwest through the hills to Bel Air, Maryland, Delta, Pennsylvania, and finally York. In its 1888 incarnation as the Maryland Central Railway the struggling company somehow found the resources to hire Baldwin to design its shingle-style Baltimore terminal at North Avenue (fig. 28), as well as a picturesque frame suburban station at Lake Avenue (plate 8). The latter building was adjacent to the grounds of the recently relocated Elkridge Hunt Club—one of Baltimore's most rarified social institutions—and it is possible that the financially strapped railroad was given help to build a proper station for the area.

Just as Baldwin's railroad work was drying up, he was plunged into a new variation of rail transportation—the electric street railway. Once again, he managed to dominate the Baltimore scene, designing virtually every modern building on the city streetcar system. Actually, Baldwin's street-railway work began in the horse-powered streetcar era, when he was hired to design two combination carhouses and stables for the Baltimore Union Passenger Railway in 1882. His patron was most likely Nelson Perin, an ambitious Cincinnatian who managed the line and who moved east in 1888 to become one of Baltimore's major nineteenth-century street-railway empire builders.

Soon afterward—and like Baldwin's later Baltimore Belt Railroad powerhouse—one of these buildings became home for a "first" in American transportation history. In 1885 inventor Leo Daft electrified the Baltimore & Hampden horsecar line, the country's first successful electric street-railway operation, using Baldwin's carhouse and stable at what is now 25th Street and Huntington Avenue to house its generating equipment and rolling stock. Daft's installation worked well enough, but the primitive early equipment wore out, and four years later the horses returned. Nonetheless, the Daft line became the grandfather of all urban electric railways, and the Baldwin carhouse, later rebuilt and expanded by him, became a technological shrine of sorts. Happily, it still stands today, although altered as a showroom for automobiles—ironically, the technology that did the most to kill the streetcars.

While Daft was slightly ahead of his time in 1885, he was soon put behind it. Electric street-railway technology developed rapidly, and by the early 1890s plodding horsecars were being replaced everywhere by electric streetcars. The new technology in turn allowed a dramatic expansion into areas that had been too difficult or too expensive to reach with horse power. Almost overnight the electric car lines began blanketing the city and creating new suburbs as lines were extended outward in all directions, in some cases reaching far into the rural outposts. In the same decade the disorganized flock of independent companies gradually coalesced into a small handful, which in turn were brought together under the single umbrella of the appropriately named United Railways & Electric Company, in 1899.

The new UR&E appeared at precisely the time that street railways were heading into their growth peak. The new company was immediately faced with the necessity of building high-capacity, modern facilities to replace and supplement the already obsolescent mishmash inherited from its predecessors. Particularly needed was a large central electricity-generating plant (commercial utilities were not yet up to handling such a load) and a single shop complex to handle the entire system's major car repair and rebuilding work.

The "United's" first president turned out to be Baldwin's old patron from the horsecar days, Nelson Perin. Perin's tenure lasted only a year, but perhaps through him, Baldwin was selected for these first two key projects. For the new central powerhouse (plate 9), located on the waterfront at Pratt Street, Baldwin designed a large addition to a slightly older structure which housed an array of thirty-two steam boilers. Since it was located near the center of the city, the plant was made as attractive as possible; its four commanding capped smokestacks and external coal conveyor system made it one of Baltimore's most memorable industrial buildings. (The Pratt Street boiler house was completed in 1901 and an addition built in 1903, but Baldwin's role in the later building is uncertain and perhaps unlikely.)

Almost by miracle, the entire complex survived Baltimore's great fire of 1904, the sale of the plant in 1921, and its final shutdown fifty-two years later—followed by two false starts at adaptive reuse. Although unfortunately shorn of its distinctive conveyor equipment in the process, it now appears to be a permanent fixture in the city's Inner Harbor.

Baldwin's real industrial masterpiece, however, was the streetcar company's vast new central repair shop, built on an open tract opposite Carroll Park (fig. 46). Actually predating the Pratt Street power house by about a year, the Carroll Park Shop consisted of two immense matched sets of four-bay monitor-roof buildings housing every type of basic shop function in a roomy, well-lighted environment. At its peak, the UR&E operated about 1,400 streetcars, all of which passed through the complex at one time or another and some of which were built there.

Finally, following the disastrous great Baltimore fire of 1904, the UR&E embarked on a large-scale program to replace its motley collection of inherited streetcars and carhouses, many of which dated to the horsecar era. Along with buying fleets of larger cars for its growing business, it planned a total of seven capacious, completely modern "fireproof" carhouses to store and service them. Baldwin produced at least three of these fortresslike structures and most likely all seven, which were built between 1907 and 1913 and scattered at various strategic locations around the city. (To the confusion of later historians, all these carhouses were actually built and owned by an odd entity called the Maryland Electric Railway. Thanks to Baltimore's great fire of 1904 and problems of its own, the UR&E was already financially wobbly, and funding had to come through a separate company.)

Modern even by late-twentieth-century industrial standards, these turned out to be Baltimore's last street-railway buildings, as well as Baldwin's last rail-related work. His death in early 1916 came less than three years after the last one had been completed. That date was symbolic, too: By at least one measure, 1916 is considered the high tide of the railroad industry; afterward began a long decline, soon accelerated by motor vehicles. Baldwin had both come and gone at the right time.

But Baldwin's work endured, as the numerous references in this book attest. As this is written in 2002, more than thirty Baldwin railroad and street-railway structures survive, many adapted for other uses but some still serving their original purpose. Among them is the nationally known and recognizable station at Point of Rocks, Maryland (cover)—

to many, the quintessential Victorian railroad station. It has been exhaustively photographed, painted, sketched, and modeled; images of it regularly appear in books, articles, posters, and calendars.

There are two other buildings that epitomize Baldwin's talents, albeit for entirely different reasons. First is the onetime UR&E's huge Carroll Park shop complex, a living testimony to Baldwin's vision and foresight. Originally built to serve the long-departed streetcar system, it has nonetheless survived for more than a hundred years as a model of efficient industrial design, still doing the same work for which it was built—now for the "United's" lineal descendant, the state-operated Baltimore regional bus system. Quite the opposite is the B&O's Mount Clare Shop "roundhouse"—innovative in its day but obsolete even by early-twentieth-century standards. Yet here Baldwin unintentionally created a different kind of monument. As the central part of the B&O Railroad Museum complex, its breathtaking interior is unrivaled in the world as the finest and most appropriate showplace for nineteenth-century railroad technology. Francis Baldwin was the consummate Catholic whose heart was always in his church work, although much of his career was devoted to the emphatically more secular railroad business. So perhaps it is not surprising that in at least this one instance he seemed to adroitly blend the two, creating what is truly a cathedral of its own kind, which symbolizes the optimistic, expansive spirit when railroading came of age.

Introduction

E. Francis Baldwin and American Architecture

MICHAEL J. LEWIS

History has always been kindest to those artists who cultivated an idiosyncratic style, making their art a vehicle of personal expression. The best-known American architects are those whose works were as distinctive as their handwriting, who provided a "signature style." We see the buildings as the physical manifestation of a personality, whether it is that of the gregarious leviathan Henry Hobson Richardson, the sharp-tongued ruffian Frank Furness, or that metaphysical dreamer Louis Sullivan.

And we are right to do so, for post–Civil War America cherished personality to an extent scarcely imaginable today. Nothing could be further from that other postwar society, 1950s America, which came to be defined in terms of the organization man, who shunned idiosyncrasy and achieved through conformity. But during the overwrought decades of the Gilded Age, when every aspect of the nation's social and economic structure was in churning, turbulent motion, a cult of personality was natural. This was an age when the titans of industry had not yet been renamed the robber barons, when public life was dominated by such swaggering figures as Commodore Vanderbilt, Jay Gould, and J. P. Morgan. Supported by Emerson's gospel of self-reliance and Whitman's belief in "spontaneous me," Gilded Age America naturally came to see the success of these men as the product of force of willpower and personality.

But not every Victorian architect developed a signature style, or even sought to do so. Most felt their task was to serve their clients ably and responsibly, to translate their programmatic requirements into durable, efficient, and fashionable designs, and to guard their clients' money zealously. As a result, their work frequently shows little stylistic unity from decade to decade as they adjusted themselves to the ever-changing vagaries of fashion. This is not to say that these were not men of imagination or originality, but that they directed their talents and time in other channels than the cultivation of an arresting signature: in planning, in problem-solving, in money-saving, and in coordinating the frenzied activity of major building enterprises. Judging architects by this standard, a very high place must be accorded to Ephraim Francis Baldwin.

Like Richardson in Boston or Furness in Philadelphia, Baldwin dominated the architecture of Baltimore, building the city's principal banks, hotels, clubs, and churches. And he did so by the same means, an unerring similarity of background and sympathy of outlook with his clients. He was also an engineer, who shared the same cultural assumptions of the railroad engineers with whom he worked. He was a Roman Catholic in the city that was the locus of the first Catholic diocese in America, and in which political and financial power was still largely in Catholic hands. On the strength of this patronage, Baldwin became the principal architect for the Catholic Church in Maryland, a practice that culminated in his seamless expansion of Baltimore's cathedral and his work for Catholic University in Washington, D.C. These Catholic ties, cemented by powerful family connections within the church, ensured Baldwin's preeminence in Baltimore but also ensured that he would remain a parochial rather than a national figure. Apart from occasional commissions in the South, his radius of action was essentially limited to the reach of the Baltimore & Ohio Railroad, the other mainstay of his career.

It was Baldwin's misfortune to preside over Baltimore architecture during the decades when it lost its national prestige. During the early nineteenth century, Baltimore possessed an architectural culture of great sophistication, initiated by Benjamin Henry Latrobe, Maximilien Godefroy, and Robert Mills and distinguished by their intelligent and forceful classicism. Such talented successors as Robert Cary

Long Jr. and John Rudolph Niernsee built upon this tradition, and in the antebellum years Baltimore was a center of architectural innovation, with significant milestones in the Gothic, Italianate, and even the eclectic *Rundbogenstil* (round-arched style) of progressive Germany theory.

But after the ordeal of the Civil War, Baltimore was more a consumer and less a generator of architectural ideas. Baldwin's own practice shows this, as his forms and motifs in the 1870s were likely to come from Philadelphia and then, in the ensuing decades, increasingly from New York. His tough and muscular essay for the Safe Deposit & Trust Company (1876) (fig. 67) shows an awareness of Furness's recent contributions to Philadelphia's banker's row on Chestnut Street, while the taut pilasters and incised pediments of the William Donnell house (1874) derive from Philadelphia's fashionable *Neo-Grec* townhouses. But his mighty central offices of the Baltimore & Ohio Railroad (fig. 34), completed in 1880, is derived from the corporate language of 1870s New York, above all, Richard Morris Hunt's Tribune Building, with its similar entrance, color palette, and overscaled mansard roof bristling with dormers. During the 1880s, Baldwin's commercial buildings were large, rangy affairs, distinguished by generously proportioned Romanesque arcades—in other words, his version of the Romanesque commercial palaces then being raised in New York by George B. Post. The Fidelity Building (fig. 70) is the finest of these, an eight-story rusticated commercial palace rising to a whimsically ecclesiastical turret. But here too the pattern holds: elegant and discerning variants of the prevailing fashions and a disdain for frivolous eccentricity for its own sake.

This amiable and agile eclecticism should not be taken as a want of principle or conviction on Baldwin's part, for in its way it was rigorously methodical. His architectural training—apart from the civil engineering background that his engineer father might have imparted—took place almost entirely in the office of Niernsee (1814–85), an Austrian émigré of considerable ability. Niernsee learned architecture and engineering according to the progressive German polytechnical model, which stressed construction, planning, and the objective components of architecture rather than inculcating a particular style. This elastic and permissive approach to architecture encouraged the designer to think of style as something of an arbitrary skin. Niernsee's work was in that vein, and his buildings invariably show a straightforward embrace of the facts of the pro-

gram, saved from utilitarian barrenness by the application of lively surface detail and by a feeling for the balanced massing of separate parts. These traits also distinguish Baldwin's work, although his walls were likely to be Romanesque or Gothic rather than the Italian Renaissance of his mentor.

Nowhere is Baldwin's inventive eclecticism more vivid than in his work for the Baltimore & Ohio Railroad. In extent and breadth it is simply stunning. Many railroad companies relied on the leading architects of the day, including the Boston & Albany (Richardson), the Reading (Furness), the Chicago, Burlington & Quincy (Burnham & Root), and the mighty Pennsylvania (Wilson Brothers). But none served a railroad for so long or did so much to establish its physical and visual character as did Baldwin, who worked for the Baltimore & Ohio from the early 1870s well into the 1890s. He designed not only its stations but also its roundhouses and stockyards, hotels, office buildings, and warehouses, and even an "emigrant house," a dormitory for immigrant laborers—in short, the full panoply of buildings that a modern railroad brought in its wake.

Baldwin's railroad structures, though straightforward and practical, never hardened into rote or routine. Spurred on by the need to project vigor and alertness at a time when America's railroads were in ruthless financial competition with one another, he constantly adjusted his architectural language, updating it in accordance with changing fashion. He moved swiftly from the eclectic Relay Station and Viaduct House (1872) (fig. 8) to the aggressively High Victorian Gothic of Point of Rocks Station (1875) (cover) to the lively Queen Anne jumble of gables at Sykesville Station (plate 2).

But for all his stylistic lunges and shifts, Baldwin remained a loyal disciple of Niernsee and his sober German classicism. He not only remodeled Camden Station in 1891–92 (fig. 22) but also took it as the model for his own Mount Royal Station of 1896 (fig. 26), the centerpiece of his railroad career. There he faithfully followed the classical composition that Niernsee, the B&O's "house architect," had taught him: the same central towered mass, the same lower wings, and the same bold and blocky pavilions that terminate the composition at either end. Even the change to Romanesque forms scarcely affected the overall sense of judicious balance and volumetric clarity. This continuity of expression from Niernsee to Baldwin, despite the superficial changes in style, is remarkable, amounting to a veritable architectural dynasty that shaped the Baltimore & Ohio for half a century.

Perhaps because of his relative disinterest in stylistic invention for its own sake, Baldwin seems to have been happy to relegate the cosmetic details to his partners. And indeed, apart from one decade, he worked in partnership with a younger man who seems to have served as the firm's chief designer: before 1873 with Bruce Price, and after 1883 with Josias Pennington. Pennington, the lesser light, was a Renaissance revivalist who contributed the blocky civic designs of the later years. But Price was a figure of national renown. Born in 1845, he was a fellow graduate of Niernsee's office, although he seems to have been more passionate in his High Victorian ecclesiology, preaching truth in materials in moralistic terms. He evidently contributed the firm's early Gothic essays, such as Saint Ann's (plate 12), with their strident banding and rambunctious rooflines. Perhaps he even designed St. Augustine's Church (fig. 48), in Washington, an unusual High Victorian Gothic church for black Catholics. Price left the firm in 1873, eventually becoming one of the nation's most accomplished domestic architects. But for this he had to move to New York—a choice that Baldwin, constrained by the bonds of patronage and clientele, could not make. Like H. L. Mencken, another chronic Baltimorean, he cast his lot with his chosen city, and there he remained until the end.

Now Carlos Avery has rescued Baldwin from the abyss of history. He has done so with ingenuity and imagination, and in twenty-five years of intrepid sleuthing has proven himself to be an Inspector Javert of the hunt. Here is the architect's work in its totality, not only the monumental civic projects but also the hundreds of secondary commissions and alterations that are almost always lost to scholarship. Here the enormous scope of Baldwin's practice is shown, and its stupefying tempo. But what is refreshing about this book is its absence of any special pleading, any attempt to make of Baldwin something he was not or to use him as a straw figure in the attempt to prove a polemical point. Of course, the work of interpreting and evaluating Baldwin's role in American architecture must now begin. But through Avery's efforts, we have a corpus of reliable documentation, the likes of which has rarely been assembled for an American architect.

In glancing over the pages one is struck by the integrity of Baldwin's approach to design. It was empirical rather than systematic, and for all the styles in which he dabbled, there always remained something of the sobriety of German academic classicism. If there was anything distinctively personal in his expression, it was a keen appreciation for the lithic solidity of the wall and the inherent poetry of masonry. Look at how deeply the piers of the Safe Deposit & Trust Company are cut, or at the assured juxtaposition of solid and void in the Maryland Club (fig. 84), one of his handsomest Richardsonian performances. In the end, Baldwin emerges as something of a signature architect in spite of himself.

PART I

E. FRANCIS BALDWIN,
ARCHITECT

CHAPTER 1

The Life and Times
of E. Francis Baldwin

The Early Years

Ephraim Francis Baldwin was born in West Troy, New York, on October 4, 1837. His father, Alonzo Clarke Baldwin (b. Nov. 24, 1807), was a civil engineer from Louisville, Kentucky. Baldwin's paternal grandparents were Ephraim and Frances (Sage) Baldwin. His mother, Mary Elizabeth Elder (b. Aug. 21, 1805), was one of thirteen children born to Basil Spalding Elder, a Baltimore merchant, and Elizabeth Snowden; a younger brother, William Henry Elder, became the Roman Catholic Archbishop of Cincinnati, Ohio, in the late 1870s. Mary Elder married Alonzo Baldwin on May 16, 1832, in the cathedral in Baltimore. Alonzo Baldwin died eleven years later, on April 18, 1843; Ephraim and his mother—and possibly his sister—subsequently moved to Baltimore, where they lived for the rest of their lives.[1]

E. Francis Baldwin received his early education in Baltimore. He attended St. Mary's College for at least one year (1851–52) and then presumably attended the newly created Loyola College for the next two years.[2] "E. F. Baldwin" is recorded as having attended Mount St. Mary's College in Emmitsburg, Maryland, only from August 26, 1854, to June 27, 1855. Had he remained there, he would have graduated with the class of 1858. (According to school records, his

uncle, William Henry Elder, graduated from Mount St. Mary's in 1837.)

At this point, the stories about Baldwin's education are conflicting. Some accounts stated that he graduated from "Troy Polytechnic Institute." According to obituaries published at the time of his death and also published biographies, Baldwin graduated in 1860 from Rensselaer Polytechnic Institute, Troy, New York, where he had studied architecture.[3]

It is now clear that Baldwin never attended, let alone graduated from, any school of higher education in New York. His name appears in no directory, catalogue, register of graduates, or class listing of students or former students of Rensselaer Polytechnic Institute, and there was no such school as the Troy Polytechnic Institute. (There was a Troy Academy, but it was a preparatory school, and Baldwin had already attended Mount St. Mary's. Troy University was founded in 1858, and its first and only class graduated in 1862.) Finally, Baldwin's name does not appear in any Troy, New York, city directories during the years 1855 to 1860—but it does appear in the 1858 *Baltimore City Directory*.

Baldwin's lack of formal education in architecture should not detract from his professional accomplishments—perhaps that should make his mark even deeper. The manner in which Baldwin developed his architectural skills was actually not at all unusual for young men seeking a career in this field in the period before the Civil War: He started as a "draughtsman" or apprentice, in the office of an established architect. In Baldwin's case, he was fortunate enough to have been taken under the wings of John Rudolph Niernsee and James Crawford Neilson, of Baltimore.

---

1. Ephraim's sister, Mary Baldwin, was born on June 11, 1842, and died on January 6, 1845.

2. St. Mary's College, on the grounds of the seminary on Paca St., was closed in the summer of 1852. Sulpician training of students for the priesthood was transferred to St. Charles College, near Ellicott City in Howard County. Loyola College was created to replace St. Mary's College; it opened in September 1852 on Holliday St. and Orange Alley. (It moved two and a half years later to Calvert and Madison Sts., where it stayed until 1922, when it moved to its present campus, on N. Charles St. and Cold Spring Lane.)

3. It is also worth noting that the first architecture curriculum in the United States was not set up until 1868, at the Massachusetts Institute of Technology.

J. R. Niernsee was born on May 29, 1814, in Vienna, Austria, and educated in Vienna and Prague as an engineer before emigrating to the United States in 1837. By 1839 he had found work as a draftsman for the Baltimore & Ohio Railroad, working under Benjamin Henry Latrobe. It was here that Niernsee met Neilson, who was employed by the B&O as an engineer. James C. Neilson, who was born in Baltimore on October 14, 1816, received his technical training in Belgium. The firm of Niernsee & Neilson was formed in June 1848 and grew to become one of Baltimore's most prestigious and influential architectural firms of the 1850s and 1860s. Niernsee & Neilson was dissolved in June 1874. Niernsee died on July 7, 1885; Neilson died on December 21, 1900.

E. Francis Baldwin was one of a number of students or apprentices of Niernsee and Neilson, then in their office at 49 St. Paul Street. Richard Snowden Andrews (1833–1903) had been associated with them for a time prior to the Civil War. T. Buckler Ghequier (1854–1910), a nephew of the architect Robert Cary Long, also was a student. Baldwin worked with Neilson or Niernsee & Neilson from 1860 to 1867. Neilson's personal records show "private accounts" with Baldwin over the years 1864–67. Bruce Price apparently began working as a draftsman with Niernsee & Neilson in 1864.

Baldwin left Niernsee & Neilson to make his own way in 1867. He apparently practiced alone in Baltimore for a couple of years until he formed what was to be a relatively short-lived and eventually troublesome association with his former fellow apprentice Bruce Price, whom he must have met just a few years before. The Baldwin & Price partnership undoubtedly began with the best of intentions and was generally successful for a time for both men. Their brief association resulted in the creation of some significant and enduring works, including Christ Protestant Episcopal Church, the Albion Hotel, St. Ann's Church in Baltimore, the Grace-Lee Church in Lexington, Virginia, and the Cathedral of St. John the Baptist in Savannah, Georgia.

Bruce Price was born in Cumberland, Maryland, on December 12, 1845, and died in Paris on May 28, 1903. The son of William and Marian (Bruce) Price, he received no formal training in architecture, and his college education at Princeton was terminated following the death of his father. Price learned his profession as a draftsman-apprentice in the firm of Niernsee & Neilson. After leaving the firm and studying for a time in Europe, Price returned to Baltimore and formed his partnership with Baldwin in 1869. They established their office at 54 Lexington

Street, on the SW corner of Charles and Lexington, in the heart of an enclave of architectural offices in Baltimore.[4] Price and Baldwin separated by 1874, and Price moved on to Wilkes-Barre and New York and earned international fame by the time of his death.

The American Institute of Architects, Baltimore

A small group of professional Baltimore architects banded together in early 1870—in what may have been a precursor to their eventual formal alliance—to protest the lack of compensation for design proposals for a new building for the Maryland Deaf and Dumb Asylum in Frederick, Maryland. The Executive Committee of the state institution had advertised for "plans, specifications and estimates" from Maryland architects, with compensation to be made only for the winning submission. The Baltimore architects collectively refused to accept these terms and openly published a letter in April to the Executive Committee deploring the proposed scheme to obtain their unpaid services and "gratis" work.[5] The group suggested the winner be compensated at the usual rates and that one percent of the estimated value of the proposed building, about $1,000, be distributed in awards of $200 to each of the five next best designs. They also suggested that all proposal drawings be to the same scale (1/8 inch to the foot) to enable a fair comparison of their merits.

The Baltimore chapter of the American Institute of Architects was formed on December 10, 1870. Its first president was J. Crawford Neilson, who had joined the AIA the previous July. The two vice presidents were Edmund G. Lind and Thomas Dixon; John Ellicott was the treasurer, and Nathaniel Henry Hutton the secretary.

E. Francis Baldwin, Bruce Price, and George Frederick were elected to membership in the AIA on

---

4. In 1886, Baltimore renumbered its streets and 54 became 1 W. Lexington St. For the text that follows, unless otherwise indicated, the building numbers are those that were reported or those that would have been in use at the time of the event being discussed.

5. The signatories were J. Crawford Neilson for Niernsee & Neilson; E. G. Lind and N. H. Hutton for Hutton & Murdoch; Thomas Dixon; J. Wilkinson; John W. Hogg; Charles E. Cassell; Frank E. Davis; Jackson C. Gott; Henry Brauns; R. Snowden Andrews; J. C. Wrenshall; John Ellicott; E. F. Baldwin for Baldwin & Price; and G. A. Frederick. The Baltimore architect (W. F. Weber) whose design was selected was not a signatory.

January 13, 1871. Price and Frederick became members of the chapter's Executive Committee. During the 1870s, some of Baltimore's best young architects were members of the local AIA chapter. And as a testimony to the close relationships between the architecture and the engineering communities of the time, civil engineers Wendel Bollman, Charles Latrobe, and J. L. Randolph were elected "non-professional" members, and William Rich Hutton (1826–1901) of Clopper, Maryland, was a "corresponding member" (fig. 1).

The Baltimore chapter hosted the ninth annual convention of the AIA in November 1875. The business meetings were held in the library of the Maryland Historical Society (the Athenaeum Building). Papers were read by Niernsee, Adolph Cluss, and others. Baldwin attended the meeting and had drawings of three of his buildings displayed at the exhibit in the nearby St. James Hotel. These buildings were the Safe Deposit Company, the Savannah Cathedral, and the Baltimore & Ohio Railroad headquarters building.

Baltimore's AIA chapter was problem-ridden, and many members seemed not to maintain their affiliation with it for very long. The chapter secretary reported that Bruce Price had been "removed" from the chapter rolls in February 1873 (not long after his marriage and apparently at about the time that he severed his partnership with Baldwin and moved to Wilkes-Barre). Price resigned in 1877. In 1875, Neilson himself was dropped for "non-payment of his dues," and Niernsee (who had been a charter member of the AIA and a signatory to its first constitution and bylaws in May 1857) allowed his membership in the Baltimore chapter to lapse in October 1875. In 1876, then-president N. H. Hutton resigned.

Chapter elections were held in October 24, 1876, in one of the many architects' offices on the corner of Charles and Lexington. The officers elected at this time were Edmund G. Lind (president), F. H. Smith and John Murdoch (vice presidents), J. B. N. Wyatt (treasurer), and E. Francis Baldwin (secretary). Mr. R. L. Poor and Charles E. Cassell were elected to the Executive Committee.

As the chapter secretary in 1876, Baldwin filed a report stating that "Mr. George A. Frederick, I regret to say, has resigned his membership of the chapter simply on account of some personal feelings. When his September dues are paid, his resignation will be accepted." Frederick did resign from the chapter in 1877, though he maintained his association with the parent AIA organization and was a fellow of the AIA. Joseph Evans Sperry, who had joined the chapter with Wyatt in December 1875, resigned from the AIA in October 1879. Baldwin apparently remained as an active member of the AIA and the Baltimore chapter—he was first vice president in 1886—until his unfortunate resignation in late 1887 or early 1888.

There is also a bit of evidence that Baldwin later took an active role in proposing a school of architecture for Baltimore. On August 19, 1890, the *Sun* reported that Baldwin and Charles E. Cassell had stated that "such a school is needed here beyond doubt and if established would be successful. Of course, like every other enterprise, it should be given time."

Architect of the B&O Railroad

The first "architect of the B&O Railroad" was Jacob Small Jr. (1772–1851), who was engaged by the company in 1831 as an architect and superintendent of depots. He is credited with the design of the B&O station at Ellicott City, Maryland. Built in 1831, it is the oldest existing railroad station in the United States. Benjamin H. Latrobe has been suggested as Small's successor, but it is likelier that this role fell to John R. Niernsee. Among the stations that Niernsee is credited with are Camden Station (original concept) and stations at Frederick, Maryland; Washington, D.C.; and Wheeling, West Virginia. Then the torch was passed, appropriately enough, to one of Niernsee's associates—E. Francis Baldwin. (After Baldwin, M. A. Long apparently assumed the position.)

E. Francis Baldwin probably assumed the position of the B&O's "house" architect in 1872 (fig. 2). The earliest known reference to this title is in a Lexington, Virginia, newspaper of August 1872. Baldwin quickly seized whatever promotional advantage he could from this appointment; in George W. Howard's book, *The Monumental City*, published in 1873, a small advertisement mentioned "E. Francis Baldwin, Architect of the Baltimore and Ohio Rail Road and the Safe Deposit Building." Baldwin is generally considered to have held this position with the B&O until about 1883, but it seems likely that it went beyond that, certainly until the mid-to-late 1890s. The Baltimore City directories for 1873 through 1883 listed Baldwin as the B&O architect, and this may be the source of the conjecture. Baldwin was not a full-time employee of the railroad and he did not maintain an office with the railroad. He was retained by the railroad for the architectural work, which was extensive, but he also maintained a vigorous private practice for a variety of other clients at the same time.

Baldwin's role with the B&O may be compared to that of Frank Furness (1839–1912), the famous Philadelphia architect and contemporary of Baldwin's, who designed numerous stations and other structures for the Philadelphia-based Pennsylvania and Philadelphia & Reading railroads. Baldwin was, with few exceptions, the architect for the B&O's lines extending from Baltimore to points west and south to Washington, D.C.; Lexington, Virginia; Cumberland, Maryland; and Wheeling, West Virginia. The major exception was B&O's newly built (in 1883–86) line between Baltimore and Philadelphia. Probably for political reasons, to help placate an unfriendly Philadelphia, the B&O hired Furness as the architect for more than two dozen stations including those at Wilmington, Chester, and Philadelphia.

Considering the large number of projects and the sheer geographic spread—as well as their timing—it is unlikely that Baldwin traveled to many of the construction sites of the railroad stations or other B&O projects he designed. Many stations were probably built directly from rather simple drawings and specifications (at least by today's standards) and according to standard masonry and carpentry construction procedures under the supervision of the railroad's own engineers or foremen. The drawings that Baldwin prepared would simply have been forerunners of what the B&O would later develop into more formalized practices. (By the early 1900s, the B&O and many other railroads had standard plans for their structures, right of way, equipment, and bridges.)

On some of Baldwin's projects (for the railroad or otherwise) the situation might have been quite different, depending upon the complexity, importance, and location of the project. On buildings such as churches, banks, schools, and hospitals, for example, the architect would probably have had the responsibility and found it necessary to make periodic visits to the construction site to ensure that the work was proceeding in accordance with his specifications. The architect would have had to monitor the progress in order to approve or disburse payments to the contractor and to see if the builder was meeting a contractually agreed-upon schedule. Because many of Baldwin's largest projects were in or very near Baltimore, visiting these sites would not have posed a problem. In some cases, such as the cathedral in Georgia, he would have had to take some time to visit a site.

One can easily imagine Baldwin taking the train on the Washington Branch, the Metropolitan Branch, or the Main Stem and the Valley Railroad into the Shenandoah Valley to monitor the progress of selected buildings. It is known, for example, that Baldwin personally visited the Forest Glen church at least six times from July to December 1893. In some cases, Baldwin kept an accounting of his rail fares for reimbursement beyond his standard fee, which was based on a percentage scale of the total cost of the project. For some more remote projects, an associate was sent to supervise on site; for example, Francis Tormey was sent on one or more occasions to inspect the construction of Henry Gassaway Davis's home in Elkins, West Virginia.

Partnership with Josias Pennington

Following the departure of Bruce Price, Baldwin again practiced alone, for about ten years. In 1883, he formed a partnership with Josias Pennington (fig. 3). Pennington had started as a draftsman-apprentice under Baldwin in the 1870s. The son of socially prominent Baltimore parents, Pennington (b. 1854) was a graduate of St. John's College in Annapolis, Maryland.

Some of the work done by the firm of Baldwin & Pennington is difficult to associate with one particular architect or the other. However, Pennington noted in his application for membership in the AIA in 1902 that he was submitting prints of buildings that he stated were designed by him and for which he had the responsibility of supervising construction. The buildings cited were the Maryland Club, the Marburg residence on West Mount Vernon Place, the front of the National Union Bank building on Fayette Street, and his own residence at 1119 St. Paul Street, which was built in 1900.

Pennington's correspondence in 1902 with Glenn Brown of the AIA is interesting. He had delayed his application for membership and—with a change in the AIA's requirements in the interim—faced the unwelcome prospect of having to take an examination. He asked if the date of his request for

Fig. 3. Baldwin &
Pennington, Architects,
March 1893. *Front row
(left to right)*:
E. F. Baldwin
W. G. Keimig
J. Pennington
Back row:
E. Herring
F. Woodward
C. Darsch
H. J. West
F. E. Tormey
L. Neal
Eugene F. Baldwin

an application could be used instead of the date of filing the completed forms, noting that if an exam were required, he would withdraw his request for membership. The AIA's records show that Pennington was made an associate member in 1902.

Josias Pennington designed three "cottages" at Deer Park, Maryland, in the 1890s. His own cottage, which is still standing, is on the National Register of Historic Places. The other two, built for Charles K. Lord (a B&O vice president) and George Small, have been demolished. Josias Pennington is reported to have been an avid golfer and was instrumental in having the B&O Railroad build a golf course in front of the Deer Park Hotel in the 1890s. Pennington was a member and a president of the Elkridge Hunt Club in Baltimore.

Pennington was the principal architect for the annex to the Maryland State House in Annapolis, which was built in the early 1900s. Baldwin had probably hit his peak well before the turn of the century, so with some exceptions, Pennington probably was the architect responsible for executing many of the commissions secured by the firm of Baldwin & Pennington from the mid-1890s on.

In contrast to the alliance with Price, Baldwin's association with Pennington was long-lasting and apparently harmonious. Their partnership ended with Baldwin's death in 1916, though the firm of

Baldwin & Pennington was not formally dissolved until 1918. After Baldwin's death, Josias Pennington formed a partnership (Pennington & Pennington) with his son, Hall Pleasants Pennington.[6] Josias Pennington passed away on March 4, 1929, and was buried in Green Mount Cemetery.

Just as Baldwin and Price received their training in the firm of Niernsee & Neilson, and as Pennington was trained in Baldwin's office, so also were other young architects trained in the firm of Baldwin & Pennington who later went out on their own to form firms and partnerships. Baldwin & Pennington may be thought of as just one of the links in an evolutionary chain or a genealogy of architectural firms in Baltimore. A chart (fig. 4) summarizes some of the known associations and relationships of the major firms in Baltimore over the second half of the nineteenth century and the first quarter of the twentieth,

6. Hall P. Pennington graduated from Princeton University in 1910 and studied architecture at the Ecole des Beaux Arts in Paris. During World War I he worked for the Red Cross, building hospitals in France. He married (and later divorced) Alice Damrosch (daughter of composer-conductor Walter J. Damrosch) and returned to the United States to practice architecture, specializing in apartments. His work includes buildings at 36 E. 72nd St., 66 E. 79th St., 10 Gracie Sq., and 1001 Park Ave. in New York City. He died in April 1942 in New York at the age of fifty-three.

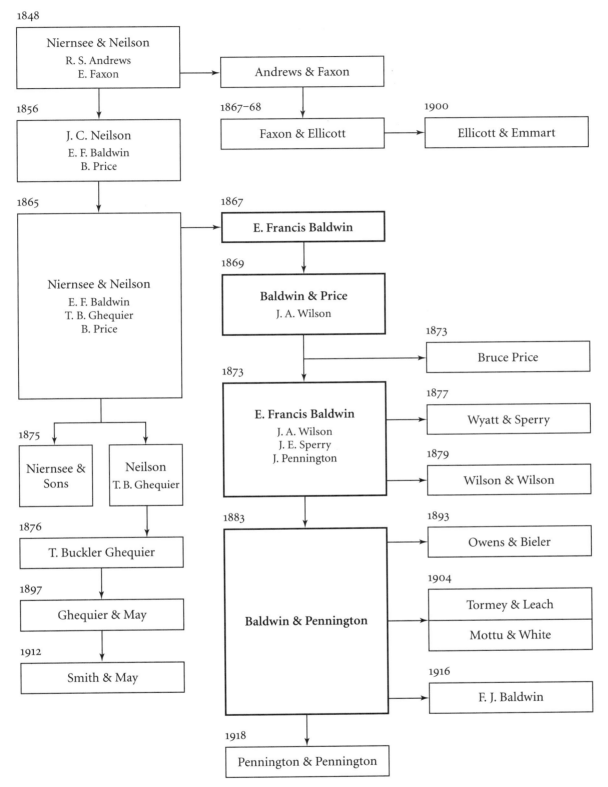

Fig. 4. Origins and
Evolution of Baltimore
Architectural Firms: The
Niernsee & Neilson
Architectural Family
Tree

1848
Niernsee & Neilson
R. S. Andrews
E. Faxon

Andrews & Faxon

1856
J. C. Neilson
E. F. Baldwin
B. Price

1867–68
Faxon & Ellicott

1900
Ellicott & Emmart

1865
Niernsee & Neilson
E. F. Baldwin
T. B. Ghequier
B. Price

1867
E. Francis Baldwin

1869
Baldwin & Price
J. A. Wilson

1873
Bruce Price

1873
E. Francis Baldwin
J. A. Wilson
J. E. Sperry
J. Pennington

1877
Wyatt & Sperry

1879
Wilson & Wilson

1875
Niernsee & Sons

Neilson
T. B. Ghequier

1876
T. Buckler Ghequier

1897
Ghequier & May

1912
Smith & May

1883
Baldwin & Pennington

1893
Owens & Bieler

1904
Tormey & Leach

Mottu & White

1916
F. J. Baldwin

1918
Pennington & Pennington

highlighting the roles of Baldwin and his partners and associates.

John Appleton Wilson (1851–1927) was trained at Columbian College and at the Massachusetts Institute of Technology. He began working in the firm of Baldwin & Price in the early 1870s. He prepared a list of buildings for which he had made drawings while employed with various architects. This list, in the collection of the Maryland Historical Society, includes four buildings known to have been designed by Baldwin and Price: the cathedral at Savannah, Georgia; and St. Ann's Church, St. Joseph's Hospital, and what he called the "marble houses" on Chase Street near Christ Episcopal Church, in Baltimore. When Baldwin & Price dissolved their partnership in 1873, Wilson must have stayed on with Baldwin until the mid-to-late 1870s. He worked for a time with W. F. Weber and formed a partnership with William T. Wilson in about 1880.

Wilson's best-known works are the houses known as Belvidere Terrace, on North Calvert Street in Baltimore. Wilson also designed the Wilkins house, 1201 Biddle Street (1877); the C. L. McKim house at Calvert and Chase (1879); and the Calvin Wilson house on St. Paul near Preston. His lesser-known works include a "summer hotel" at Rogers Station in Baltimore County (1881), the Highland Park Methodist Episcopal Church (1890), and a Baptist church in Onancock, Virginia (1890).

Sydney Williamson apparently worked in Baldwin's office in the 1870s, probably at about the same time as James Appleton Wilson. Williamson's name appears in early Baldwin accounting ledgers, but no other evidence has been found concerning him or his work.

George Welch was the delineator on a few drawings of Baldwin buildings: the B&O Headquarters building, St. Mary's Seminary, and the Rennert Hotel. Welch was listed in Baltimore City directories as an "artist," working at the SW corner of Lexington and Charles—the location of Baldwin's offices—from 1870 to 1889.

Joseph Evans Sperry (1854–1930) worked in Baldwin's office from 1872 to 1876. Sperry was the delineator for drawings of Baldwin's design for the Safe Deposit Company building in 1875. Sperry's work, well known and abundant in Baltimore, includes the Equitable Building (1889), the Provident Savings Bank (1903), the Emerson ("Bromo-Seltzer") Tower (1910), and the Emerson Hotel (1911). Sperry also designed his own residence at Guilford Avenue and Bishop Road in 1913.

James Bosley Noel Wyatt (1847–1926) worked in Baldwin's office from 1874 to 1876. It was here that he met Sperry, and the two formed a partnership in 1877. Their practice took off when they won the design competition for the church of St. Michael and All Angels. During their ten-year association, Wyatt and Sperry designed the Mercantile Safe Deposit & Trust Company on Calvert and Redwood Streets (1885–86). Wyatt formed a partnership with William G. Nolting in 1889.

William Louis Plack (1854–1944), an engineer-architect from Altoona, Pennsylvania, worked for William Rich Hutton in New York and later for Baldwin as a draftsman in the 1870s. He went on to design a number of buildings in Maryland and Pennsylvania. Plack designed the First National Bank in Havre de Grace, Maryland, in 1906.

Alphonsos Henry Bieler (1862–1951) worked briefly with George Frederick and Smith & Sons before joining Baldwin in 1883. His projects include Greenmount Methodist Episcopal (ME) Church at McKim and Chase Streets (1884) and the People's Railway Company carhouse on Druid Hall Avenue at Retreat Street (1885). He assisted Frank Furness with the 1888 B&O terminal in Pittsburgh. Bieler's name appears on drawings for the Leiperville railroad station near Philadelphia (1889), the Branchville station (1889), the Boothwyn station (1887), and the Madisonville, Ohio, station (1887). He left Baldwin in 1893 and formed a two-year partnership with Benjamin Buck Owens, whose work includes the McDonogh School gymnasium (1893) and the Harlem Park ME Church (1893). Bieler moved to New York in 1902.

Francis E. Tormey (1865–1935) was an architect who seemed to have shared Baldwin's preferences for buildings and clientele. Tormey may be regarded as Baldwin's "successor," and he designed many dozens of buildings in Baltimore and elsewhere. Tormey prepared some of the drawings for the City College building while employed by Baldwin & Pennington. Many of his—and his son's—drawings were saved by the Baltimore Architecture Foundation and placed in the Maryland Historical Society. Some of these drawings are for buildings designed by Baldwin: St. Gregory's Church, St. Michael's Chapel, St. Elizabeth's School, and St. James School. Tormey designed the Orchard Street Sunday School building (1903), St. Joseph's House of Industry on North Charles (1906), the dormitory of St. Mary's Industrial School (1908), St. Rose Industrial School in Washington, D.C. (1909), and the Cecil National Bank in Port Deposit, Maryland (1906). F. E. Tormey Jr. (1894–1971) was the architect for Pangborn Hall at Mount St. Mary's College (1954).

William G. Keimig is something of an enigma. Little is known about him, but he worked with Baldwin & Pennington for a number of years. His name does not appear on Baldwin & Pennington office stationery used in 1892, but he appears prominently in a March 1893 photo of the entire staff, along with Frank Tormey, Frank Woodward, Herbert J. West, Charles Darsch, Edwin F. ("Eddie") Herring, and

Leander Neal. Osmund Latrobe and James Cooper may also have been associated with the firm at about this time. Keimig's name appears (along with those of Baldwin, Pennington, and Frank Baldwin) in an advertisement in a 1908 *Sun* almanac.

Charles Darsch was an artist or a delineator for Baldwin & Pennington. The initials "CHD" appear on published drawings of their Hopkins Place Bank.

Herbert J. West graduated from the Maryland Institute College of Art in 1894 and was employed by Baldwin & Pennington for a time. The *Sun* reported that he had been the recipient of a sixty-five-dollar award in the architectural division of his school. West went on to form the H. J. West Construction Company. This firm worked on the high school building in Brunswick, Maryland, in 1911. It also had a number of contracts on buildings that were designed by Baldwin & Pennington, including the UR&E carbarn on Harford Road (1912), the Manufacturer's Record Building on Water and Commerce Streets (1912), and the new Hutzler Building on North Howard Street (1913).

Francis J. Baldwin (1874–1963) attended Mount St. Mary's College (class of 1893) and then studied architecture at the University of Pennsylvania. He worked with his father for a time and then went to New York for five years. He rejoined the firm of Baldwin & Pennington, where he worked on a number of projects with his father. In particular, they were jointly responsible for some buildings at Mount St. Mary's College. After his father's death, he went into business on his own and lived for a time in Ellicott City. Frank designed the Holy Rosary Church and St. Elizabeth's Home in Baltimore and LeClerc Hall at Notre Dame College (1926).

A typed list in the possession of the Baldwin family shows the following additional buildings by Frank Baldwin (whose office was then at 328 North Charles): Our Lady of Pompei Church and School, Our Lady of Lourdes Church and School, Holy Rosary School and Rectory, St. Martin's Academy, Holy Rosary Convent, Mount St. Agnes High School, St. Joseph's Hospital Nurses' Home, Archbishop's Residence alterations, Mercy Hospital Nurses' Home, Visitation Convent, St. Peter Claver's Rectory, and the Cathedral Sisters' Residence.

Henry S. Taylor White (1879–1946) was a draftsman with Baldwin & Pennington. In 1904 he formed a partnership with Howard M. Mottu (1868–1953), who had also worked in Baldwin's firm. Mottu & White designed the Baltimore Life Insurance Company building at Charles and Saratoga (1930); a post office at Hagerstown; Trinity College, at Ilchester,

Maryland; and the Church of the Messiah in Baltimore. The Second Church of Christ Scientist, at Mount Royal and St. Paul (1909), is attributed to them also. On the Eastern Shore of Maryland, Mottu & White designed the house at 115 Mill Street in Cambridge. White also designed his own home at 39 Warrenton Road, Baltimore.

Alfred Lowther Forrest was born in London in 1864, came to the United States in 1898, and worked in Boston and New York until he joined Baldwin & Pennington in 1904. He lived in Catonsville and in later years had an office of his own in the Professional Building. Among his works are an opera house in Winchester, Virginia; the Macht Building on Fayette Street (1908); and the Blue Mouse Theater (1909).

E. Francis Baldwin was obviously able to develop and maintain connections and relationships with a group of powerful and influential individuals and leaders which led to his being awarded a variety of architectural contracts and commissions. In particular, he enjoyed the association with very important client-contacts in the hierarchy of the Roman Catholic Church, the Baltimore & Ohio Railroad, and some of the leading Baltimore business, banking, industrial, and transportation firms. Some of these clients not only made contracts with Baldwin for their business or commercial ventures but also engaged him for work on their personal homes and estates.

Baldwin's links with the Catholic Church are obviously derived from his family and his own involvement in the church. He undoubtedly had a personal association with James Cardinal Gibbons, the archbishop of Baltimore from 1877 to 1921. Less well known was Baldwin's association over the years with Rt. Rev. Alfred A. Curtis, who was named bishop of Wilmington in 1886. Father Curtis had also served in high positions in the Baltimore Archdiocese. Baldwin clearly benefitted from his long-term association with the B&O Railroad and its leaders, John Work Garrett, Robert Garrett, and John K. Cowen. The Baltimore civil engineer Mendes Cohen was also a Baldwin client, as were Maj. Joseph Pangborn (the B&O's so-called promotional genius) and Henry Gassaway Davis.[7]

*Partnership with
Josias Pennington*

7. Henry Gassaway Davis worked his way up from a brakeman to a division superintendent with the B&O Railroad and went on to become an entrepreneur in West Virginia coal and timber, a railroad builder, a U.S. senator, and the 1904 Democratic candidate for vice president of the United States. He was primarily responsible for the development of Deer Park, Md., and Elkins, W.Va.

Baldwin's clients were some of the movers and shakers in the Baltimore business and commercial world and throughout Maryland, and many of them are well known to Baltimoreans and students of local and state history. These include Arunah S. Abell, Summerfield Baldwin, George Brown, Thomas Deford, J. Swan Frick, T. Harrison Garrett, James A. Gary, John Gill, John S. Gittings, T. Edward Hambleton, David Hutzler, Henry Jenkins, William Keyser, A. Leo Knott, Albert and Theodore Marburg, Thomas O'Neill, Nelson Perin, Robert Rennert, and Douglas H. Thomas.[8]

Through Bruce Price, Baldwin must have become acquainted with Lloyd Lowndes, a Cumberlander who was president of the Second National Bank there, a director of the Fidelity Trust & Deposit Company in Baltimore, and the first Republican governor of Maryland after the Civil War, from 1895 to 1899.

The "Baldwin-Frederick Imbroglio"

At the twentieth annual convention of the American Institute of Architects, held in New York City on December 1–2, 1886, Mr. George A. Frederick delivered a paper entitled "The Ethics of Architectural Practice." The paper mentions no individual by name, but it complains of an institute member who offers free drawings and reduced fees to attract potential clients and cites particularly the practice of offering "one-half commissions on all ecclesiastical work for a *certain* denomination." George Frederick, a Fellow of the AIA, has already been mentioned in the accounts of the early years of the Baltimore chapter of the AIA.[9]

8. Edward Hambleton and Nelson Perin were both major figures in building and consolidating Baltimore street-railway systems, and it would appear that both were major patrons for various carhouse commissions.

9. George Aloysius Frederick was born on December 16, 1842, in Baltimore. In 1858, at the age of sixteen, he joined the firm of Lind & Murdoch, where he began his architectural career as a draftsman and apprentice. He also reportedly was employed briefly by Niernsee & Neilson. Frederick achieved early success and everlasting fame when, at the ripe old age of nineteen, he won the design competition for the Baltimore City Hall, which was subsequently built over the period 1867–75. (Wendel Bollman designed the dome and ironwork for this building.) Frederick's work includes the Old Rennert House (1871), the Abell Building (1879), Cylburn, the Jesse Tyson mansion (1888), and the George Bauernschmidt house (1894). George Frederick retired in 1903; he died on August 17, 1924, at his home, 210 Roland Ave., and was buried in New Cathedral Cemetery in Baltimore.

Frederick was, of course, a Roman Catholic contemporary and arch-competitor of E. Francis Baldwin, the target of Frederick's attack. A Special Committee on Charges of Unprofessional Conduct concluded that "a member of the Institute has been guilty of offering his services in a case where another member was fully employed—at a rate of remuneration much below the schedule rate—and by this means not only secured the discharge from the work of the member first employed, but also, by testifying in court that the schedule rates are excessive, prevented proper compensation of the member first employed for services rendered to the date of his dismissal." While a minute of implied censure was felt to be too mild a penalty for such a serious offense against professional courtesy, the only action possible under the constitution was to request the resignation of the offending member for reasons of unprofessional practice. The committee recommended that the constitution be amended as soon as possible to enable the Board of Trustees to expel an offending member in such cases.

Baldwin was not present at the meetings in New York. He denied the charges and asked for an opportunity to disprove them. He soon responded in a letter to the editors of the *American Architect and Building News*, which was published on December 18th. Baldwin's letter, dated December 7, 1886, reads as follows:

Dear Sirs,—Appreciating your refined sense of justice and sound judgement I venture to ask of you and the members of the profession who were not present at the recent convention of the A.I.A. held in New York last week, a suspension of judgement upon the, *if truly reported*, unjust and hasty judgement passed by the convention upon me on charges preferred by a fellow member, until I have had an opportunity to disprove the acts which I scorn as I do the man who accuses me of them, and oblige,

Yours respectfully,
E. F. Baldwin

Accompanying Baldwin's letter was a letter of support from Wyatt & Sperry to the *Baltimore American*, dated December 6, 1886, noting "the utmost surprise and indignation to us and others of Mr. Baldwin's professional associates in this city" and critical that "such precipitate action should be taken by the Institute in regard to a member of such high standing as Mr. Baldwin, both as an architect and a man, without an opportunity for explanation or defence." The authors went on to state that "it is merely a public expression of our feeling in the matter, pending any more official action that the Baltimore Chapter may take later. Our opinion is shared by many others."

Frederick and the AIA seemed reluctant to explain what the real source of the controversy was. The *Baltimore Sun*, however, reported that the dispute had arisen over charges for plans for an annex to the Rock Hill College building at Ellicott City, Maryland. The newspaper went on note that the Baltimore Chapter of the AIA had sent a protest and that Josias Pennington had represented Baldwin before a board and had offered to provide affidavits from the president of the college and from the cardinal, if necessary, to prove that a charge of underbidding would not hold.

The board reportedly was of the opinion that "personal differences" had prompted the question, and their resolution not to ask for a resignation would be the end of it. But the issue was not so easily settled and forgotten. What had come to be called the "Baldwin-Frederick Imbroglio" came up again at the twenty-first annual AIA convention in Chicago, held October 19–21, 1887. George Frederick again addressed the representatives, and again Baldwin was not present. The press had been withdrawn for the closed session, so the only record is that contained in the official proceedings published by the institute. Eventually, the so-called Burnham Resolution was proposed, by the distinguished architect Daniel H. Burnham, which resolved that the Board of Trustees of the American Institute of Architects be directed to form a commission to investigate the controversy between Mr. Frederick and Mr. Baldwin and that a three-person board of arbitration be created to hear out both parties and render a finding in accordance with the facts.

Whether or not such a board of arbitration was ever convened is unknown; the issue was a controversial one within the institute. Adolph Cluss of Washington claimed to have a similar case with Baldwin, but the trustees took no action, stating that they had done as much as they could in the matter. (Cluss's animosity toward Baldwin undoubtedly stemmed from Baldwin's selection as the architect for the original building of Catholic University. Frederick may also have held a grudge over this same issue.) Some members of the AIA thought that no one person should be so singled out and made a martyr when there were other similar cases known to them.

The Baldwin-Frederick "imbroglio" eventually ground to a conclusion of sorts, though further details are unknown. An 1887 membership list of the AIA records Baldwin as an associate member in good standing. A pen-and-ink update of the membership list as of March 1888, in the AIA archives, shows a line drawn through Baldwin's name. Finally, a printed AIA membership list dated June 1, 1888, indicates that Ephraim Francis Baldwin had resigned.

This resignation did not put an end Frederick's difficulties with Baldwin, however. He lost to Baldwin in the competition in 1892 for the Maryland Building at the Chicago World's Columbian Exposition of 1893 after a protracted and complicated selection process.

One senses the undercurrents of hostility between Baldwin and Frederick even in the early 1870s. Baldwin lost out to Frederick in 1871 in a competition for a commission for St. Joseph's Hospital in Baltimore. The accounts of the interactions of the two in the AIA chapter in Baltimore are tinged with sarcasm and acrimony. The events, then, of the 1880s seem merely to be a final chapter in a saga of deep conflict and competition between two ambitious and dedicated architects struggling for professional survival in tough times. Both are probably to blame for their difficulties and the pain they inflicted on each other.

George Frederick was blessed with early success and fame for his design of the Baltimore City Hall. He may have felt the pressures of trying to live up to an early-won reputation. The glimpses we get of him suggest to this author that he was a rather vain-glorious individual, peevish and petulant, and very much taken with himself and his own importance. He tended to exaggerate his role in the design of projects in which other architects besides himself were involved.[10]

The endorsed fee schedule of the AIA was printed in the report of the Board of Trustees in the eighteenth annual convention, which was held in Albany, New York, in 1884. It suggested a 5 percent commission for "full professional services" upon the cost of the work; for "partial" services, the following scale was indicated: 1 percent for preliminary studies, 2½ percent for preliminary studies including drawings and specifications, 3½ percent

The Baldwin-Frederick "Imbroglio"

10. The "Recollections of George A. Frederick" (1912 typescript) and Frederick's drawings of many of his buildings, including structures he designed for Baltimore's parks, are at the Maryland Historical Society.

for preliminary studies, general drawings, details and specifications; warehouses and factories were at a flat 3½ percent rate. For works less than $10,000 or for "monumental and decorative work," special rates were to be in effect, regulated by special circumstances and varying according to "the skill and artistic powers" of the architect. The AIA obliged its members to adhere to the fee schedules; such adherence was, in fact, a condition of membership. The use of fee schedules by the AIA dated back to the early 1860s and was viewed as an important legal basis to prove the worth of the architect's services.

Baldwin was clearly a shrewd and capable businessman, as well as a talented architect. With his accounts with the railroads, Baltimore businesses, and banking establishments, he might well have been able and inclined to offer rates for ecclesiastical work for a particular denomination that were below the AIA's suggested scale. Baldwin might well have concluded, too, that his work on churches could fall in the category of "monumental or decorative" and that he could offer special rates at his own choosing.

Some information is available on Baldwin's notions of structured fees. An entry in one of his ledgers, dated July 1889, indicates that he and the B&O Railroad had agreed upon the following fees for his work: 5 percent of the total cost of construction for alterations to buildings; 4 percent for "new work" erected, and 3 percent for "sheds and plain work." Other kinds of work were to have what Baldwin described as "special rates." (These percentages, by the way, aid in determining the type of building involved when it no longer exists and for which there is no information other than a cost of construction.) Baldwin's work for the Western Maryland Railway was done at a commission of 3½ percent plus expenses, whereas his agreement for the Rennert Hotel was scaled to 5 percent on the first $50,000 and 4 percent on the balance of the total cost of construction.

The Pocket Notebooks

E. Francis Baldwin was a dedicated and perhaps compulsive record-keeper, if the records he left behind are any indication. His penmanship was beautiful; his ledgers and records are a pleasure to read. In addition to the office records and business ledgers, Baldwin carried a small pocket notebook with him at all times and used it to record miscellaneous information about the projects he was working on. He recorded his trips to the construction sites, notes on the progress, rail fares, drawings and sketches of portions of buildings or construction problems, computations of the cost of various buildings based on their floor area, and so on.

Baldwin also used small pocket notebooks to record personal finances and investments as well as family matters. Allowance payments, loans, and records of receipts of letters and correspondence from his children appear in these notebooks. In one book that he took with him on a European trip, he recorded the daily temperatures. He noted the dates when the boiler in his house was fired up for the winter and when it was shut down in the spring. An assortment of names and addresses of some of his family members were scattered throughout some of the notebooks. One even had a safe combination.

Some of the notebooks contain tabulations or summary lists of the work on hand at a given time or of buildings of a given type (specifically, churches). One such undated list of churches and their costs—assumed to be in dollars—is shown below.

St. Elizabeths	18,000
14 Holy Martyrs	22,000
St. Ann's, Wilmington	19,000
Cape Charles, Va.	13,000
St. Patrick's	60,000
St. Augustine's, Elkridge	
Ch. at Cambridge	5,600
Forest Glen	12,000
St. Mary's Washington	58,500
St. Gregory's	45,000
St. Anne's	57,000
Our Lady of Good Counsel	28,000

Several building and project lists were found in these small notebooks for the period 1889–1907. These lists, which provide a glimpse of the scale of the business being done at these selected points in time near the peak of Baldwin's productivity, are included in Appendix C.

Baldwin's notes and journals occasionally refer to costs of buildings and the calculations of costs based on their volume (see table). Perhaps it was an accepted tradition of the time or of the profession, but Baldwin almost consistently misused the units, citing "area" in "feet" when volume (in cubic feet) was meant. For Gibbons Hall Annex, for example, he recorded an "area" of 732,000 (actually cubic feet), and a cost estimate of 9 cents per cubic foot, for an estimated total cost of $65,880.

	Building	Area	Price per Ft.	Cost
1888	City Hospital	768,000	13½ ¢	$103,250
1886	Hotel Rennert	1,050,000	29	305,000
1892	Hotel Rennert Annex	260,000	27	270,000
1888	F & M Bank Bdg.	420,000	25	104,000
1887	Orphan Asylum	733,760	10	73,376
1883	Seminary N. Wing	482,000	9½	40,600
1891	Seminary N.W. Wing	298,000	12½	49,000
1891	St. Agnes Hospital	520,000	15	79,000
1889	Divinity Bdg.	620,000	18½	300,000
1890	St. Catherine's	201,000	10	20,300
1893	McCoy Hall	1,625,000	10	163,000
1894	Md. Gen'l. Hospital Stores	347,000	10	347,000
1886	Abell's 9&11 Howard	500,000	13	65,250
1889	Abell's 320&18 Balto	570,000	11½	65,120
1886	Jenkins			14,062
1886	Gittings German St.	720,000	8½	60,000
1893	St. V. Sanitarium	282,000	11	32,000
1893	Mt. Hope Kitchen &c.	388,600	11½	44,700
1893	Bon Secours	19,000	10	19,600

The Baltimore Fire of 1904

The Baltimore Fire of 1904

The great fire that swept through downtown Baltimore in early February of 1904 was a tragic milestone in the city's history. The fire began on Sunday morning, the seventh, and by the time it had burned itself out some thirty-six hours later, more than thirteen hundred buildings in an area of one hundred forty acres had been destroyed. The fire certainly had a major effect as well on the life and the work of E. Francis Baldwin.

Many business buildings that Baldwin & Pennington designed and built in the downtown area were destroyed. The B&O's massive headquarters building, which was barely twenty-five years old, was completely gutted and beyond restoration. (This could account for the loss of some of the drawings and records of Baldwin's work for the railroad.) Of the twenty banking, savings, and financial buildings that were severely damaged or destroyed, seven were works of Baldwin: Hopkins Place Savings Bank, Farmers & Merchants National Bank, Farmers & Planters National Bank, Maryland Trust Company, Merchants National Bank, National Bank of Commerce, and National Union Bank.

Though the Maryland Trust (the Guardian) Building on Redwood and Calvert Streets suffered considerable damage, it was restored. Hopkins Place and Merchants National were completely gutted but were rebuilt. The Farmers & Merchants Bank building was a total loss and was replaced by a totally new structure. On the other hand, some Baldwin buildings did survive, the most significant of which was the Safe Deposit & Trust building on South Street. It met its eventual end, however, when a high-rise was built on the site.

The foremost consequence of the fire for Baldwin & Pennington was that it totally destroyed their architectural offices, which were then located on the fifth floor of the Farmers & Merchants Bank building on the NW corner of South and Lombard Streets, near the center of the "burnt district" (fig. 5). The architects found temporary office space in a building at 311 North Charles for about a year; then they moved to the fifth floor of the American Building for the next year, and finally to the suite on the sixth floor of the Professional Building at 330 North Charles—a building that they designed themselves.

There apparently was time, however, for the architects to get to their office before the eastward-moving fire reached the building on Sunday night. Critical records were saved, but very few of the drawings. Baldwin's personal records contain a listing of the drawings that were saved, but unfortunately the whereabouts of these drawings is unknown and they are now presumed to be lost forever.

Fig. 5. South and Lombard Streets, Baltimore, 1904

Some insight into the circumstances surrounding the probable rescue of Baldwin's drawings comes from an article in the *Sun* a few years after the fire. The Hutzler company reportedly had engaged Baldwin & Pennington to prepare plans for an annex to their Palace Building on North Howard Street, and Hutzler's general manager had returned the plans to the architects' office only the day before the fire. It was reported that the plans were among those taken to an unidentified warehouse on North Avenue on Sunday night and that they were later used to build the annex to the store.

A hand-written tabulation entitled "Drawings Saved from Fire, Feb. 1904" was found in Baldwin's personal notes and records. For each of the seventeen buildings in this list, the nature of the surviving drawings—scale, detail, original, or blueprint—was itemized. The entries are:

—Merchant's Nat. Bank
—National Union Bank
—Hambleton & Co.
—Fidelity Building
—O'Neill & Co Store
—Rev. E. J. Horning
—Md. State Building
—Soldiers Home
—Baltimore City College
—Bank of Commerce
—Farmers & Merchants
—Guardian Building
—Safe Deposit & Trust Co.
—Hutzler Bros.

—Wheeling Depot
—Md. State House
—German Savings Bank

Everything on the list is familiar except for the reference to Rev. Horning [sic], which may pertain to St. Wenceslaus Bohemian Church or its rectory or school building. A footnote specifically noted the loss of all drawings of the Maryland Club—perhaps an indication of the significance of this particular building to the architect.

A few of Baldwin's drawings have survived, scattered about in various public and private collections. The Smithsonian Institution has drawings of a number of his Maryland railroad stations: Boyds, Brunswick, Brooklyn, Hagerstown, Hyattsville, Ilchester, and Woodstock, as well as a large office building for the B&O at Locust Point. The B&O Railroad Museum in Baltimore has drawings of Gaithersburg's station and freight house, the station at Skagg's, and the "signal cabin" at Bailey (on the corner of Ostend and Eutaw, Baltimore). The B&O Museum also has Baldwin's drawings for the very buildings it is housed in—the Mount Clare Passenger Car House and the Library.

The Catholic University archives has drawings of its first two main buildings, Caldwell and McMahon Halls. St. Vincent's Seminary in Germantown, Pennsylvania, has some of the drawings of its buildings and church. The Sulpician Archives in Catonsville is a repository for Baldwin's work on St. Mary's Seminary on North Paca Street and the Chapel at Mount St. Mary's College in Emmitsburg.

A list (which appears to be in Bruce Price's handwriting) of "drawings saved in a chest" was found in one of the ledgers and hints at the tantalizing possibility of a collection of drawings. The location of this mysterious chest and its contents is unknown. The list of drawings in the chest includes some of Baldwin and Price's earliest works:

—St. Vincent's Seminary, Germantown, Pa.
—W. Lee, Stables and Conservatory
—School House, Cumberland, Md.
—Grace Church, Lexington, Va.
—Mrs. S. Hillen
—P. de Murguiondo
—Jones Falls and Balto City P. Railway Co.
—St. Augustine's Church, Washington
—M. H. Bogne[11]

11. Of the works and names on this list, all but this one are known or familiar clients or buildings, and most of these are described in more detail elsewhere in this volume.

—William Kennedy

—Savannah Cathedral, Savannah, Ga.

—John Gill, 35 W. Eager St., Balto.

—John S. Gittings, Richmond and Cathedral Sts.

—Burwell Bank, Richmond St.

—W. M. Price

—Baldwin and Holland

—Safe Deposit Company

—James E. Tyson, Eutaw Pl.

—A. A. White, Madison Ave.

—Henry Tyson

—Keyser Bros. and Co.

—Christ Church, Baltimore

—Saint Ann's Church

—St. Agnes Hospital, Balto. County

—James Forbes

Laurence Sangston, an architect who worked in the New York offices of Pennington & Lewis in 1927 and 1928, recalled that at that time Josias's son had the drawings or blueprints for the Maryland State buildings at Annapolis. Over the years, Mr. Sangston, who later became an architect for the State of Maryland, has searched for these important drawings, but without success.

The Ones That Got Away: Proposals

Architects in the last century lived in a highly competitive world—as they do today—and from time to time even the best of them lost out in competitive bids on building projects and commissions. Baldwin, Price, and Pennington were no exceptions. There were instances in which these architects' designs never got past the drawing board and design stage.

We get glimpses of the clients and contracts that got away from the various accounts in the newspapers of the day, from the architectural trade journals, and from the architect's personal records. In addition to losing out on competitive bids, architects knew that some projects would not reach fruition because a client changed his mind, for personal or professional reasons, or could not secure the necessary fundings.

George A. Frederick was the architect for St. Joseph's Hospital, located on the corner of Caroline and Hoffman Streets in Baltimore. Built by John Stack, this 80-by-170 foot, three-story facility opened in late 1872. Its cornerstone was laid on October 8, 1871, so the bidding and competition would have taken place a year or so earlier. St. Joseph's Hospital was included, however, on the list of drawings that J. Appleton Wilson compiled of drawings he had prepared while working with Baldwin & Price.

Though the date is not given, one can only conclude that Baldwin & Price lost out in a competition to Frederick; if true, this was their first significant loss. This could have been the origin of the ill will between Baldwin and Frederick that led to unfortunate ends nearly twenty years later.

The next "failure" was one that was not the architect's fault. Baldwin and Price submitted a proposal to the city of Cumberland for a "Market House and City Hall." According to the *Alleganian* of December 20, 1871, Baldwin & Price submitted a $50,000 building proposal. A man named Gorsuch had one for $46,000 and Frank E. Davis submitted two ($40,000 and $50,000).[12] No award was made, however, and the city dropped or postponed the project. (The newspaper noted the following June that the city was bankrupt and taxes would have to be increased.)

On October 14, 1871, Bruce Price wrote to H. I. Johnson in Cumberland, tendering his services as architect for the Academy of Music building there. Price proposed to make the necessary design drawings and to take his chances for compensation with the success of the building. In January 1872 Price sent his drawings for the proposed "opera house" to his father, William M. Price. His efforts came to naught.

The Academy of Music building, which was erected in 1876 on Centre Street in downtown Cumberland, was designed by Frank E. Davis and built by J. B. Walter of Baltimore. It was a four-story Second Empire-style structure with a farmer's market on the ground floor, city offices, a 1,300-seat theater, and a lodge hall on the top floor. This building was destroyed by a fire on March 14, 1910.

At the request of John Gittings, a proposal for plans, detail drawings, specifications, and superintendence of the construction of "improvements" to be erected at the corner of Charles and Centre Streets was submitted on April 13, 1872. Dixon & Carson won the job for the building, which became the St. James Hotel.

12. Francis Earlougher Davis was born in Ellicott City in 1839, apprenticed under Edmund Lind, and worked for a time as a partner with Thomas Dixon. He was elected to membership in the Baltimore chapter of the AIA in December 1870. Among his familiar works are the Western Police Station in Baltimore (1871), St. Michael's Church Convent, the Bayview Insane Asylum, Clifton School, the Montgomery County Courthouse, and Christ Episcopal Church in Rockville, all on the National Register of Historic Places. Davis died in Los Angeles in 1921. The other architect was probably Daniel Henning Gorsuch of Baltimore, who had worked in Norris G. Starkweather's office.

In July 1879 Baldwin received an invitation from Charles D. Fisher, chairman of the Building Committee, to submit plans for the new Corn & Flour Exchange Building. Baldwin was to be teamed with the firm of Wyatt & Sperry, in a competition with Niernsee & Neilson and Mr. Miller from Chicago. Fisher agreed to pay each competitor $125. Baldwin began work on the plans by mid-July. Niernsee won, and the building, known as the Chamber of Commerce Building, was built on the corner of Holliday and Second Streets.

In mid-1884, Baldwin & Pennington entered the competition for the Mercantile Trust & Deposit Company building to be erected on the NE corner of German and Calvert Streets. They received $200 for their effort, losing out to Wyatt & Sperry, who saw the building to its completion in 1886.

Baldwin & Pennington prepared plans for the A. F. Dulin Warehouse, which was to be constructed on Garrett Alley at Howard Street. It must have been a fairly large structure, because the plans cost $360. But the lot was sold and the Dulin warehouse was never built.

Baldwin & Pennington entered the 1892 competition, against five other firms, for the design of the Baltimore Auditorium, to be built on the corner of Cathedral Street and Mount Royal Avenue. Drawings were prepared with the understanding that the architects would be paid $200 if they were not accepted. Baldwin received his money on June 29; the *Sun* announced the selection of Griffin & Randall of New York as the winners. The other losing architects were Carrere & Hastings, Bruce Price, Wyatt & Nolting, and J. A. Wilson.

In 1893, Baldwin & Pennington prepared plans, sketches, and cost estimates for the Maryland Life Insurance Company building, which was to be built at 8–10 South Street. They received $100 for their efforts but lost to Baldwin's former pupil, Joseph Evans Sperry.

The *Architects and Builders Journal* cited proposals by the firm of Baldwin & Pennington in 1901–2. These included a two-story building for Crook, Horner & Co., Saratoga Street; a residence for William A. House, General Manager, UR&E; a new chapel for St. Mary's Seminary; and the Polish Catholic church at Chesapeake and O'Donnel Streets.

In 1903, Baldwin & Pennington competed against ten other architectural firms for the commission on the new United States Custom House, which was to be built in Baltimore. This was the fifth building in which architects outside the U.S.

government were engaged to design large public buildings. A congressional act authorized the Secretary of the Treasury to invite submissions of drawings in a competition to be judged by a jury drawn from the ranks of practicing architects. At the suggestion of the Treasury Department, the competitors agreed that the winner would pay $500 to each of the losing competitors. Hornblower & Marshall won. The losers, in addition to Baldwin & Pennington, were Charles E. Cassell, Ernest Flagg, Ellicott & Emmart, J. E. Sperry, Jackson C. Gott, Wyatt & Nolting, Frank Miles Day & Bro., S. S. Beman, and Winston, Wetherell & Bigelow. Construction of the Custom House was begun in 1903 and completed in 1908.

The drawings that Baldwin & Pennington prepared for the Custom House included front and rear elevations, side view and cross-section, a basement plan, and plans for the first and second floors. These drawings, along with those of the other competitors, were on display in 1900 at the Baltimore Architecture Club (the Charcoal Club). All of the drawings were later sent to the "T-Square Club" in Philadelphia for another viewing there.

Baldwin & Pennington prepared drawings in 1904 of new buildings for the Egenton Female Orphan Asylum, which was to be built near Roland and Merryman Avenues in Baltimore. A Baldwin & Pennington sketch of the proposed structure, which was exhibited in the Baltimore Architectural Club, is in the AIA archives. (J. A. Wilson also competed for this job and lost.)

In 1905, Baldwin & Pennington were unsuccessful in the competition for the design of the Maryland Institute, on the corner of Lanvale Street and Mount Royal Avenue. The building was expected to cost about $350,000. All competitors were given a standard set of prescribed floor plans, so the designs were only for the exterior. The drawings for the front elevations for all the entries, which were all quite similar, were published in the May 1905 issue of *American Architect and Building News*. The design by Pell & Corbett was selected. The other entrants were Davis & Davis, Rankin, Kellogg & Crane, Martin C. Muller, and Owens & Sisko. Also in 1905, Parker & Thomas won a competition over Baldwin & Pennington and Hiss & Weeks for a laboratory and a museum building for the Johns Hopkins University.

Personal Matters and Family Life

During the 1850s and 1860s, Baldwin lived with his mother at various locations (132 Madison and 57 W.

Biddle Streets) in Baltimore. In the *Baltimore City Directory* for 1872 he was listed at 50 McMechen Street; a year later (after the death of his mother on August 10, 1872), at 57 Mosher Street.

On May 1, 1873, thirty-five-year-old Ephraim Francis Baldwin was united in marriage to Ellen Douglas Jamison of Baltimore. The twenty-one-year-old bride, born on November 11, 1851, was a daughter of William Douglas Jamison, a surgeon in the United States Marine Corps and a great-grandson of George Mason of Virginia. In January 1874, Baldwin purchased a house at 198 Division Street from John Anderson for $3,000. He and his wife lived here for the next six years. (The house, which was renumbered to 1534, was retained by Baldwin for rental income until at least 1894.) In 1881, the Baldwins moved to 359 (later renumbered to 1524) Druid Hill Avenue, where they would reside for more than twenty years. This row house was one of four that the young architect had designed and built a few years earlier. The Baldwins were devout Roman Catholics and they joined the congregation of the Church of the Immaculate Conception, located just a short distance away, on Mosher and McMechen Streets.

Seven sons and two daughters were born to the Baldwins (fig. 6) over a twenty-one-year period: Francis Joseph (1874–1963), Mary Elizabeth (1876–1948), William Douglas (1878–1935), Alonzo Charles (1881–1957), Joseph Aloysius (1883–1959), Thomas Abbott (1885–1973), Ellen Douglas (1889–1962), Lau-

rence Aloysius (1892–1966), and Eugene Francis (1895–1975).

Only the first-born son, Frank, followed in his father's footsteps in architecture. The daughters never married. William was a businessman. Alonzo became a Vincentian priest. Laurence married a granddaughter of the contractor John Stack. The youngest child, Eugene, lived in Baltimore and was engaged in the construction business.[13]

Outside of his business and professional work, relatively little is known about E. Francis Baldwin as an individual. In his politics, Baldwin was reportedly a Democrat. His obituary notice mentioned that he enjoyed swimming, driving and riding horses, and motoring. Religion was obviously an important, perhaps central, element in his life, ranking with his family and his work. It has also been reported that he was a personal friend of Cardinal Gibbons (1834–1921), the renowned prelate. Baldwin was

13. The contractor and builder John Stack (1828–1907) was responsible for the erection of many of Baldwin's works. His sons became partners in his firm, which was located for many years at 250 W. Preston St. Stack was active from the 1860s and also built structures designed by Niernsee, George Frederick, and other contemporaries of Baldwin. Those buildings include St. Mary's Star of the Sea (L. I. O'Connor, architect, 1871); St. Joseph Hospital (Frederick, 1872); St. Thomas Church, Hampden (1874); Episcopal Church of the Atonement, Preston and Chester St. (J. A. & W. T. Wilson, architects, 1895).

awarded a gold medal—the Bene Merenti—by Pope Leo XIII in 1889 for his work on the first buildings at the newly founded Catholic University. Baldwin was a member of the Loyola Alumni Association, the St. Vincent de Paul Society, and the Young Catholic's Friend Society.

An interesting glimpse into what Baldwin's early life and work were like is obtained from portions of a letter he wrote in 1876 to his uncle, William Elder, then a bishop in Cincinnati:

> Father Rolando told me Sunday that he had seen you and my uncles in New Orleans but a short time ago. I hear that Uncle Basil and family are in great distress fearing every day that their furniture would be sold for rent and they be turned out of a home. Basil has no employment and the girls can get little or nothing to do.

Fig. 7. Ephraim Francis Baldwin, circa 1914.
Eugene F. Baldwin

> What are they coming to! Times are so bad now that the few of us are able to spare anything to help one another. My business has been good but at present I have scarcely any work in the office and no more this summer unless from unexpected sources. Still I will try to send them a little assistance. Julia is well and always busy in the church. My little boy is near 26 months old, bright and well but cannot talk yet. Pray for him and send him and *all* of us your blessing. My wife joins me in much love and many thanks for your affectionate blessing.
>
> Your afft nephew
> E. Francis Baldwin

After the 1870s, Baldwin's business and personal investments improved. His records show an active and steady accumulation of wealth through stocks, bonds, and rental properties from the 1880s onward. From 1908 to 1912, for example, he recorded total monthly rents of $700–800 on some twenty dwellings. Many of these properties—on Druid Hill Avenue, Carey Street, and Mosher Street—he had owned for twenty years or more. A 1910 summary of his personal financial assets in bonds, property, insurance, and accounts in his children's names amounted to over $218,000. His stock and bond holdings tended to be in utilities and streetcar or railroad lines, many going back to the 1880s.

In August 1911, Baldwin purchased a new automobile from the Baldwin-Chandlee Supply Company for $852. (This company was co-owned by his son William, who also owned a supply company in Elkins, West Virginia). He carefully recorded—to the penny—the total expenditures on gasoline, oil, repairs, parts, accessories, and licenses for himself and Laurence for the rest of the year.

A tally of letters that Baldwin received in the period 1908–11 is interesting. His son Abbott, who was in his mid-20s at the time, apparently moved a lot and wrote to his father at the rate of one to four times a month, while the older sons, Douglas and Alonzo, wrote less frequently. The other children must have been living at home or very close by because they are rarely listed. The many letters received from his wife and youngest sons, Laurence and Eugene, during August suggest that they were vacationing at that time outside of Baltimore. One gets the impression that Baldwin did not take many vacations and that he traveled only as necessary for his work.

In 1904, the Baldwins moved from their inner-city rowhouse on Druid Hill Avenue to a larger house in the Dixon Park section of Mount Washington, an upper-northwest suburb of the city. The architect of his house on the north side of Poplar Avenue (now 1808 Dixon Road) is not known, and it seems curious that Baldwin did not design a new house for himself at a time when he could well afford to do so and as many other architects of his time were wont to do. In Mount Washington, the Baldwins became members of the congregation of Sacred Heart Church, just a few blocks down the hill from their home.

It is fitting—and perhaps poetic—that the Sacred Heart Church was Baldwin's last project. Baldwin was reported to have been working on the drawings and plans for a new church building on Saturday, January 15, 1916, when he contracted the illness that would prove fatal. He was supposedly working in front of an open window in his office in the Professional Building and caught a cold. He repaired to his home that day, but his condition progressively worsened. Ephraim Francis Baldwin died at 2 A.M., on Thursday, January 20 (fig. 7).

Baldwin was survived by his wife and children and four grandchildren. Funeral services were held on January 22 in Sacred Heart Church, and he was laid to rest in the Baldwin family plot in New Cathedral Cemetery, Baltimore (sec. H, lot 268). His wife died nearly twenty years after her husband, on March 16, 1935. She and some of their children were also buried in the family plot.

PART II

THE B&O AND OTHER RAILWAY PROJECTS

❧ CHAPTER 2 ❧

Victorian
Railroad Stations

In terms of sheer numbers, railroad stations alone account for almost a quarter of the structures that E. Francis Baldwin designed during his long career, and though railroad stations may have contributed but a small fraction of his earned income over the years, the work was appreciable and significant in the stage of his career in which it was done. In many respects, the Baltimore & Ohio Railroad was a bread-and-butter client for Baldwin in the early years and in the lean 1870s. Thus, it is appropriate for objective, as well as subjective, reasons to begin the discussion and review of Baldwin's works with the Victorian-era railroad stations, and specifically with the stations built for the B&O.

The Baltimore & Ohio Railroad

The hundred-plus B&O stations that Baldwin designed can be classified relatively simply and reasonably. I have divided the major groups as follows: (1) railroad station–hotels, (2) brick stations of the 1870s, (3) early wood-frame stations, (4) brick stations of the 1880s, (5) a late series of frame stations, and (6) the "Richardsonian" style stone stations of the late 1880s and the 1890s. Stations originally designed by other architects for which Baldwin designed significant additions or modifications over the years are also included.

Station-Hotels

The concept of station-hotels was common in Europe but less so in the United States, especially in the East. Herbert Harwood points out that in the early years of U.S. railroads, before the widespread use of sleepers and diners, railroad station–hotels were built at some major way points, but they were less necessary by the 1870s, and Garrett's station-hotel program for the B&O (which also included

several lesser station-hotels in Ohio) was a bit of an anachronism by this date.

Relay Station–Viaduct House (fig. 8) was a very early—if not the first—Baldwin project for the B&O. This hotel complex was built in 1872 at the north end of the massive stone Thomas Viaduct over the Patapsco River near Elkridge. Any doubts as to Baldwin's association with this Gothic station-hotel are dispelled when one considers a list of drawings prepared by the architect J. Appleton Wilson. This list, in the Maryland Historical Society collection, cites the buildings that Wilson drew while employed by various architects. It explicitly cites "Viaduct Hotel, Relay" and an attribution to E. F. Baldwin. (Other buildings on the list included St. Ann's Church, the Savannah cathedral, St. Joseph's Hospital, the Deer Park Hotel, the Silver Spring railroad station, Elevator A and the Coffee Warehouse at Locust Point, and a B&O repair shop in Cumberland—all attributed to Baldwin.)

Construction of Relay Station–Viaduct House (also sometimes called the Washington Junction Hotel and Station) was begun in July 1872. The B&O annual report of 1873 provided a detailed description and an announcement that it would open in October of that year:

It is a station and hotel combined, built in the gothic style, of Patapsco granite, with red Seneca stone trimmings; it consists of a main building 55 feet by 70 feet, three stories high, with rooms in the roof of wings, and a station building 43 by 52 feet, two stories high, the second story being constructed with the hotel. The whole is covered with a slate roof of variegated colors and patterns and finished with iron crestings and finials. The waiting room is 23 by 40 feet, and the dining room 25 feet by 50 feet.

The building is heated by steam and lighted by gas manufactured on the site.

The B&O's expenditures reported for this project in 1872 and 1873 were $7,721 and $50,078, respectively. The B&O station was closed in November 1938; the Viaduct Hotel was demolished in 1950.

Queen City Hotel. It is rigorously correct to state that E. Francis Baldwin was the architect for a number of additions and modifications to the magnificent B&O station-hotel in Cumberland, Maryland (fig. 9). But it is also possible that he had more to do with its original design than is generally known. Others have claimed that the Queen City Hotel was designed by a virtually unknown individual by the name of Thomas Heskett, who was presumed to be on the B&O's engineering staff of the Road Department and whose signature appeared on an 1864 drawing for a bridge at Harpers Ferry, West Virginia. Baldwin, however, seems more likely as the architect for this station-hotel. According to the *Cumberland Alleganian*, an official visit was made to Cumberland in 1872 to discuss the landscaping of the grounds of the then nearly completed structure. The visitors named were Mr. Keyser (a B&O vice

president), Mr. Bolling (an engineer), Mr. Wilkinson (a "landscape gardener"), and Mr. Baldwin, the architect of the company.[1] (Interestingly, no mention was made of Heskett, who might have been only a local construction superintendent.)

After a decade-long struggle by Cumberlanders and various preservation groups, the Queen City Hotel was demolished over a four-month period in late 1971, just short of its centenary. (Its construction had begun in July 1871 and it was opened on November 11, 1872.)

Brick Stations of the 1870s

According to the Montgomery County *Sentinel*, when the B&O's Metropolitan Branch (from Washington, D.C., to Point of Rocks, Maryland) opened in May of 1873, stations were to be built at nine locations. At four of these—Rockville, Silver Spring,

1. Bolling may actually be Wendel Bollman. Herbert Harwood agrees that it is possible that Bollman was the engineer. He points out that while Bollman had resigned from the B&O many years earlier he did occasionally work for the B&O, building bridges on the Cumberland-Connellsville line in the early 1870s. The landscaper is probably John Wilkinson, of Baltimore.

Fig. 9. Queen City Hotel, Cumberland, Maryland. *Smithsonian Institution, Transportation Collection*

Germantown, and Dickerson—so-called first-class brick stations, 53 by 41 feet and two stories high with slate roofs, were to be built. For various reasons, however, only two were ever built as advertised.

Rockville Station (plate 1) was built first, in late 1873. It was also the first in the series of brick stations that Baldwin designed in the 1870s. The Rockville station is still standing, though it was moved a few dozen feet in 1981 to avoid destruction when the Metro subway station was built. Restored and in use as an office, it is on the National Register of Historic Places.

Silver Spring Station was a mirror image of the Rockville station. Built in 1878, it was demolished in 1944. These stations have been described as "Ruskinian Gothic," with pointed arch windows, jerkin-head roofs, and variegated polychrome slate roof tiles, pierced by dormers and octagonal chimneys.

The designs of the Rockville and Silver Spring stations bear a remarkable resemblance to the 1869 stone station that the Philadelphia architect Joseph M. Wilson designed for the Pennsylvania Railroad at Bryn Mawr, Pennsylvania. (Wilson was an 1858 graduate of Rensselaer Polytechnic Institute and the architect of the Baltimore & Potomac station, which stood on the SW corner of Constitution Avenue

and Sixth Street NW, where the National Gallery of Art is now.) The Bryn Mawr freight house is still standing, and it too shows so many similarities that one is compelled to suggest that Baldwin copied Wilson's designs for both the station and the freight house at Rockville.

Point of Rocks. In 1875 Baldwin designed the imposing and photogenic station (cover) still standing at this junction of the Metropolitan Branch and the Main Stem from Baltimore. Its salient feature is the high square tower, steeplelike in appearance. Like Rockville, it has the arched windows, decorative brackets and bargeboards, dormers, and polychrome slate jerkin-head roof. This station received special attention in the B&O's annual report, but no mention was made of its architect:

At Point of Rocks a new station, with accommodations on the second floor for residence of the Agent, and a freight house adjoining, 25 by 50 feet, has been erected and is now occupied. The station is built of pressed brick, with trimmings of light Ohio and brown stone, covered with an ornamental slate roof, and contains on the first floor a waiting room, 18 feet by 27 feet 10 inches; ladies' room, 11 feet 2 inches by 12 feet; ticket office, 11 feet 2 inches by 13 feet 10 inches. On the second floor are five chambers, with a kitchen over part of the warehouse, besides a fine store room in the tower, which is finished with a signal lantern, forming an attractive feature in the building. It is a handsome and commodious station.

The warehouse section of the station is believed to be the predecessor station. The available Baldwin records do not contain accounts of the 1875 work, but they do show later work at Point of Rocks. There is a reference to a "signal tower" here in the early 1890s as well as "station alterations" amounting to $1,236 in 1896.

The Point of Rocks station was closed on July 2, 1962. It still stands, however, recently refurbished in cream and black trim. It was added to the National Register in 1973. Seeing it now, it is hard to imagine that it was struck by lightning in the late afternoon of June 27, 1931, and gutted. Everlasting credit is due the officials of the B&O who ordered the full restoration of the station.

Keyser, West Virginia's B&O station (fig. 10), was later attributed to Baldwin. Built in 1875, the annual report for that year described it as a 48-by-

25-foot building, two stories in height, with a 32-by-33-foot wing in the rear, built of red brick with bands and arches of yellow brick. This station is still standing, and plans were begun by a local group in 1999 to restore it.

Hancock (Brosius). Baldwin probably designed the B&O station for Hancock, Maryland, which actually stands on the other side of the Potomac River in Brosius, West Virginia. It is a one-story freight and passenger depot, 25'-8" by 51'-10", built in 1876. Baldwin's records show his work on minor alterations at a cost of $269.

Mount Airy Station (fig. 11), built in 1876, was described as a one-story brick freight depot, 25'-8" by 51'-10". The station was extended at both ends in 1882. Still standing, it has been nicely restored and is now used as a commercial building.

The station in **Paw Paw**, West Virginia (fig. 12), is interesting because it has a jerkin-head roof and a vague similarity to the Rockville station. The 1882 B&O annual report states that "at Paw Paw a new station 36 feet by 60 feet, one story, 14 feet 3 inches high, brick, with a slate roof has been built." Remarkably, the station is still standing.

The **Charles Town**, West Virginia, station was described in the annual report of 1880: "Brick with

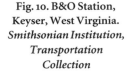
Fig. 10. B&O Station, Keyser, West Virginia. *Smithsonian Institution, Transportation Collection*

Fig. 11. B&O Station,
Mount Airy, Maryland

Fig. 12. B&O Station,
Paw Paw, West Virginia.
*Smithsonian Institution,
Transportation
Collection*

black mortar; Cheat River stone trim, variegated slate roof crowned with a wood and slate ventilator. It is 57 feet long by 21 feet deep, with a general waiting room, 19 feet by 20 feet, a ladies' room 17 feet by 21 feet, a ticket office 10 feet by 17 feet, an express office 10 feet by 17 feet, and a porch in front, 10 feet by 57 feet, covering the platform." This station has been demolished.

Early Frame Stations

The B&O annual report of 1873 mentions that "a small frame station house was built at **Scagg's Crossing**, 14 by 20 feet, one story high." Drawings of this very station, which was located where Branchville, Maryland, is now, are preserved in the B&O Museum archives in Baltimore and bear the name of E. Francis Baldwin.

On the basis of timing and structural similarities, we can assume that a number of the B&O stations erected in Maryland in the 1870s and 1880s are also attributable to Baldwin. These include **Deer Park Hotel** (1873), **Savage** (1875), **Muirkirk** (1875), **Elkridge** (1875), **Germantown** (1877), **Mount Winans** (1877), **Annapolis Junction** (1877), **Halpine** (1878), **Bridewell** (1880), **Hanover** (1880), **Tuscarora** (1882), **Linden** (1887), **Derwood** (1877 and 1887), and **Brentwood** (1888). These stations were typically of board-and-batten construction with a metal roof. Most had a sort of Baldwin trademark decorative finial (acroterion) and scrollwork (bargeboards

or vergeboards, sometimes referred to as "carpenter's lace" or "jig-saw gingerbread").

The B&O annual report for 1873 described the **Deer Park Hotel Station**: "The large number of persons attached to the hotel at this place demanded proper railway station accommodations: accordingly a station house was built at a convenient point. This building is 28 by 57 feet, one-story high, and contains a general waiting room 27 feet by 32 feet 6 inches. A ladies' room 13 feet 3 inches by 23 feet, a baggage room 13 feet 3 inches by 14 feet, ticket office 8 feet by 13 feet 3 inches, and a telegraph office 5 feet 6 inches by 9 feet. It has a slate roof, a projecting hood on ornamental brackets for the protection of passengers against the weather, and is a neat and convenient structure. The expenditure on this account was $2,937." This station has been destroyed.

Two stations—probably both designed by Baldwin—were built at **Derwood**. The first was a 10-by-14-foot "waiting shed," erected in 1877. The second, 16 by 20 feet and built in 1887, was nearly identical to the stations constructed at about the same time at Linden and earlier at Hanover, Maryland (fig. 13). It was destroyed in a fire on June 7, 1952.

Brick Stations of the 1880s

In the relatively short period from 1883 to 1887, Baldwin designed a series of brick stations that are distinctively different from those of the previous decade. This burst of productivity came at a time when the B&O was expanding its service, and stations were being built or upgraded throughout the company's rail system.

The brick stations of the 1880s are fondly thought of as examples of quintessential Baldwin designs. They remind one of the stations of the same period designed by the more eccentric architect, Frank Furness of Philadelphia, though the stations that Baldwin designed are "toned down" from what Furness might have done. Each of these Baldwin stations is unique, while sharing many common design features and dimensions with one another, as if they had been assembled from collection of standard parts. Half of these stations are still standing; many are on the National Register.

Probably the first station of this series was the one erected in **Terra Alta**, West Virginia, in 1883. The B&O annual report for that year described it as follows: "At Terra Alta a new depot has been built of brick with a slate roof and a stone foundation, containing a general waiting room 16'-6" by 20', a ladies waiting room 15' by 21', a freight room 18' by 21'-6", and a telegraph office 10' by 21'-6"." This station was damaged by a fire in April 1992; it was razed in 1999 by CSX at the request of the City Council.

In November 1883, the Valley Railroad from Harrisonburg was extended down the Shenandoah Valley to **Lexington**, Virginia (fig. 14). (The Valley Railroad was an aborted B&O-financed project that John Garrett intended to use as an entry into the Deep South.) This large, 22-by-142-foot brick station has a massive, transversely positioned central gable. The date of its construction appears in the pediment of this gable. This station is still standing.

Staunton Station, on the Valley Railroad, does not appear in the available Baldwin records, but its design clearly warrants its inclusion in the list. This B&O station was built circa 1884, probably to replace the smaller 1876-vintage station, when the Staunton to Lexington trackage was completed; it is no longer standing.

According to the B&O annual report for 1883, a 30-by-102-foot passenger depot, with a slate roof and terra cotta trimming, was constructed in **Zanesville**, an eastern Ohio town. There is no hard evidence that Baldwin personally designed this station, but its general appearance and detailing strongly suggest that it was built according to a Baldwin design. It seems reasonable to assume that the B&O simply used or adapted one of Baldwin's plans and that a local architect or a railroad employee supervised construction. The brickwork was by C. P. Evans of Philadelphia; the stonework was by Jacob Young. The Zanesville station, on the National Register of Historic Places, was demolished in late 1998.

Detailed working drawings by E. F. Baldwin of the brick B&O station in **Woodstock**, Maryland, are in the Smithsonian collection, dated 1883. The B&O annual report for 1884 notes its construction as a one-story building, 14 feet high, measuring 60'-9"

The Baltimore & Ohio Railroad

Fig. 14. B&O Station, Lexington, Virginia. *Edward H. Weber*

by 18'-6". The date shown in the gable in the drawings is 1884.

The Woodstock station was one of seven stations that were announced in the 1884 report as being under construction or completed. The other brick stations mentioned were at Sykesville, Duffields, Gaithersburg, Summit Point, and Oakland. The remaining station, at Mountain Lake Park, was not brick, but all of these stations were designed by Baldwin.

The station in **Sykesville** (plate 2) is a large asymmetric brick building, 85 feet long and 18 to 26 feet wide. The central section was two and one-half stories high with an agent's office, waiting room, and lavatory on the first floor and a stationmaster's apartment above. The east section was an office or waiting room; the west end a warehouse or baggage room. The station was placed on the National Register and has been adaptively restored for use as a restaurant—"Baldwin's Station and Pub"—appropriately named after the architect.

The **Hyattsville** station (fig. 15) was one of the larger varieties in this series of Baldwin stations. The main building was 25 by 30 feet, with a tall domed tower in one corner. A frame waiting shed, 33 by 49 feet, was attached at one end. The station opened in August 1884. The following year a small companion brick freight house was built nearby. The entire station no longer stands, though it appears that a portion of it may be imbedded in a structure that is still standing.

The station and matching freight house at **Gaithersburg** (plate 3), the mid-point on the Metropolitan Branch, was built in mid-1884 on land purchased from the prominent engineer William Rich Hutton. Baldwin's original drawings for these structures are in the B&O Museum archives in Baltimore. The original station was a symmetric structure with a cruciform floor configuration, 44'-4" long by 21'-8" wide. Identical waiting rooms flanked the office on both ends. The red brick building with slate roof is set off by a high peaked transverse gable over the central agent's office. The building has elaborate brick dentil work, a massive corbeled chimney, and fish-scale shingles on the curved recessive end gables. The east end of the station was extended near the turn of the century to form a baggage room, and the new end wall faithfully reproduced the architect's original designs. Gaithersburg station, which is on the National Register, serves today as a rail commuter station.

Hazelwood, a unique and ornate station near Pittsburgh, bears such a strong resemblance to the Gaithersburg station that it had to be a Baldwin design. The feature that made this station so unusual was the very large, transverse second-story living quarters over the central office. Built in the mid-1880s, it is no longer standing.

Fig. 15. B&O Station, Hyattsville, Maryland. *Smithsonian Institution, Transportation Collection*

McKeesport, another Pennsylvania station, about fifteen miles from Pittsburgh, has been attributed to Baldwin on the basis of its appearance. Built in the mid-1880s, it is no longer standing.

The station in **Morgantown**, West Virginia, was very much like the Terra Alta station. It is still standing, though it is barely recognizable as an original Baldwin design: Its upper gables have been removed and the overhanging roof has been shorn off and replaced with a hip roof.

Duffields (fig. 16). The 1884 station at this small West Virginia stop about six rail miles west of Harpers Ferry was 40 feet long and 18 feet wide. It bears a strong resemblance to the Gaithersburg station, though Duffields (or Duffield's) is a "combination" type station (with a central office flanked on one end by a baggage or freight room and a passenger waiting room at the other).

Laurel Station (plate 4), on the Washington Branch midway between Baltimore and Washington, is nearly identical to the Gaithersburg station in its basic dimensions and plan. This is not immediately evident because of the station's setting on a fill adjacent to an underpass and because the roof design is markedly different. This station has been on the National Register for some time. It suffered from a serious fire a few years ago and has been repaired, but it was not restored to its original specifications.

Summit Point Station, a few miles from Winchester on the Valley Railroad, was 78 by 25 feet, according to the B&O annual report for 1884. It no longer stands.

Oakland (plate 5), in Garrett County, in Western Maryland, was completed in 1885 and is probably one of the largest of this series of brick stations. It has a two and one-half story center section, featuring a circular tower with a domed cap, very much like the one that was on the station in Hyattsville. Always well cared for, this station is listed on the National Register of Historic Places. In 1998, the city bought the station from the railroad and, with support from the State of Maryland, completely restored it in 2000.

Parkersburg (fig. 17). This very large station in West Virginia should be attributed to Baldwin because of its appearance, though again no hard evidence exists to prove this. As it was described in the B&O annual report for 1885, it was "a brick passenger station, 37 by 116 feet, two stories high, with a slate roof." This station was demolished in 1973.

The last station in this series was apparently the one built at **Boyds**, Maryland, in 1887. Baldwin's drawings in the Smithsonian collection, which are dated September 24, 1886, show a building that is the

mirror-image of the structure that was actually built. The Boyds station was 22 by 59 feet, with a tiled octagonal tower over the central agent-office section. It had a waiting room at one end and a baggage room at the other. The "stodgy" appearance of the Boyds station is somewhat out of character with the other brick stations in this series. It was demolished in 1927, when the Metropolitan Branch was double-tracked in the Boyds area.

Many of Baldwin's original drawings of these brick B&O stations of the 1880s fortuitously survive and thus positively identify him as the architect. Yet none of the Baldwin ledger-journals has any reference at all to these stations. In light of Baldwin's meticulous record-keeping, it must be concluded that some records or ledgers have been lost.

Late Frame Stations

The wood-frame stations that Baldwin designed in the 1890s can be grouped into three categories, based mostly on their size. There are three known stations in the smallest and least adorned group, all nearly identical in appearance and probably built from one set of plans. One was at **Randolph**, Maryland, on the Metropolitan Branch just south of Rockville. It cost $797. The other two, at **Engle**, West Virginia, and at **Quicksburg**, Virginia, cost $870. These three stations were built in 1892.

The late frame stations of the second group were slightly larger, with a central office and waiting rooms on either side. These were designed and built

between 1890 and 1896. Though these stations all had the same basic floor plan and dimensions, they varied somewhat in the style of roof and agent's bay and in some decorative details. Most of these stations had a gable in the slate roof over the central agent's bay, and the date of construction was shown in the triangular panel in large wooden numerals, with the 8 and the 9 intertwined.

Most of the known stations of this group were built on the Washington and Metropolitan branches of the B&O. The locations of these stations, their dates of construction, and their costs (if known) are tabulated as follows:

Branchville, Md.	1890	$2,116
Riverdale, Md.	1891	$3,008
Claggett's, Md.	1891	$1,466
Kensington, Md.	1891	$3,271
Germantown, Md.	1891	$1,419
Morgans, Md.	1891	$1,419
Dickerson's, Md.	1891	$1,419
Langdon, D.C.	1891	$3,000
Deer Park, Md.	1891	—
Lansdowne, Md.	1892	$1,419
Woodside, Md.	1892	$2,500
Glendale, W.Va.	1892	$1,800
Garrett Park, Md.	1895	$2,511
St. Denis, Md.	1896	$1,620

Only the stations at Kensington and Dickerson (plate 6) are still standing, though the latter was rebuilt after a vandal-set fire in July 1982.

The third group or variation of late frame B&O stations that Baldwin designed consists of some relatively large and rather disparate structures. Built between 1884 and 1895, they tend to be in locations far to the west of Baltimore—in Western Maryland, West Virginia, and into Ohio. Some are more like wood versions of the brick stations discussed above. The attribution of these stations to Baldwin is in some cases positively based on existing drawings; in others, it is based on the dating and location of the station and its obvious similarity in appearance and details to known Baldwin stations. Several large frame stations are very similar to the designs executed in brick.

One of the more elaborate and decorative of these stations was the one erected at **Mountain Lake Park** (fig. 18), between Oakland and Deer Park in Western Maryland, in 1884. It measured 25 by 50 feet, with a central tower. It is still standing. The tower has been chopped off, its once-open baggage area has been enclosed, and many of its original decorative features have been removed or built over during the years it was used as a commercial warehouse. It has recently been beautifully restored and is now used for a small collection of shops and stores.

The **Ilchester**, Maryland, station was built in 1885. Baldwin's original drawings of this somewhat brooding and bulky building are in the Smithsonian archives. It appears somewhat like a distorted version of the Gaithersburg station, measuring 18 by 50 feet. It was demolished in the mid-1960s.

The **Takoma Park** station, on the Maryland-District line, was built in 1886. This station measured 17 by 31 feet and was one of the most attractive stations in this series, with a circular agent's bay under a tower capped by a conical roof and sheathed in fish-scale shingles. Though it had only one floor, the dormers gave the illusion of a larger, two-story building. Baldwin's original drawings are in the Smithsonian; his records show only his work here in 1890 on the addition of a portico (later enclosed) at one end, at a cost of $1,567. The Takoma Park station was destroyed by arson on August 17, 1967.

The Smithsonian has drawings of the B&O station at **Madisonville**, Ohio, drawn by A. H. Bieler in May 1887. This station is 22 by 53 feet, but otherwise identical in all of its features, including the conical tower and fish-scale sheathing, to the Takoma Park station. These drawings may have been prepared by Bieler while he was employed by the B&O, or they may indicate his employment with Baldwin.[2] In any event, the design of the Madisonville station must be attributed to Baldwin.

2. Bieler is probably the architect for the B&O's 1887 station at Forest Glen, Md., a station that is anomalous because it is the only one on the Metropolitan Branch that was *not* designed by Baldwin. (Others have credited T. F. Schneider with this station, partly because he was the architect for the nearby "Ye Forest Inne," now part of the Walter Reed Army Medical Center Annex. Schneider (1859–1938) was an associate of Cluss & Schulze; a remaining work is the Cairo Hotel, 1615 Q Street—the building that triggered the present 160-foot limit on the height of buildings in the nation's capital.)

Fig. 18. B&O Station, Mountain Lake Park, Maryland. *B&O Railroad Museum, Hays T. Watkins Research Library*

Fig. 19. B&O Station, Brunswick, Maryland

Blueprints by Baldwin & Pennington for the station at **Brunswick**, Maryland (fig. 19), are dated July 10, 1891. This is a frame structure with stone walls up to the window sills. It was built in 1892; Baldwin's records for that year show a cost of $4,640. This station replaced an earlier brick station, also possibly an early Baldwin design, which had been built in the 1870s. The present station is unusual in that it has Palladian windows in the roof dormers, perhaps an indication that Josias Pennington may have taken the lead in its design. The station suffered from neglect for a number of years, but it has now been restored and refurbished.

The **Weston**, West Virginia, station (fig. 20) was built in 1892 for the West Virginia & Pittsburgh Railroad, which was a leased or proprietary line of the B&O. The president of the WVa&P was none other than Henry Gassaway Davis, so Baldwin's work on this station is not surprising. He received a 3 ½ percent commission for this two-story stone and frame station, whose total cost was estimated as $8,000. The station has been restored and is used for police and municipal offices.

In 1893, Baldwin designed the 23'-6" by 90'-10" frame station at **West Newton**, Pennsylvania. Costing $5,421, it replaced a station that had been destroyed by a fire in December 1891.

The **Harpers Ferry** station (fig. 21), with a signal tower at one end overlooking the bridgehead, was a

Baldwin design. His records show a cost of $6,562 in 1896. This station has been shorn of the tower and relocated, but it is still standing in this town's historic district.

Other stations that were Baldwin-designed include **Brooklyn**, a suburban station in southeastern Baltimore (1886); **Eckington**, at New York Avenue in Washington, D.C. (ca. 1890); **Millville, West Union** (1887), and **Romney**, West Virginia (1885); **Pataskala**, Ohio (1891); and **Keedysville** and **Weverton**, Maryland. All of these stations—except the one in Ohio—are gone; the small (20-by-30-foot) Millville station survived until the mid-1980s.

Station Additions and Modifications

Baldwin was also engaged to design or supervise additions or modifications to several B&O railroad stations that had been designed by earlier architects. One of these could have been a "depot" in **Wheeling**, West Virginia, perhaps the one that Niernsee designed about 1852, because drawings of this station were in Baldwin's possession for a time and were saved from destruction in the 1904 fire. There is no documentation to prove it, but it is obvious that Baldwin was responsible for the improvements and the modifications in stylistic details that were done in the mid-1880s on the nation's oldest surviving railroad station, in **Ellicott City**, Maryland.

Fig. 20. B&O Station, Weston, West Virginia. *Postcard*

Newspaper accounts, Baldwin's personal records, and a few surviving drawings do provide evidence, however, of this architect's involvement in work on a number of interesting and important stations that he "inherited" from architects of an earlier era.

An item in the *Baltimore Sun* in February 1876 mentions that the B&O depot-hotel in **Martinsburg**, West Virginia, was being remodeled and enlarged by a two-story, 40-by-50-foot addition. The structure was to be completed by mid-March; the contractor was J. P. Towson, and it was "constructed under the supervision of E. F. Baldwin, the company's architect." This station is an early example of reverse adaptive reuse: built originally in 1849 as a hotel, it was converted to a station-hotel in 1866. It was in active use until 1992. This building is on the National Register of Historic Places. Restoration of the station with a modern addition for use by commuters and Amtrak was completed in 1997.

Fig. 21. B&O Station, Harpers Ferry, West Virginia. *B&O Railroad Museum, Hays T. Watkins Research Library*

In January 1882 Baldwin prepared drawings for an addition to the **Hagerstown**, Maryland, station. The existence of these drawings, in the Smithsonian collection, answers the question as to whether or not there was a station at this terminus of the B&O's Washington County Branch when it opened in December 1867. The main building, again a likely adaptation, was a two-story, Federal-style building 39 feet across, for which Baldwin drew up a plan for a small (19'-10" by 16'-0"), one-story frame addition.

Grafton. The large Italianate station-hotel in this West Virginia railroad town was probably originally designed by Niernsee. It underwent many additions and expansions over the subsequent years, and those that occurred during the last quarter of the nineteenth century were undoubtedly under Baldwin's supervision. The 80-by-23-foot addition mentioned in the 1884 B&O annual report, for example, was surely Baldwin's work. Though the architect's records are incomplete, one entry in the ledgers is for Grafton Station in 1893, for minor alterations that cost $508.70.

Entries in the architect's records for 1890 make reference to a trip to Philadelphia (for which Baldwin charged the railroad $7.25 in expenses) for work on an unidentified B&O station there. It is not very likely that the station was Furness's just-completed Chestnut Street Station; it may have been one of the suburban stations. The work involved a partition in a baggage room ($344), an express shed ($3,601), and a storehouse on 58th Street ($1,138).

Joseph F. Kemp's **Camden Station** (fig. 22) also underwent many additions and expansions during the years of Baldwin's tenure as the architect of the B&O. The *Sun* mentioned that improvements were being made in November 1875, for example. A 38-by-600-foot warehouse was added along Howard Street in 1881 and a baggage house was added in 1888. Work on Camden Station was particularly extensive from 1889 to 1892, all under the supervision of Baldwin & Pennington. According to the B&O annual report for 1890,

by far the greatest improvement in building stations was made at Camden Station; general alterations were made in the lower part of the building, where it has been practically remodeled, making it a first-class depot, with largely increased space for waiting rooms, adding greatly to the comfort of the traveling public. A large room has been arranged especially for excursion parties, so that the comfort of those waiting to take their regular trains will not be disturbed by a rush of excursionists. Entirely new and additional plumbing has been put throughout the building, and new gas fixtures,

Fig. 22. Camden Station, Baltimore. *B&O Railroad Museum, Hays T. Watkins Research Library*

incandescent lights, and additional heating service in some of the old departments and all of the new ones. The drainage has been entirely changed and renewed. The rear platform has been enclosed and lighted with a skylight, and offices were erected in connection with the outgoing baggage-house, giving accommodations for the Station Master, Conductors, Train Masters, Train Starter, and Operator, so that trains are now started by means of signals in a modern way, as against the old way, and the control of gates and the movement of trains from the depot thoroughly systematized. Above the baggage-room, accommodations for the passenger conductors, of the most ample character, have been provided. The main tower of the building has been remodeled, the roof repaired, and a new baggage-house built.

Baldwin's ledger-journal records for the next three years show continuing work on Camden Station as well. In 1891, charges of $27,392 were made for remodeling and alterations; in 1892, new work amounting to $42,475 was charged to the B&O, and in 1893 a building costing $5,350 was completed. Remodeling work that was done here as late as 1897 may possibly have been carried out under Baldwin & Pennington's supervision. It is doubtful, however, that they were involved with work here or on any other station after this date.

Washington Depot, at New Jersey Avenue and C Streets in the nation's capital, is another instance in which Baldwin took over a building originally designed by his mentor, Niernsee. This station (fig. 23) was originally built in 1852 to replace the very first station here, which was nothing more than an old house. The 1852 station was of Italianate design, as were most of Niernsee's stations. Baldwin was responsible for a major addition to this station, a two-story brick building on the south end of the old building in the period 1888 to 1890. Baldwin's records reveal some of the costs: $21,710 for work before 1889; $3,947 for 1890; $1,175 for 1891; $960 for 1892; and $663 for 1893.

Operations at the Washington Depot ceased on October 27, 1907, and the station was replaced by Daniel Burnham's magnificent Union Station, which opened for business the very next month.

Fig. 23. Washington Depot, Washington, D.C. *Smithsonian Institution, Transportation Collection*

The old Niernsee/Baldwin-designed station was destroyed in 1908.

The original B&O station in **Frederick**, Maryland, was an Italianate building designed by Niernsee in 1854 and built at a cost of about $5,500. It is located on the corner of All Saints and Market Streets, in downtown Frederick, at the end of a stub siding. In 1891–92 Baldwin was responsible for an addition to the east end of this station which cost $8,475.50. B&O floor plans for this station are in the Smithsonian collection. Railroad operations to this station ceased in 1948; the building still stands, in restored condition, and is on the National Register of Historic Places.

Miscellaneous Stations

There are a number of entries or references in Baldwin's records and notes, and in other sources, to stations that deserve mention—if only for completeness—but for which so little data is available that the nature of their construction is unknown and their actual existence cannot even be confirmed. This fragmentary data is most easily presented, what little of it there is, in tabular form:

Mt. Moriah, Pa.	1891	$4,724	Near Philadelphia
Kirkersville, Ohio	1891	—	—
Bascom, Ohio	1891	—	Pass. depot (B&O RR)
Willock, Pa.	1892	$896	Depot built (B&O RR)
Milmont, Pa.	1892	—	"Waiting shed"
Harrisonburg, Va.	1892	$4,467	—
Coburg, Ohio	1893	—	—
Sonora, Ohio	1893	$1,231	Depot built (B&O RR)
Broadway, Va.	1893	$300	Repairs
Capon Road, Va.	1896	$1,000	—

The *Sun* noted in November 1892 that a depot was to be built by the B&O at **St. George Terminal** on Staten Island, New York. Plans were reportedly prepared by the architects Baldwin & Pennington, and bids were solicited for the project, whose cost was estimated at $100,000–150,000. Baldwin ledgers show entries in the period 1895–97 and a total fee of $4,008, which would be consistent with the above cost estimate. This was a large rail-ferry-streetcar transfer terminal operated by a B&O subsidiary, the Staten Island Rapid Transit company. The terminal was destroyed June 25, 1946, by a fire started by a spark from a SIRT electric train, but its successor remains the terminal for the legendary Staten Island ferry.

Lombard Street Station. Baldwin & Pennington was apparently involved in designs for an underground station in Baltimore, near Howard, Lombard, and Liberty Streets, in 1894. This station, along the Howard Street tunnel, between Camden and Mount Royal stations, had originally been proposed in 1892, but it was never completed. At least until a few years ago, the cavern for the station still existed.

The *Sun* of March 1894 reported that a station had been completed on the Washington Branch, at **Har-Wood**, 2.8 rail miles south of Elkridge. It was in a Romanesque style, 54 by 28 feet, with wide platforms and overhanging eaves, set back some forty feet from the tracks. The timing and location suggest a Baldwin & Pennington association, but there is no solid evidence that the station was ever built; if it was, it must not have lasted long.

Richardsonian Stone Stations

From 1890 to 1896 Baldwin & Pennington designed at least eight railroad stations that were constructed of stone and very definitely in the style introduced about a decade earlier by the famous architect Henry Hobson Richardson. Richardson had made a radical departure from tradition in the design of a few stations he created in the early 1880s, shortly before his untimely death at the age of forty-eight, in April 1886. His architectural style in general and the railroad stations he designed at Auburndale, North Easton, Holyoke, Wellesley, and Woodland (all in Massachusetts), were beginning to have a real influence on many American architects by the late 1880s.

Baldwin and Pennington sensed what was popular and fashionable and began to design stations in the "Richardsonian" style for the Baltimore & Ohio Railroad (and also the Western Maryland Railway). Five such stations are known to have been built by the B&O: University Station, Washington, D.C.; Hagerstown, Maryland; Washington, Pennsylvania; Winchester, Virginia; and Mount Royal Station in Baltimore.

University Station (fig. 24). In late 1889, the B&O began negotiations to provide a station for the new Catholic University on the Metropolitan Branch. Charles K. Lord wrote to the rector of the university and indicated that the B&O would be willing to build a "neat and convenient" station house if the trustees of the university would deed the land for it

to the railroad. Lord approached Cardinal Gibbons about the matter and received his approval. Drawings of the station were prepared in January 1890. The proposed station was to be built of blue Georgetown stone and would "harmonize with the handsome university building." That harmony was ensured, of course, because E. Francis Baldwin was the architect for both buildings. Built in 1890 at a cost of $5,423, the station was razed in the mid-1980s to make way for the Metro subway line.

The B&O annual report for 1890 stated that a new stone station and a corrugated-iron freight sta-tion had been built at **Hagerstown**, Maryland, on the Washington County Branch. This Baldwin-designed passenger station with a porte cochere cost $8,252. This station was demolished shortly after the end of World War II.

The B&O annual report for 1892 described the new stone station at **Washington**, Pennsylvania, as having a slate roof and measuring 99'-5" by 29'-0" (fig. 25). This passenger station originally cost $9,794. Passenger service here ceased in 1956. After falling into near ruin, the station was purchased by the county in 1996 and renovations were begun.

Fig. 26. Mount Royal
Station, Baltimore.
*Smithsonian Institution,
Transportation
Collection*

Despite a minor fire set by vandals in November 2000, a beautiful restoration appeared to be nearly complete in July 2001.

The station at **Winchester**, Virginia, was built in 1892 (plate 7). The railroad's annual report described it as being of stone construction, measuring 23'-6" by 90'-10", with a slate roof, steam-heating apparatus, and gas and electric fixtures. A distinguishing feature of this fine station is its octagonal tower over the agent's bay. Baldwin's records show that it cost $6,581. The contractor was Brady & Sons of Baltimore. The city initiated an effort in 1999 to repair the station and plans to use it for a museum and tourist information center.

The "zenith" in stations by Baldwin & Pennington was reached in 1896 with the opening of the **Mount Royal Station** (fig. 26), at the north end of the Howard Street tunnel in Baltimore, on September 1. Built in one year by the contractor J. J. Walsh of Baltimore, this large, three-story stone station, which is described as Romanesque with strong elements of Renaissance Revival, is set off by a 150-foot clock tower and a porte cochere in the front. The 420-foot, four-track train shed—a magnificent engineering structure in its own right—was designed by a famous Baltimore engineer, John Edwin Greiner.[3] Mount Royal was the last railroad station designed by Baldwin & Pennington.

Rail service at Mount Royal ended in 1961. The building was sold to the Maryland Institute, College of Art. It was extensively remodeled internally in 1967, but its exterior is virtually unchanged from its appearance at the turn of the century. The Mount Royal Station is listed on the National Register of Historic Places.

The Valley Railroad of Virginia

According to rail historian Herbert Harwood, after the Civil War B&O president John Garrett attempted to establish a B&O-controlled route into the Deep

3. John Edwin Greiner was born in Wilmington, Del., on February 24, 1859. After graduation from college, he joined the B&O as a draftsman and eventually rose to become engineer of bridges in 1893. His offices were relocated to Mt. Royal Station when it was completed. Greiner resigned from the B&O in 1908 and formed his own engineering consulting company. Among his many works are the Howard Street Bridge and the Pennsylvania Turnpike. He died in Baltimore on November 15, 1942.

South, beginning with a route up the Shenandoah Valley from Harpers Ferry to Salem, Virginia. This line began with fifty-one miles of B&O-owned track between Harpers Ferry and Strasburg Junction, Virginia, then forty-nine miles leased from what later became the Southern Railway between Strasburg Junction and Harrisonburg, Virginia, and finally a B&O-financed line called the Valley Railroad, from Harrisonburg to Salem. But by the time the line was completed to Lexington, Virginia, the dream had died and no more track was laid. The leased Strasburg Junction–Harrisonburg section later reverted to the Southern Railway, leaving the Harrisonburg-Lexington segment isolated from the rest of the B&O system.

The Valley Line of the B&O Railroad, which ran 162 miles from Harpers Ferry, West Virginia, to Lexington, Virginia, comprised four segments. The first segment was completed in 1836. The Valley Railroad was the last segment to be completed. Begun in the early 1870s, it reached Staunton in 1874, but work stalled for nearly ten years; the last 36 miles to Lexington were finished in November 1883. (It was at this time that the B&O constructed the Baldwin-designed brick stations at Staunton and Lexington, cited above.) A number of other Baldwin-designed stations on the Valley Line have

already been mentioned: Millville, Summit Point, Winchester, Quicksburg, Capon Road, Broadway, and Harrisonburg.

A stone station was built by the B&O in 1888 at Woodstock, Virginia, but it was hardly in a style that could be called Richardsonian. It had a curious resemblance in its basic arrangement, however, to the station built at Forest Glen, Maryland. It is now believed that Alphonse Bieler was the architect for Forest Glen and so possibly also for Woodstock.

A few additional stations on the Valley Line should probably be attributed to Baldwin as their designing architect. These attributions are based on the time at which these stations were constructed, Baldwin's known responsibility for other stations along the branch, and in some instances, strong similarities in dimensions, style, and detail among these and other known Baldwin-designed stations elsewhere. The one-story, 18-by-51-foot brick passenger depot and the 32-by-51-foot brick freight house that were built in Winchester in 1876 are possible Baldwin designs. So too are the Strasburg freight and passenger depot (1878), the Willow Grove waiting shed and the Cowans station house (1885), and a waiting shed at Capon Road (1887).

Close examination of the stations at **Timber Ridge** (fig. 27), **Daphna**, and **Raphine**, which were

The Valley Railroad of Virginia

Fig. 27. Timber Ridge, Virginia.
Edward H. Weber

built between Lexington and Strasburg, reveals not only their commonality of design but also a strong similarity to the stations at Duffields and West Union. It is suggested that all of these stations were designed by Baldwin or built from Baldwin plans for other B&O stations.

It is tempting—but still premature—to credit Baldwin also with the design of the stations at Pleasant Valley, Mount Crawford, Weyer's Cave, and Mount Sydney. These stations show some remote resemblance to other Baldwin stations, but their similarities are not strong enough to make an attribution without independent evidence.

The Maryland Central Railway

The Maryland Central Railway was a narrow-gauge line that meandered from Baltimore to Bel Air, Maryland, and then on up to Delta, Pennsylvania. Formed in 1888 as a successor to the Maryland Central Railroad (which was itself a result of a merger with the Baltimore & Delta Railway in 1882), it was transformed into the standard-gauge Maryland & Pennsylvania Railroad—the much beloved Ma & Pa—in 1901. The Baltimore terminus of the Maryland Central was at North Avenue and Oak (now Howard) Street. From here, the line climbed north to Lake Avenue on the present-day city boundary and on to Towson and beyond to Pennsylvania. E. Francis Baldwin designed two unique stations on this colorful and quirky local short-line railroad.

North Avenue Station (fig. 28) was a 36-by-43-foot stone and frame building in the then-current shingle style. It apparently replaced a wooden structure built by the Baltimore & Delta in 1882. Bids for the station were received by Baldwin in August 1886, and the contract was awarded to Philip

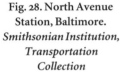

Fig. 28. North Avenue Station, Baltimore. *Smithsonian Institution, Transportation Collection*

Walsh & Son for their low bid of $9,300. The station was completed and opened on February 23, 1887.

The North Avenue station, also referred to as the Oak Street station, may have the curious distinction of being the tallest railroad station Baldwin ever designed. Built into a steep hillside on a cramped triangular lot bounded by streets and the railroad tracks, this four-level structure is estimated to have had a total height of nearly seventy feet (from the tracks to the chimney). The ticket office and waiting room were at street level, and the floor above was used for the railroad's corporate office. Restrooms were located on the floor below, and the boiler room on the floor below that. Passengers had to thread their way down four flights of covered wooden stairs to a 25-by-100-foot wooden train shed at track level well below the main building.

According to the newspapers, there were plans in 1912 or 1913 to replace this station with a new one that was to be designed by the architects Wyatt & Nolting, but the plans fell through. Baldwin's North Avenue station managed to survive until 1937, when it was razed to make way for the construction of the new Howard Street Bridge.

Homeland Station, 4.3 rail miles north of the North Avenue station, was built according to plans prepared by Baldwin in 1888, at a cost of $1,240.[4] This small (22-by-31-foot) frame structure served until 1954, when, sadly, passenger service on the Ma & Pa was discontinued. In 1958 the line in Maryland was abandoned and the track removed. Today the physical evidence of a colorful little railroad is mostly gone and continues to disappear, but Homeland station survives. It has been converted into an attractive private residence on West Lake Avenue, with only minimal changes in its external appearance (plate 8).

The Cumberland & Pennsylvania Railroad

In the 1850s, the Cumberland & Pennsylvania Railroad, a short-line mountain railroad, began to serve coal-mining interests in Western Maryland. Its thirty-one-mile main line ran from Cumberland to Mount Savage and then down the western border of Allegany County through Frostburg to Western-port, Maryland. In its heyday, it also ran up to eight passenger trains a day with a stop for nearly every mile of track. It is highly likely that there was some kind of personal relationship between Baldwin and the Cumberland & Pennsylvania, which was then owned by the Consolidation Coal Company, whose principals had close connections with the B&O.

E. Francis Baldwin designed at least four stations for the C&P: Mount Savage, Frostburg, Lonaconing, and Barton. All are similar in many respects to the small or medium-sized stations that he designed at about the same time for the B&O.

Lonaconing (fig. 29) was the first in this series of stations, built in 1887. It was the only station of the four that was brick. C&P records show that the total cost of this station was $2,274, which probably includes Baldwin's standard 3½ percent fee. The Lonaconing station was demolished in 1960.

The **Frostburg** (fig. 30) and **Mount Savage** stations were built at almost the same time in 1891. The Frostburg structure was the largest of the four C&P stations, with an office and waiting rooms at the south end and a large freight and baggage section at the other end. Passenger service on the C&P ended in 1942; the tracks were removed in 1976. For a time this decrepit structure stood nearly abandoned at the mouth of the old 1857 tunnel under the town, its future bleak; but it was restored and refurbished as a popular restaurant. It is also a terminus and an attraction for passengers on seasonal rail excursion trips, which operate between Frostburg and Cumberland, mostly on old Western Maryland Railway trackage. The Mount Savage station was torn down in May 1955.

Barton, Maryland's small frame station, was very similar to the B&O stations at Dickerson and Germantown and was probably built at the same time (1891); it is no longer standing.

The Western Maryland Railway

Over a very brief period, Baldwin designed a number of stations for the Western Maryland Railway, one of the B&O's competitors. Four stations are known, without a doubt, to be Baldwin's; a fifth is highly probable. Three of these stations were built of stone, in much the same style as the B&O stations that Baldwin worked on in the same period. One station was brick and one was a wood-frame structure.

In September 1891, Baldwin & Pennington received the proposals for a fine stone station that

4. Herbert Harwood opined that the construction of the Homeland station coincided with the development of the relocated Elkridge Hunt Club just to the north. He suspects that a club member or the club itself may have paid to have the station built here; at the time, the area was sparsely populated by large estates, and a station may not have been warranted.

Fig. 29. C&P Station,
Lonaconing, Maryland.
*W. Raymond Hicks
Collection*

Fig. 30. C&P Station,
Frostburg, Maryland.
*W. Raymond Hicks
Collection*

Fig. 31. WMRR, Mount
Hope Station,
Baltimore.
*W. Raymond Hicks
Collection*

was to be built at **Mount Hope** (fig. 31), adjacent to the hospital in upper northwest Baltimore. The contractors and their bids were John Stack & Sons (station with privy), $4,400; John Cowan, $4,138; Edward Brady & Son, $3,944; and Philip Walsh & Son (no privy), $3,200. Walsh presumably got the job. The WMRR Valuation Department records confirm that Baldwin & Pennington were the architects for this station, which opened in 1892. The cost was $3,440, and the architects earned a standard 5 percent fee of $172 for this 22-by-50-foot station. The Mount Hope station was demolished in 1931.

In January 1892 Baldwin agreed to provide the railroad with drawings and specifications for three additional stations for a fee of 3½ percent of the cost of construction: New Oxford, Frederick Junction, and Cherry Run.

The **New Oxford**, Pennsylvania, station measured 21 by 62 feet and cost $4,287, according to Baldwin's records. Made of stone, it was gutted by a disastrous fire on December 17, 1902. The railroad restored it to its original appearance the next year at a cost of $7,615. That station is still standing.[5]

Frederick Junction, which the railroad also called Bruceville, is now known as **Keymar**, Maryland (fig. 32). The cost was $6,445, according to

Baldwin's ledger, for this large (23-by-65-foot) stone structure with a huge octagonal tower over the bay. The WMRR's records for the final cost show a somewhat higher figure ($7,008). The station was demolished in 1959.

In August 1892 the Western Maryland Railway opened a strategic rail link from Williamsport, Maryland, to Cherry Run, West Virginia. This connected the B&O system with the Philadelphia & Reading Railroad, creating a new freight route to Philadelphia, New York, and other eastern cities. A station was then required for the junction at **Cherry Run**. The records show that Baldwin designed a passenger station and a freight house there, at a cost of $4,451 and $2,540, respectively. The WMRR records are in total agreement, showing the contractor (Edward Brady) and a total cost of $6,991. The Cherry Run station was a 21-by-85-foot frame building and the freight house was 24 by 26 feet, with a portico at one end. The railroad's records also list the cost of the lot ($1,000) and architect's fees paid to Baldwin & Pennington in the amount of $244.68 (precisely the 3½ percent in the agreement).[6]

There is at least one other station on the WMRR that should be attributed to Baldwin, and perhaps there are more. The station, which predates the ones

5. Herbert Harwood has noted a strong similarity in appearance between the New Oxford station and the Western Maryland station in Glyndon, Md., which was built (of brick) in 1904. The Glyndon station, however, has been attributed to Jackson C. Gott.

6. The corroboration of the Baldwin records with those of the railroad serves as a useful calibration of sorts for the accuracy of the architect's records and enhances the confidence that can be placed in them in interpreting other entries in those records.

Fig. 32. WMRR Station, Keymar, Maryland. *W. Raymond Hicks Collection*

cited above, is the large two-story brick station built at **Blue Mountain**, Maryland, to serve the Pen Mar resort hotel, which had been built in the Catoctin Mountains in 1883. This station is remarkably similar in style and detailing to the quintessential Baldwin stations built for the B&O in the 1880s. Another fact in support of Baldwin as the architect of this station is his service as the architect for the railroad's hotel. Blue Mountain station cost $5,713. It was demolished in December 1929 (fig. 33).

Fig. 33. WMRR Station, Blue Mountain, Maryland. *W. Raymond Hicks Collection*

❧ CHAPTER 3 ❦

B&O Railroad Projects

In addition to railroad depots or stations, E. Francis Baldwin was the architect for many dozens of other buildings for the Baltimore & Ohio Railroad from 1871 to about 1900. These works included resort hotels, maintenance and right-of-way structures, elevators, freight houses, warehouses, and a stockyard. But one building deserves special attention and should be considered first, even if it was built somewhat later than some of these other projects. That building was the so-called Central Building—the B&O's headquarters building, in Baltimore.

The B&O Headquarters Building

Planning for the new headquarters building for the B&O Railroad must have begun in the early 1870s; the etching of a proposed building prepared by the young architect E. F. Baldwin appears in George Howard's *Monumental City* (1873). The headquarters was to be located on the NW corner of Baltimore and Calvert Streets, on a site formerly occupied by the old Baltimore Museum, which had been destroyed by fire in that same year.

Work on the building, which was of great personal interest to the B&O's President John Work Garrett, must have proceeded by fits and starts. Mr. Garrett had decided to use Cheat River stone from the quarries of Senator Henry G. Davis of West Virginia. In March 1875 the *Baltimore Sun* reported that work was under way by the builders, S. H. & J. F. Adams of Baltimore.[1]

In July 1875 work was reportedly suspended after the foundations had been laid, and there was some question then as to whether brick or stone would be used. The matter was said to have been set aside pending Garrett's return from a European trip. John R. Niensee was appointed as "consulting architect" for this project. (This is somewhat confusing because the *Sun* later reported that the B&O had not purchased the land until 1876 and that construction began in 1880. Moreover, the architectural trade journal *American Architect and Building News* reported that the permit for this building was applied for in 1881.)

The design of the building itself was undergoing changes as well. The original scheme was a rather boxy five-story building. In November 1875 it was reported that a decision had been made to increase the granite building, which was to be 60 by 104 feet, to seven stories by adding a two-story mansard roof and a tower. The artist's sketch of the new building was printed in the August 14, 1880, issue of *American Architect and Building News*, and it did indeed show a high tower on the Baltimore Street side of the building and massive pavilions emerging from the mansard roof on the other side(s). This drawing was prepared by Josias Pennington in 1879, and his name and designation ("Del," for delineator) appear in one corner. The building also appears more square in its base dimensions than previously depicted, as indeed it was when completed. Work began in earnest in 1880.

The B&O Central Building was completed in 1882 (fig. 34). When finished, however, it did not have the tall, steeplelike tower. In its place was a prominent pavilion, much like those on the other sides. The October 14 issue of *American Architect and Building News* that year had an article on recent building activity in Baltimore and it described the new B&O building in part as follows:

1. The builder S. H. Adams died on June 11, 1875. The *Sun* reported that the buildings he had worked on included St. John's Church, the Mount Hope Insane Asylum, the YMCA (Morris) Building, the Convent of Notre Dame, and the B&O roundhouse at the Riverside shops. Adams apparently had a long association as a builder, first with Niernsee and subsequently with Baldwin.

The first story is of fine hammered granite, the others of red brick and dark bluestone. Panels of terra cotta are used below the windows, in the brick dormers, and in the main piers. The color of the entire mass is dark, while the second tier of dormers, the angles of the roof, and the elaborate cornice at its top, are colored in two shades of very light brown; the lighter exactly the tint of the yellow terra cotta cresting, crowning the black slate roof. The windows are square and round-arched in alternate stories, the fifth having mullion shafts of polished granite. The carving, of which there is considerable, is distributed over the entire building, as large rosettes, and as capitals to brick window-pieces, which are generally continued as string courses, though in the third story the line of stone caps is continued on the walls by a band of flat terra cotta tiles. The effect of the building is massive, until dispelled by the fanciful coloring of the roof work. The execution of the work of the exterior is apparently faultless. The architect is Mr. E. F. Baldwin.

Scharf described the B&O building in his book, *History of Baltimore City and County*, noting that the base dimensions were 102'-6" on Baltimore Street, 104'-2" on Calvert. He reported that the first floor was to house passenger, ticket, freight, and express services; the offices of the president, vice president, and treasury department were to be on the second floor; the board of directors and the general freight department offices on the third floor, and the auditor's department on the fourth. The staircases, window frames, and joists were of iron, and the building had fire- and burglar-proof vaults. The building was made "fireproof" throughout—an ironic statement in light of its demise less than a quarter-century later.

There are no Baldwin records from the early years that cover construction or work on the B&O headquarters; these were presumably lost in the 1904 fire. The only references by Baldwin to this building are in the period 1889–91, when he noted supervision of a few thousand dollars' worth of work on roof repairs and other alterations or minor improvements.

The B&O headquarters building, which for a time was the tallest building in Baltimore, was gutted by the great fire of 1904. It stood, blackened and hollow, for many months awaiting its fate. Finally, it was razed. The last vestige of this fine building was not removed until February 1906. (The Emerson Hotel, designed by Sperry and eerily reminiscent of the B&O building, was built on the site in 1911; it was razed in 1971.)

Resort Hotels and Pavilions

The Gay Nineties are remembered as a time of gaslights, Chatauquas, and summer resorts. Residents of cities like Baltimore, Washington, Pittsburgh, and Wheeling escaped the summer's heat and humidity by vacationing in the mountains. Very wealthy families were able to live in their mountain retreats over the entire summer; in some cases, the father would commute to the city for the week and return on weekends.

Admittedly self-servingly, the railroads undertook to develop resort complexes in the mountain-

ous regions their lines passed through in order to stimulate passenger revenue on these lines. John Garrett's plans to develop the B&O's resorts in Western Maryland were delayed by the Civil War, but in the 1870s he developed and promoted two large hotels in Garrett County near Oakland and Deer Park. At Deer Park he also built an enclave of "cottages" near the hotel for individuals and families who wished to enjoy the resort's amenities but did not want to live in the hotel itself. A decade later the B&O developed a resort complex on the Chesapeake Bay, near Annapolis. E. Francis Baldwin appears to have played a role in the design of most of these buildings.

Ground-breaking ceremonies for the **Deer Park Hotel** were held on the Fourth of July 1872. The *Cumberland News* noted that "Mr. William Keyser, Hon. H. G. Davis, Mr. Baker, and Mr. Baldwin (architect) laid it off." Construction was soon under way, and the hotel opened its doors for business the following Independence Day, 1873. The buildings and 400-acre grounds reportedly cost $106,139. The B&O annual reports provided detailed descriptions of the complex: the main building was 56 by 48 feet, four stories high, with three-story wings (55 by 40 feet), a dining room (36 by 50 feet) in the rear, and a kitchen and servant's extension (30 by 63 feet). Its mansard-style roof was metal and slate of different (variegated) colors (fig. 35).

The first floor of the hotel contained a main hall, a reading room, a sitting room, an office, a parlor, and the dining room. There were 104 sleeping rooms in the hotel. It also had its own laundry, bakery, pantry, and icehouse. The railroad built adjacent buildings for a billiard room, ten-pin alleys, a stable, and a carriage house. A 16-foot-square music pavilion was built on the front lawn for band concerts. The hotel also had its own railroad station just down the hill from the main buildings.

In 1882 the hotel was enlarged by the addition of two annexes, each 40 by 111 feet and three stories high, separated from the main building by 125 feet for fire-safety reasons. Additions were also made to the main building. In 1886 a natatorium (swimming pool) measuring 86'-6" square was built. Baldwin's records show additional work here of a general and unspecified nature until 1896. The B&O Railroad's operation of the Deer Park Hotel was discontinued in 1911. The building (and grounds) eventually fell into disrepair or ruin, and it was finally torn down in 1944.

The B&O's **Oakland Hotel**, opened in 1876 (fig. 36), was located at the base of a hill across the tracks

and a meadow from the Oakland station. The contractor was Julius C. Holmes of Charles Town, West Virginia. Like the Deer Park Hotel, the Oakland was built of wood with stone foundations. The main building was four stories high, 109 by 42 feet, with a 72-by-40-foot wing. The first floor contained a grand hall, an office, a reading room, dining rooms, a billiard room, a barber shop, baths, a kitchen, a bakery, a serving room, and a storeroom. On the upper floors there were 110 sleeping rooms. The cost was estimated to be about $40,000.

In 1882 another wing and an extension on the first wing were added, making the total length an imposing 321 feet. Additional modifications and

improvements were made over the next decade or more, some of which were noted in Baldwin's ledgers. The B&O Railroad discontinued its operation of this hotel in 1907; in 1911 it was demolished.

Deer Park Cottages. Henry Gassaway Davis owned much of the land around Deer Park, and he built a home there in 1866. He also built five cottages in the area, which he rented to summer vacationers and later sold to the B&O Railroad.

Between 1881 and 1884, John Garrett built five additional cottages near the Deer Park Hotel. The 1885 B&O *Annual Report* notes that three cottages had been built at Deer Park the previous year. One was 28 by 53 feet, and two were 32 by 39 feet, two stories high. Though called "cottages," these were fairly large houses, some multistoried. The house that Garrett built for himself had fifteen rooms. He died there on September 26, 1884. The Garrett house was destroyed by a fire on Christmas Day, 1939.

Considering Baldwin's extensive connections with the B&O Railroad, Henry G. Davis, and other Garrett projects, it is difficult to imagine these cottages being designed by anyone other than E. Francis Baldwin. (His records make some reference to the plans for the hotel and the cottages, and Baldwin recorded charges for work on them in the early 1880s. He also designed a cottage for J. Swan Frick here in the early 1890s.) A number of the cottages at Deer Park are still standing and occupied now on a year-round basis (fig. 37).

Pavilions. There are occasional references in Baldwin's records to "pavilions" for the B&O in three locations. The word *pavilion* is difficult to interpret because it can legitimately be used in various ways—all of which are plausible in the context of work for the B&O at these locations. In a strict architectural sense, a pavilion is a technical term used to denote a projecting portion of a larger building, such as the pavilions that Baldwin designed on the roof of the B&O headquarters building.

Pavilion can also refer to a simple shelter or waiting shed. This term was used to describe a passenger shelter at Washington Grove, Maryland, for example. The term can also mean a covered area, such as a covered platform or portico. It can refer to a large structure used for some special purpose, such as an exhibit or a performance. A mention by Baldwin in 1889 of work on the "Bay Ridge pavilion" may refer to a part of the B&O's resort on Chesapeake Bay near Annapolis. The B&O had undertaken the development of this resort in 1885; it included a "Grand Hotel" and a "pavilion," which was used for musical performances and exhibits. This resort was linked to Annapolis by the 4.5-mile Bay Ridge & Annapolis Railroad (built by the B&O). It seems doubtful that Baldwin's entry is referring to the large pavilion—it may have been to a waiting shed for the rail connection or possibly the pier on the Bay.

Baldwin cited work on an "Island Park pavilion" in 1890, at a cost of $1,710 and a fee of 4 percent,

Fig. 37. Deer Park Cottage, Deer Park, Maryland

indicative of new work. This was probably a small passenger waiting shed on the B&O main line near Harpers Ferry, West Virginia. Rail schedules and reports show a stop at Island Park, just a short distance above Harpers Ferry.

A pavilion could also be a dancing pavilion, and this seems to be precisely what Baldwin's 1890 entry for the "Irving Park pavilion" meant. It was built at a cost of $881.65. This conforms with the statement made in a B&O annual report: "In 1881 a dancing pavilion, 30 by 75 feet and 14'-6" high, with a metal roof was built." Irving Park is near Annapolis Junction on the B&O's Washington Branch. In 1890, the annual report noted that a new frame dancing pavilion had been erected at Irving Park.

Shop, Yard, and Right-of-Way Structures

The **shops at Mount Clare** in Baltimore were the oldest, and probably one of the largest, railroad equipment construction and repair facilities in the United States in the 1880s. For a ten-year period,

from about 1884 to 1894, Baldwin played a significant role in the design and construction of many buildings here. The best known, and certainly the most impressive, of these is the building located at the eastern vertex of this triangular complex, on the corner of Pratt and Poppleton Streets, Baltimore.

The permit for the construction of a new B&O **Passenger Car Shop**—oftentimes erroneously referred to as a "roundhouse"—was granted to the railroad in June 1883 to replace the shop that had burned on January 3. Built under the supervision of Colin McLean, a B&O engineer, and completed in February 1884, this great "rotunda" (as it is also called) was the largest passenger car shop in the world, and for many years it had the distinction of being the world's largest circular industrial building. It cost $100,472 when it was constructed (fig. 38).

The Passenger Car Shop is a twenty-two-sided brick structure, 245 feet in external diameter. The height to the top of the central cupola is 123 feet. A detailed contemporary description and dimensioned plans of the shop were published in the August 22, 1884, issue of the *Railroad Gazette*:

Fig. 38. Mount Clare Passenger Car Shop and Library, Baltimore. *Smithsonian Institution, Transportation Collection*

The building is divided into 22 stalls, and as it measures 235 feet diameter inside, the longest passenger or sleeping cars can be easily accommodated. The whole building is completely roofed in, and is very well lit by the central lantern or clerestory, some 80 feet in diameter. The roof rises sharply from the outside walls to the base of the lantern, and is carried on lattice girders, which with the lantern are supported by wrought-iron pillars composed of two 9-inch and two 12-inch channel irons riveted together. The lantern is trussed, a precaution which is very generally thought to be unnecessary, the sloping sides being treated as struts, whose thrust is counteracted by a ring at the base of the cone. The great height and size of this remarkably handsome structure are enhanced by the tasteful manner and light color in which the interior is painted.

In 1884 a two-story annex was designed by Baldwin and added to the Passenger Car Shop building in the NE quadrant. The annex, which is 119'-6" by 71'-10", was originally an employee library; it was later converted to a print shop. These two connected buildings became a part of the B&O Transportation Museum in 1953 and currently house the B&O Railroad Museum. The buildings were repaired and restored in the mid-1970s. In February 2003, the southern half of the car shop roof collapsed under a record-breaking snowfall; the building is being rebuilt.

In 1892, Baldwin & Pennington did some minor work on an unidentified office at Mount Clare, which cost $856, and a "Hopper Shed," which cost $4,972. The 60-by-300-foot Tender House was designed by these architects in November 1891 and constructed in 1892; its cost was $7,793, according to the Baldwin records. Also in 1892 a large "Store House" was built at Mount Clare, at a cost of $20,157.

In the early 1890s the B&O developed a small facility in the **Trinidad** section of Washington, D.C., for the service and minor repair of locomotives and rolling stock. A roundhouse and a sandhouse designed by Baldwin were constructed between P and R Streets, along the boundary of the Columbia Institution for the Deaf and Dumb (now West Virginia Avenue and Gallaudet College). The roundhouse was built in 1890; the 20-by-85-foot sandhouse was built two years later. This facility was closed and demolished after Union Station was completed in 1907.

The railyard and employee housing, as well as the station at **Brunswick**, Maryland, were considerably improved and enlarged in the early 1890s. A building, which Baldwin described as a "work building," was built in 1891. It was most likely the large locomotive roundhouse. The cost was $23,207 and the architect earned a 3 percent commission. After a temporary reprieve from the wrecking ball in 1988, the 104-year-old structure was demolished in November 1995 by CSX Transportation.

In 1892, a fire occurred in the frame powerhouse building at Brunswick, and Baldwin oversaw its repair, which cost $1,725. Baldwin's records also show charges of $3,836 for a Trainmen's House, a blacksmith shop, and a water supply (for $11,949) in the period 1892–93.

Brunswick was a "railroad town"—a fact that is vividly underscored by the references in Baldwin's ledgers to a number of "cottages" he designed for the B&O here in 1892. In this instance, *cottages* probably means something different from what it meant at Deer Park. At Brunswick, the meaning is more literal, and the structures were most likely small, quite unlike the large and sumptuous homes in the resort areas. Fifteen such cottages—actually B&O employee dwellings—were built first at a total cost of $10,250. They must have been rather plain, simple structures. An additional series of twenty-one were built by the contractor Edward Brady at a cost of $26,438, and five more were built by Maier & Miller. Some attempt at variety was made in the design of these houses because the architect notes that eight different sets of plans were prepared for them. The precise locations of these forty-one Baldwin-designed houses in Brunswick have yet to be determined, but it is quite likely that many of them are still standing.

Baldwin apparently had a long and continuing involvement with the B&O's maintenance facilities in **Cumberland**. The first and earliest evidence of this is J. Appleton Wilson's reference to having made drawings under Baldwin for the Cumberland Repair Shops, in the early 1870s. Baldwin & Pennington were engaged in the mid-1890s to design a very large roundhouse and additional repair shops.

The B&O annual report for 1895 reported that a contract had been awarded to J. Walsh & Son for the construction of a roundhouse, an oil house, a freight house, and a machine shop. The *Railroad Gazette* described these shops, which were to be completed in late September 1896, and stated that Baldwin & Pennington had been selected as the architects. The roundhouse was to be 306 feet in diameter, with forty-four stalls and a double-tracked entrance. It had an iron truss roof covered with slate. Baldwin's records show a cost of $80,980 for the roundhouse. The machine shop was 60 by 80 feet. The oil house cost $7,123. These buildings have all been destroyed.

Baltimore Belt Railroad Power House. In the 1890s, the B&O Railroad constructed the 7.2-mile link between the rail system south and west of Baltimore with its lines up the northeast corridor to Philadelphia. This Baltimore Belt Line Railroad incorporated a double-tracked, 7,341-foot tunnel beneath Howard Street, from the Mount Royal Station to Camden Station. Baldwin & Pennington's effort in this development was their crowning and probably final work for the B&O, which included the Mount Royal Station (and the never-completed underground station at Lombard and Howard Streets), improvements and expansion of facilities at Camden Station, and the "Power House," which supplied the electrical power for the General Electric locomotives that pulled the trains up the 0.8 percent grade in the tunnel from Camden to Mount Royal Station.

The 69-by-300-foot stone and brick powerhouse (fig. 39) was built by J. J. Walsh & Son in 1894–95. The powerhouse—the heart of the world's first mainline railroad electrification—had five 500-kW electrical generators. The architect's ledgers cite a cost for the powerhouse of $51,895. The building was used as a powerhouse until 1914, when it was converted to a repair shop. Located on South Howard Street between Henrietta and Montgomery Streets, it was razed in the mid-1970s.

Freight Houses. In the mid-1880s, Baldwin designed at least four brick freight houses that were relatively elaborate and, in most cases, matched the brick railroad stations they accompanied. These freight houses are distinguished from those discussed elsewhere; these particular houses are general-purpose buildings that were closely associated or co-located with a companion station and sometimes built at the same time as the station. Because these particular freight houses were architecturally quite decorative, they deserve special attention.

The four known examples were at **Gaithersburg**, **Hyattsville**, **Rockville**, and **Ellicott City**. The Rockville freight house has a jerkin-head roof; the others all had a simple gable roof. The Hyattsville and Gaithersburg houses were relatively small; the other two were large. All were quite impressive brick buildings, but the one at Ellicott City was the most elaborate of the lot (fig. 40). It seems likely that freight houses similar to these four were built by the B&O elsewhere, but none has so far been identified.

The Gaithersburg freight house as built originally was 21'-2" by 24'-2". It was built in 1884 along with the station, but it was enlarged to twice its original size about 1904. Drawings of the Gaithersburg station and its freight house are in the B&O Railroad Museum. The Hyattsville freight house was nearly identical to Gaithersburg's and built at about the same time. Ellicott City's freight house is 20 by 50 feet and was built in 1885. Finally, the 21-by-40-foot building at Rockville, with its eyebrow dormer roof

Fig. 40. B&O Freight House, Ellicott City, Maryland

vents, was built in 1887. All of these freight houses except Hyattsville's are still standing, though the Rockville building and station were moved to make way for the Metro subway station.

Baldwin prepared plans and a report for a freight house in Columbus, Ohio, in 1889; it may well have been the large (307'-6" by 80'-8") brick building mentioned in the B&O annual report for that year. In 1891, he prepared plans for a small freight house in nearby Higbee, Ohio, and also for a new freight house (built at a cost of $3,471) in Hagerstown, Maryland, to accompany the railroad's new stone passenger station that had been built there. Small freight houses at Claggett's (now called Gapland) and Van Bibber, Maryland, were erected in 1892 and 1893, respectively. The latter cost $1,230.

The B&O annual reports of 1895 and 1896 detail the construction of a large freight depot at Alexandria, Virginia. Baldwin's records for the same time period show billings to the B&O for a freight depot there which is undoubtedly the same structure.

The small frame freight houses that were built in the 1870s and 1880s to accompany the frame stations of that same period were also very likely Baldwin designs. These buildings were erected adjacent to, or across the tracks from, the stations at Elkridge, Muirkirk, and Washington Grove—and perhaps elsewhere.

A photograph of a particularly elegant two-story brick freight station was found in the Smithsonian collection; it bears the familiar features of a product of Baldwin, with the detailing and delicate brickwork characteristic of his stations of the 1880s. Its location is unknown, but Baltimore seems to be a good guess.

The earliest known example of a building that Baldwin designed for the B&O Railroad—other than a station, hotel, or warehouse—is **Bailey's Interlocking Cabin** (fig. 41), the small interlocking signal tower that was located at the NW corner of Ostend and South Eutaw Streets in Baltimore. (The railroad's name for the location was *Bailey*.) Drawings for this structure, called a "cabin," were prepared by Baldwin in 1880, and it is believed that the structure was built in that year. In 1888 the B&O's *Annual Report* cited expenditures that were probably for an extension of the upper floor to house interlocking equipment. This may account for the change in the appearance of the structure from the plans; the drawings show a board-and-batten substructure, whereas later photographs show that brick was used.

Baldwin's records indicate that he did some work on a signal tower for Washington Junction (Point of Rocks) in 1892. In the same year he also prepared plans for a series of thirteen small signal towers on the B&O's Philadelphia Division. He received a flat fee of $10 for each building; the design and actual locations of these towers are unknown.

Elevators, Warehouses, and a Stockyard

Although the B&O reached the ports of Philadelphia and New York, Baltimore was always its principal export-import port, so large facilities for bulk products such as coal and grain, general freight, and associated goods storage were required. And for much of the nineteenth century Baltimore was also an entry port for European immigrants, and the B&O erected special facilities to accommodate those passengers heading inland.

Baldwin's work for the Baltimore & Ohio Railroad included a number of buildings in the Baltimore harbor area, on Locust Point and Henderson's Wharf (Fells Point). He also designed a few large warehouses in Washington and Philadelphia. Early in his career, he took on the offbeat project of designing a stockyard, and—as a valedictory of sorts to his long association with the B&O Railroad—he and Pennington designed the monumental warehouse at Camden Station.

The scene at **Locust Point**, the heart of the B&O's link with deep-draft ocean-going vessels, was dominated in the 1870s by construction of three huge grain elevators on the northern shores of this peninsula. These were described in the annual reports simply as Elevators "A," "B," and "C." By the 1880s, this trio of buildings, jutting out into the bay on their piers, loomed as huge sentinels over the rail yards and the waterfront on Locust Point (fig. 42).

Elevator A, begun in 1871, opened in January 1872, on 4,400 piles and a granite foundation. The superstructure was 150 feet long and 80 feet wide; its overall height was approximately 140 feet. Built of wood with a slate roof, its interior was divided up into 120 bins, each 9'-6" square. The reported capacity was over one-half million bushels of grain. Aside from the circumstantial evidence associating Baldwin with the B&O in this time frame, J. A. Wilson's list of drawings that he worked on with Baldwin includes Elevator A. Elevator A was destroyed in a fire on October 4, 1891.

Elevator B, presumably also a Baldwin design, was built in 1873 and 1874. An even larger building than its predecessor, it was 324'-10" long, 96'-10" wide, and 168 feet high. It required 11,750 piles to support it and contained 228 square bins, 11'-6" on a side. It had a capacity of over 1,500,000 bushels.

Elevator C was the largest of all. According to B&O's annual report for 1881, the main building measured 409'-6" by 86'-6" and was 171 feet high. Its 254 storage bins provided a capacity of 1,800,000 bushels. The engine and boiler house was 64'-6" by 33'-10", and 45 feet in height; its smokestack was 180 feet high and 14 feet square at the base. Constructed under the supervision of B&O engineer Colin McLean, it was completed on September 8, 1881. This gigantic structure was destroyed in a spectacular fire in 1922.

The **B&O Tobacco Warehouse** on Locust Point (fig. 43) was built in 1879 and 1880. Architect Baldwin received bids in 1879 from six builders (John Stack, Hopkins & Marshall, Markland & Bros, Philip Walsh, S. H. & J. F. Adams, and J. P. Towson) for the proposed 77-by-800-foot building. The bids were all near $25,000, varying according to roof (iron or slate). No winner was indicated in Baldwin's records. The building may have been redesigned, because newspaper and journal accounts and the B&O annual reports referred to this as either a tobacco or coffee warehouse and described it as three stories high, 80 feet wide, and 317 feet long. It was built under the supervision of Ichabod Jean at the corner of Fort Avenue and Harper Street. In

Fig. 42. Locust Point
Elevators, Baltimore.
*B&O Railroad Museum,
Hays T. Watkins
Research Library*

1993, attempts were made unsuccessfully to turn the warehouse into a museum honoring European immigrants. This building was destroyed in a six-alarm fire (suspected arson) on New Year's Day, 1996.

The **Coffee Warehouse** was also on Wilson's list of buildings, and the 1873 annual report does record the construction of such a building at Locust Point, beginning in August of that year. It was 267'-11" by 77'-4". Baldwin's records for 1892 mention a "coffee roasting warehouse," which may be the same structure for which repairs amounting to $8,252 were made. Baldwin also refers to considerable work that same year, amounting to $27,418, on piers for the

Fig. 43. B&O Tobacco
Warehouse, Locust
Point, Baltimore

B&O at Locust Point. There is also a record of a fee of $100 paid to Baldwin in 1893 for work on the B&O's Spears Wharf.

In the Smithsonian collection there are drawings by E. F. Baldwin, dated January 1881, of an **Agent's Office** at Locust Point. This was a large, three-story brick building, approximately 52 by 60 feet, with a mansard roof. Whether this rather elegant structure was ever built according to Baldwin's plans is not known, because the drawings of the Locust Point Agent's Office by Colin McLean are of a more austere design. A single mention in a Baldwin journal, about ten years later, of an "appraiser's office" at Locust Point, may refer to the same building.

Tobacco Warehouse. This huge six-story, 283-by-204-foot structure was built in the mid-to-late 1890s at Henderson's Wharf. Its interior was wood on a framework of thick pine beams. According to the B&O's *Book of the Royal Blue*, it cost about $150,000. Baldwin's records show receipts for this building amounting to at least $7,700, which corresponds to a total final cost of nearly $200,000 based on his established fee of 4 percent for a building of this type. The warehouse, at 1000 Fell Street, has been converted into an apartment building.

Only fragmentary information is available on a few additional B&O warehouses designed by Bald-

win & Pennington. In 1883, Baldwin recorded the award of a contract to Charles R. Heddon for $24,069 for an "Express Stable" in Jersey City. An 1896 entry mentions repairs on a Washington, D.C., warehouse for a brewing company amounting to $3,150. And there is a reference to new work on the Philadelphia Transfer freight shed on Lehigh Avenue in 1896, which cost $2,921.

Camden Station Warehouse (fig. 44). There are no references to this building in any of the Baldwin records. Other researchers have concluded, and it is generally acknowledged, that Baldwin & Pennington were the architects for the enormous B&O warehouse along South Eutaw Street at Camden Station. Built between 1898 and 1905, this four-block-long (1,116 feet) and 51-foot-wide eight-story brick edifice has some 430,000 square feet of floor space.

After this building ceased to be used as a warehouse in the mid-1970s, it faced an uncertain future. Demolition seemed inevitable when the Maryland Stadium Authority acquired the property west of Camden Station for a new baseball stadium, but the owners decided instead to preserve the old warehouse and use it for Oriole offices. The stadium's architects then capitalized on the warehouse, integrating its imposing brick facade into their design so

B&O Railroad Projects

Fig. 44. Camden Station Warehouse, Baltimore. *Smithsonian Institution, Transportation Collection*

Fig. 45. Claremont
Hotel, Baltimore.
*Photography Collections,
University of Maryland,
Baltimore County*

that it now provides the impressive right-field back-drop for the award-winning ballpark which opened in 1992. With high attendance and national TV coverage of the baseball games, the warehouse is now one of Baldwin's most visible buildings in Baltimore, even though few people know of Baldwin or his role in its creation.

An 1892 entry in a Baldwin journal is for work on an "**Emigrant House,** Cumberland" and a cost of $1,278. The B&O annual report for that year corroborates the building of such a structure. Why such a railroad project? It has been suggested that the B&O enjoyed a large and profitable business for many years after the Civil War transporting immigrants from the ships docking at Locust Point to the interior of the United States.[2] Because Cumberland was then about a day's rail journey from the port of Bal-

timore, lodgings would have been required for the passengers there. And because the Queen City Hotel was either too expensive or otherwise unacceptable, second-class quarters were provided by the railroad in the form of the "emigrant" houses, in much the same way that the railroad provided second-class passenger cars.

It is possible that Baldwin was also involved with another "emigrant building" that the B&O built at Locust Point in 1888. This two-story structure was 60 by 165 feet, 27 feet high, built of brick with an iron roof. According to the B&O annual report for that year, it cost $3,095.

Baldwin's journal records also contain entries for the following unidentified buildings: a B&O

2. John Hankey, personal communication.

office building in Washington, D.C. ($1,343 in alterations); two section houses on the Pittsburgh Division in 1892; new buildings at Riverside Shops, Baltimore ($2,983); a small pump-house on the Ohio River (1892); and (drawings for) a "swing trestle" for the Monongahela River Railroad near Fairmont, West Virginia (1893).

In 1880 a company was formed to organize and construct a stockyard in Baltimore on the B&O line in the area between Wilkens and Washington Avenues near Brunswick Street. The company was called the **Claremont Stock Yard** by the *Sun* and in the B&O's annual reports. Baldwin referred to it in his records as the "Baltimore Stock Yard Company," as did the *American Architect and Building News*, which announced his responsibility for the preparation of drawings in September 1880. It also was reported that the architect was engaged in plans for a three-story brick hotel (42 by 122 feet), a three-story stable and carriage house (38 by 214 feet), a frame sheephouse (272 by 336 feet), a brick feed-storage house (40 by 100 feet), and several other stock buildings for the yards. The stockyard was obviously not a trivial project.

On October 4, 1880 (his forty-third birthday), Baldwin received bids for the structures from four contractors: P. Walsh, S. H. & J. F. Adams, Henry Smith & Son, and H. E. Loane. The Adams brothers were chosen with their bid of $41,082 for four items: hotel ($21,590), stable ($7,993), feed house ($3,074), and hog house ($8,425). Through additional negotiations a sheephouse and a "back building" were included, and the contract was rounded to an even $50,000, work to be completed by April 1, 1881. A scale house and additional work was added, bringing the final contract to $54,179. The yard began operations under the railroad in late 1881; in 1891 it was sold to the Union Stock Yard Company with the B&O retaining a part interest. The **Claremont Hotel** building (fig. 45) survived until the 1970s.

❧ CHAPTER 4 ❧

Street-Railway Structures
in Baltimore

In the last quarter of the nineteenth century a revolution of sorts in mass transportation systems began in American cities, and Baltimore was no exception. Beginning with horse-drawn cars on rails, Baltimore's street-railway system evolved in a relatively few years in to a rail network with self-propelled cars powered by electricity provided by centralized power-generation plants. Baldwin's contributions to these street-railway ventures consisted of the design of a number of stables, carbarns, shops, and powerhouses. As Baltimore's public transportation system grew, Baldwin went with the flow and designed buildings for successive generations of equipment, within a given company and among competitive companies.

The North Baltimore Passenger Railway was formed in 1872 (it would later be absorbed into the Baltimore Traction Company) and E. Francis Baldwin was hired in 1882 to design stables and a carhouse for the Cross Town Line at Edmondson Avenue between Fulton Avenue and Mount Street. The buildings were brick with terra cotta trim. The carhouse was 30 by 140 feet and the stable was a two-story, 56'-7" by 140-foot structure. The facility was built to accommodate 112 horses and 20 passenger cars. The adjoining buildings were constructed by John S. Hogg under a contract for $13,727. Hogg completed the job ahead of the July 15 target date.

In the early 1880s street railways in Baltimore were expanding rapidly. In April 1882, Baldwin was engaged by the newly chartered Baltimore Union Passenger Railway Company for three carhouse and stable facilities. The BUPR would eventually become a part of the United Electric system. Baldwin's patron, Nelson Perin, the controlling force behind the BUPR, created and controlled the City & Suburban Railway and, subsequently, the Baltimore Consolidated Railway. The three Baldwin projects were

—a 97-by-202-foot brick carhouse and stable on the corner of Huntingdon Avenue and Oak Street (now Howard and 25th Street). It was built by Lewis C. McCusker for $15,605. The building had waiting rooms and conductors' rooms and could house 150 horses and 25 cars. It was completed in July 1882. In 1885 this was also the terminal of the country's first regular electric street-railway operation—Leo Daft's electrification of the Baltimore & Hampden horsecar line.

—a small carhouse and stable on Washington Avenue, also built by Lewis C. McCusker, for a cost of $5,995.

—a carhouse and stable on Frederick road, near Pratt and Smallwood Streets, built by J. J. Walsh for $9,575. Baldwin was probably the architect for the two-story brick addition to this facility in 1883.

When the Baltimore Union was absorbed into the City & Suburban Railway Company, Baldwin was employed to make the necessary alterations to the two old carbarns. In 1892 a 51-by-200-foot brick addition was made to the Huntingdon Avenue structure. (The carhouse, stripped of its facade, still stands as part of an automobile dealership.) Baldwin's records show continuing work on these buildings into 1896, when City & Suburban merged into the Baltimore Consolidated Railway. The Frederick Road carbarn was apparently renovated or replaced. Baldwin's records indicate that John Hiltz was selected as the contractor for the carbarns on Frederick Road, winning over five other bidders with a proposal for $55,065.

In 1899, the Consolidated Railway became part of United Railways & Electric Company. As its name suggests, the UR&E united all of Baltimore's street railway companies under a single management. Baldwin seems to have been almost a fixed part of the deal, because he was retained for some very large UR&E projects over the next few years.

The UR&E's formation resulted in a requirement for a large, centralized shop to handle car storage, maintenance, and repairs. Plans were begun in 1899 to create such a complex on Washington Boulevard near the Carroll Mansion in southwest Baltimore. To familiarize themselves with such large shop complexes, Baldwin and Pennington visited the Chester Park car shops of the Cincinnati Street Railway Company.

Baldwin & Pennington prepared drawings and specifications for the **Carroll Park Shops** and invited proposals from builders. Ten proposals were received, ranging from $539,000 to $580,000. John Waters was the lowest bidder and a contract was signed on September 26, 1899. The shops were constructed in 1900–1901.

The Carroll Park shops were in the form of two huge, four-bay buildings, each 475 feet long and 360 feet wide. The 342,000 square feet of covered area was divided up into various shop and servicing areas, including a paint shop (240 by 310 feet), a motor-erecting shop (130 by 210 feet), an erecting shop (270 by 260 feet), a cabinet shop (85 by 270 feet), a mill shop (130 by 270 feet), two blacksmith shops (each 90 by 200 feet), two machine shops (90

by 285 feet and 90 by 368 feet), an armature room (80 by 90 feet), a storeroom (175 by 180 feet), and a powerhouse (80 by 100 feet). A lumber yard and the necessary yard trackage completed the facility. The main building of the Carroll Park shops is still standing (fig. 46).

Baldwin's records are scanty on the matter, but they make reference to a "Boiler House" for the UR&E, dated 1901, at a cost of $302,426. This is undoubtedly the huge **Pratt Street Power House**, which still stands at 601 East Pratt Street on Dugan's Wharf on the Baltimore Inner Harbor. Its massive hulk and four huge smokestacks are a landmark in the area, though less pronounced of late with all the tall skyscrapers surrounding it (plate 9).

The facility was used to generate steam heat until 1973. The City of Baltimore purchased it in 1979, and several attempts were made to adapt this massive structure for other uses. Its incarnation as the Six Flags entertainment center failed, and a nightclub (P. T. Flagg's) was short-lived. Circa 1998 it became the home for a Barnes & Noble bookstore, a Hard Rock Cafe, a Gold's Gym, and an ESPN Zone entertainment complex.

No mention at all is made in any of the available Baldwin notes or records of the **Edmondson Avenue Car House**, which opened in May 1907, but the design of this building is generally attributed to Baldwin.

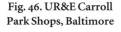
Street-Railway Structures in Baltimore

Fig. 46. UR&E Carroll Park Shops, Baltimore

Beginning in 1906, the Maryland Electric Railways (a company used to finance the UR&E's carhouse program) hired Baldwin & Pennington as the architects for a series of carhouses. Three are known:

—**York Road Car House.** Baldwin started the plans on September 21; he received thirteen bids from builders for this project in November 1906. The contract was awarded to the Noel Construction Company, and construction began on November 23. The final negotiated price was $115,685, which excluded a sprinkler system. This 140-by-404-foot carhouse opened on February 24, 1908. It was taken out of service in the early 1960s and converted to various commercial uses.

—**Park Terminal Car House,** on Druid Hill and Fulton Avenues. Baldwin started preliminary plans in February 1907; by the end of March the design had been accepted and plans completed. Ten proposals were received on June 21, 1907, and the contract was awarded to J. Henry Miller for a final price of $215,593.88. This concrete building with brick facing and terra cotta trim opened in 1909.

—**Harford Road (Montebello) Car House.** West Construction Company was the lowest of nine bidders. After negotiations, the final price was $74,997. This one-story, 140-by-320-foot structure was built in 1912–13.

Street-Railway Structures in Baltimore

PART III

OTHER WORKS IN BALTIMORE AND BEYOND

❧ CHAPTER 5 ❧

Churches and Rectories

Baldwin seems to have preferred ecclesiastical work, on churches in particular, perhaps as a way of melding his religious devotion with his professional architectural interests and his livelihood. Some of his very earliest work—and his last—was on the design of houses of worship for the Roman Catholic Church. Baldwin's family provided an obvious and natural connection to this church, which led to many commissions for Baldwin and his firms. Through his partnership with Bruce Price, a member of the Protestant Episcopal Church, Baldwin obtained a lesser—but interesting—number of commissions for churches of that denomination. (In the following discussion, all churches, unless otherwise noted, are Roman Catholic.)

Churches are buildings that command respect and care, and they are the most enduring and survivable category of Baldwin's work. If Baldwin were alive today he would likely derive no small measure of satisfaction from knowing that four-fifths of the churches and rectories that he worked on from 1869 to 1916 are still standing. All told, there are more than sixty such structures or projects. Many are major buildings, but some are additions or alterations to existing structures. Most of the churches are in or near Baltimore, but there were important commissions some distance away—one as far as Savannah, Georgia.

Baldwin & Price (1869–1873)

Five churches were begun or completed during the relatively brief period that Baldwin and Price were partners in Baltimore.

In the first year, the young architects secured an important commission for the **Christ Episcopal Church** (fig. 47), to be built on the NW corner of St. Paul and Chase Streets. This large project must surely have been a boost for the new firm. By early 1870 the plans had been drawn and approved, and builders were put under contract. Peter Snyder was hired for the stonework and excavation, with a contract for $43,795; McComas & Paine were hired for general construction. On March 22, Price recorded that the builders had commenced laying stone. The cornerstone was laid in ceremonies on May 24. By July 1, the building was "under roof" and plastering was nearly finished. On July 26, Peter Snyder "topped out" the main tower in the SE corner of the building. The church was structurally complete and opened for use on January 7, 1872. The total cost was $112,136.

On September 28, 1870, Robert E. Lee made his last public appearance at a vestry meeting in **Grace Episcopal Church**, on the campus of Washington & Lee University in Lexington, Virginia. Upon his return home that evening, he suffered the stoke that led to his death, on October 12. Lee's death provided a strong incentive for the erection of a new church building in his memory (plate 10). The Building Committee resolved on October 19 to request plans and specifications for a church capable of seating 1,200 persons. The church records show that by the next February the size had been reduced to 800 people and the cost limited to $20,000. On March 23, a new plan was presented to the committee, which resolved, in April 1871, to proceed with the erection of the new church, "upon the general plan submitted by Messrs. Baldwin and Price." How it came about that Baldwin and Price were invited to bid on this church is not known, but James C. Neilson was a friend of Washington Lee, then president of the college. In any event, this is the only reference to Baldwin or Price, or any other architect for that matter, in the church records.

Because there were many changes in the plans of the church in the ensuing years of its construction, the identity of the architect has been the subject of

debate and discussion. In addition to Baldwin & Price, arguments have also been put forth for R. Adams Cram and James C. Neilson. Both can now be discounted. The records are incomplete, but Price was probably primarily responsible for executing the commission and preparing the original design of the church in Lexington, and Baldwin was left to complete the work alone after the first year or two. The journals of the architects, coupled with the evidence unearthed by others in Lexington from local sources, allows the formulation of a clearer interleaved chronology of the origins and construction of the Lee church.

The first entry in the Baldwin & Price journal on the "Grace PE Church, Lexington, Va." is in Baldwin's handwriting and dated July 5, 1871. Baldwin noted that Price had visited Lexington in February and on his return prepared the design of the church. The drawings were forwarded early in March and accepted by the vestry. Price visited Lexington again in April and received orders to proceed with working drawings and specifications, with a fee for full charge and superintendence of 5 percent.

The next record is dated November 13, 1871, when a meeting of the vestry decided to reduce the number of seats to 450 and the cost still further, down to $15,000. On December 16, 1871, Baldwin recorded that a sheet of drawings had been for-

warded to General Custis Lee which had been carefully designed so as to not exceed $15,000.

The church records for April 15, 1872, indicate that the vestry had voted to abandon the new church and accept the design of the architect for an enlargement of the present church. This was not met with approval by the congregation. On April 30, the previous decision was rescinded and orders given to proceed with the new church, at a cost of $15,000 or less.

By May 30, demolition of the old church and salvage of some materials was under way. The local paper reported that the new church would be built of stone. In this regard, the August 30, 1872, issue of the *Lexington Gazette* contained an advertisement for a slate quarry of a C. C. Baldwin, Amherst county, which included the endorsement of "E. F. Baldwin, Esq., the architect of the B&O Railroad and also of the new Episcopal Church in Lexington, Va." (This is not only additional evidence of Baldwin's responsibility for this church but also the earliest known published reference to Baldwin as architect of the B&O Railroad.)

The church records on the construction of this church over the next few years are almost as silent on the subject as are the architects' records. Progress was slow. The walls were completed in July 1880; repairs to the foundation had to be made in 1881. Baldwin noted payments in March 1882 to Joseph Thomas & Son for interior wood finishing ($2,723) and to Otto Duker & Company for doors, pews, wainscotting, communion table, and so on, for $1,963. In June 1882, Baldwin noted that John G. Hetzell had agreed to furnish the galvanized ironwork on the spire for $355 and to cover the spire with metallic shingles for $165.

The church was consecrated on May 30, 1886, though it had essentially been completed in December 1883. The final cost was given as $54,480. The name of the church was changed in 1886 to Grace Memorial and again in 1903 to the "R. E. Lee Memorial."

Savannah Cathedral (plate 11). Plans for the building of a new Roman Catholic cathedral for the Diocese of Savannah were put in motion in 1870 by Bishop Ignatius Persico, who acquired the land on Abercorn Street in Savannah, Georgia, for this purpose. Baldwin's first entry in his journals on this cathedral was made on August 9, 1871: "Bishop Persico being in town we consulted with him in regard to the competition for his new cathedral. Made him some sketches and agreed to furnish plans and specifications in competition to be in by Oct. 15th."

Clearly both Baldwin and Price were involved in these early stages. On October 13, Price recorded that he had forwarded the designs to Bishop Persico.

On November 7, 1871, the architects received a telegram from the bishop stating that their design had been selected and that one of them must go to Savannah immediately. Price wrote that a telegram was sent the next day advising of a visit on the following Monday. An official letter of confirmation was received from the Building Committee in Savannah on the thirteenth. Baldwin then wrote that he went to Savannah on November 16 and stayed with Persico and that he had signed a contract at 3½ percent of the cost. He received $500 as the premium for their adopted design, and he obtained information on the prices of labor and materials in the Savannah area. Baldwin returned to Baltimore on November 22.

In February 1872, Baldwin sent drawings and specifications to the bishop and gave drawings to Philip Walsh, a contractor, to use in preparing estimates for construction. Also in February, it was noted that 140,270 paving bricks were sent on the Schooner *A. H. Edwards* to Savannah, at a cost of $13 per thousand. In April, Baldwin forwarded the two proposals that had been submitted: one for $165,000 by Walsh, the other for $145,000 by John Kelly. Other proposals were submitted for specialized work (e.g., ironwork by Bartlett, Robbins & Co. for $33,977).

The cornerstone was laid on November 19, 1873, by Bishop William H. Gross, who had replaced Persico in February of that year. Nearly three years later, on April 30, 1876, the cathedral was dedicated. The total cost was about $150,000. (The two spires were not added until 1896, at an additional cost of about $35,000.) Other interior furnishings remained to be installed. Baldwin noted proposals for the main altar, communion rails, etc., in the years 1881 and 1882. The *Baltimore Sun* article on the new cathedral mentioned that architect Baldwin had personally designed special candlesticks for it.

The **Episcopal Residence** adjoining the cathedral was designed by Baldwin in 1889. The original bid was by W. F. Chaplin for $25,717, which was later negotiated down to $22,175. The final cost of the residence was closer to $26,000.

The cathedral, officially known as the Cathedral of St. John the Baptist, was almost entirely destroyed by fire on February 6, 1898. Baldwin was summoned to Savannah to take on the task of rebuilding the great church. Later that month he

reported to the committee in Savannah that he had inspected the ruins and that the towers (which were suspect) were not beyond repair. He agreed to do the work for 2½–3 percent depending upon the requirements imposed on him as to superintendence. The committee insisted that the cost be held to less than $100,000. By November, Baldwin had received the proposals for the rebuilding: Miles & Bradt received the basic contract for $83,500; other bids were accepted for electrical work (D'Olin Engineering, $1,190), the electrical fixtures (George Walther, $1,820), and the altars (Mullan, $3,077 and $2,890). Baldwin penciled in a total estimate of $92,477, which appeared to meet the committee's requirement. The figure given for the rebuilding in the literature published by the church was $150,000. The second dedication of the cathedral took place on October 28, 1900. The structure had been used, however, for its first mass the previous December. In 1912, the interior was redecorated and the twin spires were finally completed.

Baldwin and Price both appear to have worked on **St. Ann's Church** (plate 12), Greenmount and 22nd Street. Baltimore plans were begun in 1872 or 1873. John Stack was the builder with a proposal for $32,000, exclusive of the "spire tower." Work began in March 1873 and the cornerstone was laid on April 15. By the time the church was dedicated, on January 30, 1874, responsibility for it had fallen totally to Baldwin. Baldwin's accounting of the costs totaled $42,790: contract ($32,000), completion of tower ($9,000), marble cornice ($550), and side altars and pews ($460).

Baldwin was commissioned for several alterations and modifications to St. Ann's in 1879, and it is probable that the proposals he recorded receiving in 1884, for an "extension" to the church, were for the transepts, which were completed in 1888. Philip Walsh was the builder, at a cost of $14,300, bringing the total cost to about $57,000.

Also in the 1880s, Baldwin designed additional buildings for St. Ann's parish. On June 26, 1883, proposals were submitted for a "Sister's House" and a "Pastoral Residence." Henry Curley was given the contracts, for $4,250 and $5,750, respectively, work to be completed by the end of 1883. In 1887, Baldwin designed a two-story granite parochial school building adjacent to the Sister's House; it was built by Philip Walsh & Sons for about $14,000.

St. Augustine's Church (fig. 48), on 15th and L Streets NW, in Washington, was the district's first church for black Catholics, and Baldwin was chosen as the architect. Work on the building began in 1873,

Baldwin & Price
(1869-1873)

Fig. 48. St. Augustine's Church, Washington, D.C.
Laurence V. Baldwin

in part with the labor provided by the members themselves in order to defray costs. One of the builders may have been a man by the name of Rawlings. The cornerstone was laid on June 14, 1874. The church, which could seat 1,500 persons, was completed and dedicated on June 11, 1876.

In 1890, Baldwin prepared the plans for a pastoral residence for St. Augustine's. Proposals were

Fig. 49. St. Teresa of Avila, ("Uniontown Church"), Washington, D.C.

received in March from John Stack ($11,921) and Edward Brady ($11,384), but a month later Baldwin noted in his records that "the plans were modified and reduced and the residence was erected by a Washington man for $8,000."

St. Augustine's Church was last used for the Christmas mass in 1946. The Washington Post purchased the vacant church and applied for a permit for its destruction, which was carried out in 1947.

Baldwin and Pennington (1874–1916)

Most, if not all, of the churches that were built from 1874 onward were probably designed by Baldwin, even during his partnership with Josias Pennington. Baldwin took a personal interest in ecclesiastical work, while Pennington's interests tended toward secular works for businesses and for a private clientele. Baldwin's ledger books have brief entries on four churches in the latter half of the 1870s; only two of these may actually have been built.

—In 1877 Baldwin sent sketches for eight sheets of drawings to Reverend Luizelle in Memphis for **St. Joseph's Church**, which measured 50 by 100 feet and would cost about $9,500. The cost of a tower, sanctuary, and sacristy was an additional $5,000. Baldwin received $150 for his work.

—In 1878 Baldwin prepared plans for Rev. George Bradford, **Chestertown Church**, in Kent County, Maryland, for a small frame church 35 by 65 feet. Baldwin received a payment of $25.

—In 1878 Baldwin submitted proposals to Rev. J. A. Walter for the "**Uniontown Church**" in Washington. Drawings for a building that would cost about $6,500 were sent in June and returned with a request for a less costly design. Revised plans for a small brick church that would cost about $5,000 were sent in July. The church—Saint Teresa of Avila—was built in 1879 by Isaac Beer and still stands at 13th and V Streets, SE (fig. 49).

—A proposal was prepared for Bishop Gross of Savannah, Georgia, for **St. Patrick's Church**, which Mr. Towson would build for $38,700. This was probably the church that was built in downtown Savannah at Liberty and West Broad Streets. Its cornerstone was laid in 1879 and it was dedicated on St. Patrick's Day, 1882. This structure was demolished in 1941.

Woodville Church. In April 1879, Baldwin records that he made plans and detail drawings for a small frame church for Rev. Henry Volz in Woodville, in Prince George's County, Maryland. The church was to cost about $2,800. A builder, William Murphy, estimated that the church would cost closer to $3,400, but on May 2 he signed a contract to build it for $3,200, with a completion date of August 1. Baldwin provided additional details to Murphy for the porch entrance, belfry, rose windows, and gable brackets. Woodville is now called Aquasco. It has a small church with a cornerstone dated 1879. Though it is made of brick, this may be the church mentioned in Baldwin's journals, even though the journals originally specified a frame structure.

There is no question about Baldwin's responsibility for **St. Leo's Church** (fig. 50) in Baltimore's "Little Italy," on the corner of South Exeter and Stiles Streets. Baldwin's role was dutifully reported in the *Sun* and in the *American Architect and Building News*. In June 1880, Baldwin had prepared the drawings for the 53-by-95-foot brick structure. The foundations were laid in July, and Cardinal Gibbons himself presided over the cornerstone-laying ceremony on September 13, 1880. The church was completed and dedicated on September 18 of the next year. Edward J. Brady was the builder. The church is on the National Register of Historic Places.

In May 1881 Baldwin recorded a contract for a "temporary chapel" for Rev. W. E. Starr; the builder was Philip Walsh for a cost of $11,882. This could be the **Starr Methodist Episcopal Church**, which was located on Poppleton Street, just one-half block north of the B&O's Mount Clare Station.

St. Gregory's Church (fig. 51), on North Gilmore Street, was founded in 1883. A schoolhouse was built for the church in 1884, which Baldwin may have designed, but it is certain that he was the architect for the church and rectory. In May 1885 a contract was given to John Stack for $42,000 for the church building. The cornerstone of this 60-by-120-foot stone church was laid on September 13, 1885. The marble altar was built by Hugh Sisson for $1,995. The church, which was completed in 1886, was closed in the early 1970s. The adjacent rectory, or "pastoral residence," was built in 1896 by Cornelius Sheehan under a contract for $8,300.

Our Lady of Good Counsel Church was built under the pastorate of John Hagan in 1889 and 1890. Baldwin received bids for the building in April 1889, and Buckley & Winn were chosen as the general contractors for a sum of $26,298. Hanrahan & Sons

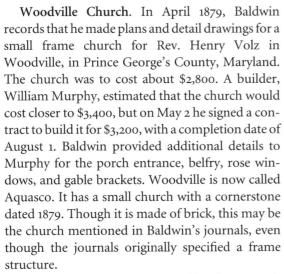

Fig. 50. St. Leo's Church, Baltimore

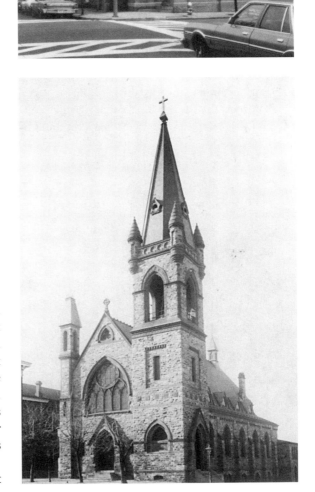

Fig. 51. St. Gregory's Church, Baltimore. *Laurence V. Baldwin*

were the subcontractors for the stonework. The cornerstone was laid in May 1889. The 57-by-110-foot structure with a 107-foot tower was completed and dedicated on June 1, 1890. This church is still standing on the NW corner of Fort Avenue and Towson Street in Locust Point.

The *Baltimore American* reported the dedication of St. Lawrence Church on Fort Avenue in September 1867. This small, 30-by-75-foot wood and stucco building was erected by the builder John Stack. Baldwin designed its conversion to a school building in 1889. The structure was razed in the late 1920s to make way for the present school building.

Baldwin's records indicate that in February 1889 he was engaged by Rt. Rev. A. A. Curtis for a church in **Cape Charles** (fig. 52), Virginia. In March, a contract was signed with John Stack for $11,848 for the brick structure. Mullan & Sons provided the altar and steps for $864. Baldwin recorded a total cost for the church of $13,000. This church, which is still standing, is the only known Baldwin-designed church on the Virginia Eastern Shore. Nine years later, Baldwin was the architect for a school and a Sister's residence for the Cape Charles church. The contract was awarded to Thomas M. Sleinous of Salisbury, Maryland for $8,330.

St. Michael's Church, on Lombard and Wolfe Streets in East Baltimore, was extensively rebuilt by

Churches and Rectories

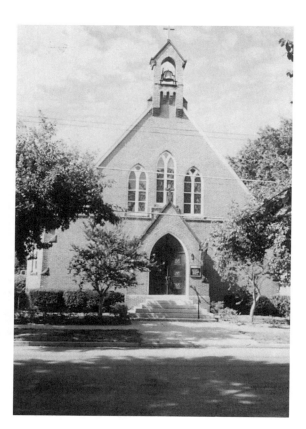

Fig. 52. Church, Cape Charles, Virginia

Baldwin & Pennington in 1889 and 1890. A new front with a tower, a spire with a clock and bells, and stone veneer completely restyled the original Louis L. Long church. Bryan Hanrahan had the $27,267 stonework contract.

The extent of Baldwin's involvement with **St. Ann's Church**, in Wilmington, Delaware, is not known; nor do we know the nature of the work here that the architect referred to in his journal in June 1891. Eleven proposals were submitted to him, and a contract for $18,975 was awarded to the McCloskey Brothers on July 6, 1891.

St. Mary's Church (fig. 53), at 727 Fifth Street NW, in Washington, was designed by Baldwin. Seven proposals were submitted for the work, and John Stack's low bid of $61,700 earned him the contract for this stone church. The articles of agreement between Stack and Rev. George Glaab were signed on April 5, 1890, with the expectation that the church would be completed by June 7, 1891. Mullan & Sons built the altar for $1,998; William E. Wood built the heating plant ($1,400), and separate contracts were made for the communion rail ($265) and two confessionals ($220). Mr. Bryan Hanrahan may also have done some of the stonework. The cornerstone was laid by Bishop A. A. Curtis on July 27, 1890; the dedication took place on June 30, 1891, with Cardinal Gibbons presiding. Baldwin's small pocket notebooks record the final cost of this church as $70,000.

The Church of St. John the Evangelist in **Forest Glen**, Maryland (plate 13), was built over the period 1892–94, for the parish of Rev. Charles O. Rosensteel. On July 6, 1892, six bids were submitted for construction of this red stone building; Baldwin's records fail to indicate who was selected, but the low bid of $14,000 was submitted by Edward West of nearby Rockville. Baldwin gave personal attention to this church; his notebooks show that he visited the construction site at least six times in the latter half of 1893. The church was completed and dedicated in April 1894. It is still standing, its appearance virtually unchanged.

Bon Secours. In October 1893 a contract was awarded to the builder John Carey for a small chapel and a house for "Bon Secours," which may be the hospital in West Baltimore. No location or specifics are revealed in the architect's records. The contract for the chapel was $5,013; the contract for the house was $12,332.

St Mary's Church, Cambridge. Baldwin was engaged by Rt. Rev. A. A. Curtis again in 1894 for this small brick church on the Eastern Shore of Maryland. The contract for $5,610 was given to Thomas Quimby of Skipton, Maryland. A rectory for the church was built in 1896 by A. W. Norbeck & Company for $3,288. These buildings are still standing, at 300 and 302 Mill Street.

Bishop Curtis also commissioned Baldwin for a church in Ridgely, Maryland. On March 24, 1896, a contract was given to Thomas Quimby for $2,750. The small white frame church still standing there is believed to be the building that Baldwin recorded in his journals.

Baldwin was the architect for **St. Martin's Male School** on North Fulton Avenue. This three-story, 36-by-62-foot school was built in 1883 by J. F. Adams and opened on September 10, 1883. In 1896, Father Broydrick of St. Martin's hired Baldwin to design a rectory and a school called Foley Hall. On May 15, 1896, a contract for them was awarded to Cornelius Sheehan, for $4,460 and $12,330, respectively. The final cost of the work was $25,076.

St. Patrick's Church (fig. 54). The first church of St. Patrick, on the NE corner of Broadway and Bank Street, Baltimore, was built in 1806 and 1807. It was replaced by a church designed by E. Francis Baldwin. On April 8, 1897, the architect received seven proposals for general construction and five for stonework. On April 22, Baldwin rejected them all, "on account of the informality of some of the proposals," and decided to invite new bids after certain changes in the drawings and specifications had been made. On April 29, three general and five stonework contracts were submitted.

The contract for St. Patrick's was awarded to Cornelius Sheehan for $45,144; he won additional contracts for the confessionals. Contracts were given to J. P. Mullan for the main altar ($2,387), the communion rail ($1,591), side altars ($1,274), and statues ($942). George Walther provided a brass altar gate for $160. The heating plant was by Wells & Newton ($2,600). Baldwin's rough figure for the total cost was $60,000. The cornerstone was laid by Cardinal Gibbons on July 25, 1897, and the church was dedicated on November 20, 1898. A 2,500-pound bell from the old church was installed in the tower for the new church, along with a clock. The church was badly damaged by a fire on August 16, 1983, but it has since been rebuilt.

Hampden church rectory. Baldwin's journal references to "St. Thomas Church in Hampden" are probably for the church of St. Thomas Aquinas, in upper Baltimore. The contract with Father Cunningham for the church rectory on 37th Street near Roland Avenue was awarded in April 1899 to Glad-

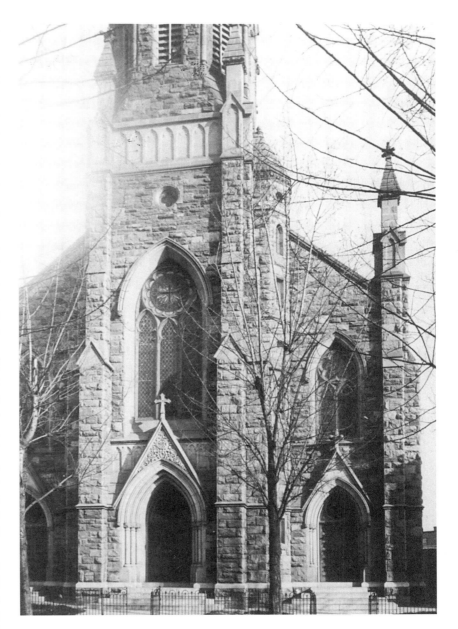

Fig. 53. St. Mary's Church, Washington, D.C. *Laurence V. Baldwin*

felter & Chambers for $8,900 and completed in November, at a final cost of $9,801. The rectory is still standing.

St. Augustine's, Elkridge (plate 14). Baldwin & Pennington were the architects for a schoolhouse and a church located in Elkridge, Maryland. Werner Brothers obtained the $4,100 contract for the school in February 1900. Work was completed in June. The contract for the church was given to George A. Blake on February 20, 1901, for $21,408. The contract for the main altar was awarded to J. P. Mullan for $1,330. The final total cost, according to Baldwin's records, was $29,090. The church is still standing, at 5976 Old Washington Road.

The **First German Baptist Church** is a rare instance of a non-Catholic church designed by Baldwin & Pennington. This 80-by-90-foot stone church was located on the NW corner of Patterson Park Avenue and Monument Street in East Baltimore. Built in 1902–3, it has long since been demolished.

The church of **St. Anthony of Padua**, on Frankford Avenue near Belair Road, in Gardenville, was built in 1885. In 1902, Rev. Henry S. Nagengast engaged Baldwin to design a rectory adjoining this church. The contract was given to C. R. Parlett on September 3 for $6,719; the cornerstone was laid on the nineteenth. Baldwin's jottings in his ledger indicate that the rectory was made up of two units: one

was 33 by 40 feet, 37 feet high; the other was 16'-6" by 23'-6", and 32 feet high. The final cost of the brick rectory came to $7,445. It was demolished in 1961.

St. Katherine's Church, on the south side of Preston Street near Luzerne, was designed by Baldwin in 1902. The contract was awarded to Elmer A. Parrish on September 6 for $23,800. Monitor Company did the steam heating for $1,382. Ground was broken on October 13 and the cornerstone laid on November 30. Excluding the vestibules, the 40-by-75-foot Falls Road granite church had seating for 400 people. Over a decade later, Baldwin & Pennington drew the plans for the three-story brick and stone rectory for this church; the builders were Monmonier & Sorrell at a cost of about $15,000. Both of these buildings are still standing.

St. John's Church Rectory, Frederick. Rev. William Kane was appointed to St. Johns, Maryland, by Cardinal Gibbons in July 1902. Kane had been born, raised, and educated in Baltimore and had held posts in the Baltimore Archdiocese before going to Frederick, so he may have known Baldwin and been responsible for commissioning him to design a new rectory there in September 1902. A contract was given to Harry W. Bowers for $7,640. Baldwin's calculations for the volume and estimated cost give some idea of the size of the rectory building: two units, one 23 by 52 feet, 46 feet high, and the other 17' by 20'-6", 40 feet high. The rectory is still standing, and it still has the front porch, which was allegedly the contribution of Father Kane himself, over the objections of the builders. The rectory was dedicated by Cardinal Gibbons on May 14, 1903.

The architect's available records show no entries for **McGovern Chapel**, but others have attributed this chapel near Mount St. Mary's College in Emmitsburg, Maryland, to Baldwin. This small, one-story brick and terra cotta trimmed structure was built in 1906 on the hill overlooking the college campus. It is also known as the Grotto Chapel.

In 1908, Baldwin and his son Francis designed the **Chapel of the Immaculate Conception** (plate 15) on the campus of Mount St. Mary's College. The architect's records that are available do not include this work. The cornerstone was laid on April 24, 1908, in ceremonies presided over by Bishop Curtis; the large stone church was completed in 1910.

By 1910, the chapel of the seminary of **St. Vincent's** in Germantown, Pennsylvania, was too small for its congregation, and plans for a new church were begun. Funds were limited, so only a "basement" church could be taken on at first. E. Francis Baldwin was selected as the architect, and excavation began at the site at 1020 East Price Street soon thereafter. Eight contractors bid for the church and a small rectory (which was not built), and the work was given to Thomas Reilly for $60,640 on February 11, 1911. The heating plant was installed by Finn & Jennings for $6,194. Baldwin himself apparently made an average of three trips a month to Germantown to oversee this work during 1911.

The "lower church" (as it was also called) was completed on December 3, 1911; the superstructure, or "upper church," was not completed until 1927. In 1915, Baldwin recorded the receipt of eight bids for a rectory for Immaculate Conception, ranging from $30,000 to $35,500. It is not known if Baldwin was involved in the completion of this rectory.

According to the *Sun*, Baldwin & Pennington were selected as the architects for the **Church of the Blessed Sacrament** on Old York Road and 42nd Street in Baltimore. The semi-Gothic brick and stone church was let for bids in May 1912. Baldwin's records show only that a contract was awarded to David M. Andrews in June 1912 for the basement level of the church, for the sum of $15,865. Any further involvement of Baldwin with this church is unknown.

Baldwin worked on **St. Wenceslaus**, on the SW corner of Ashland Avenue and Collington Street, in the early 1900s. In 1903, he designed a rectory and a "convent building" that were erected under contracts to John F. Buckley for $12,996 and $8,350. These were dedicated on July 23, 1903.

Ten years later, Baldwin was called upon to prepare plans for an addition to the rectory and a new church building. On November 10, 1913, contracts were signed with David M. Andrews, builder. The church was to be 134 by 72 feet, at a cost of $116,000; the 44-by-105-foot rectory was to cost $15,200, according to Baldwin's records. (The *Sun* reported a total cost of about $125,000.) The cornerstone of the Byzantine-style church was laid on February 28, 1914, and the building was dedicated on January 24, 1915. Baldwin's final tally of the costs for the church and rectory addition amounted to $116,474 and $14,348, respectively.

Sacred Heart Church in Mount Washington was truly Baldwin's final work. He was working on the plans for this church at 1701 Regent Road when he became ill and left his office in the Professional Building for the last time, in January 1916. The church was completed after his death. In March the *Sun* reported that bids for the $30,000 church had been submitted by J. J. O'Connor, Monmonier & Sorrell, William T. Harris & Company, and Edward

Brady & Sons. Ground was broken on April 7 and the cornerstone laid July 2, 1916. Mass was first offered there on June 24, 1917.

Additions and Alterations (1871–1902)

Over a thirty-year period, 1871–1902, Baldwin's work included additions and alterations to more than a dozen churches. Of these, only two are sufficiently important to warrant detailed discussion; the remainder will simply be tabulated with a few comments. Though not the first of such tasks, the most important was the work on major additions to the Basilica of the Assumption, or the Baltimore Cathedral.

Basilica of the Assumption. This Catholic cathedral—the first in the United states—was originally designed by Benjamin Henry Latrobe and built between 1806 and 1821. The twin towers were added in 1831 and 1837; the portico was completed in 1863 under the direction of the architect Eben Faxon (1821–68).

Baldwin was requested by Father Lee in December 1877 to make drawings of a proposed addition to the cathedral and an enlargement of its sacristy. Rev. Father Dubreul also requested plans for an extension of the cathedral. On December 17 Baldwin noted that, at the request of the archbishop, he had made three plans with drawings of their elevation and section. He estimated that the cost would be about $50,000, but if a basement chapel was not required the cost would be about $5,000 less.

On February 24, 1878, Baldwin attended the first meeting at the archbishop's residence to discuss the work. A committee was set up to evaluate the proposed plans. Baldwin must have been asked then to prepare more detailed estimates of the costs, because a month later he did so, and the new total was $35,000. On March 31, 1878, Baldwin attended the second meeting at the archbishop's residence; the committee recommended a plan and a "subscription" for $9,000 was opened. It was also decided at this meeting to pay the two architects who had been involved—Baldwin and Niernsee—$175 for the plans they had furnished.

Much of the next year must have been taken up with the preparation of detailed drawings and specifications and the submission of these to contractors to obtain bids for the work. On March 29, 1879, a contract was awarded to Henry R. Curley for the sacristy work for $6,000. But Curley found an error in his estimate and withdrew. The contract was then awarded to John Stack. On April 3, at the archbishop's request, Stack prepared an estimate for the work in which the outside walls of the proposed addition would be faced with stone like the rest of the cathedral, rather than being "roughcast." The new estimate was $8,000.

Construction was undertaken and additional contracts were let through Baldwin for heating (Thomas C. Basshor, $700), tiling and altar steps (Hugh Sisson & Sons, $1,925), and the stalls for the choir (Otto Duker, $360). Bartlett, Robbins & Company did the ironwork, and Hall's Safe & Lock Company installed a 2'-6" by 5'-0" by 6'-6" iron and steel vault for $900. The work was completed for the most part by the end of 1879, at a total cost of $19,625, according to Baldwin's personal records.

E. Francis Baldwin was the architect for the 33-foot extension of the east end of the cathedral in 1888–90.[1] This work is not reflected in those records of Baldwin's that are available, but there is a reference to the addition of "building vaults and crypt" in 1896, which was done by Bryan Hanrahan & Sons at a cost of $1,526. Baldwin's commission on that job was $75.

The original Italianate church of **St. John the Evangelist**, on the corner of Eager and Valley Streets in East Baltimore, was designed by John R. Niernsee in 1856; the 1882 additions were designed by E. Francis Baldwin. In May of that year Baldwin received proposals for the work, and a contract for $7,955 was awarded to John Stack. The separate $450 contract for the remodeling of the main altar was given to Mullan & Son in June. J. G. Hetzell & Son did the ironwork for $336. The stained-glass windows were provided by H. G. Gernhardt for a cost of approximately $1,050. According to the *Sun,* the final total cost of the work amounted to $28,000. The church reopened on September 23, 1883.

1. James Wollon notes that the addition to the cathedral was a major commission for Baldwin, *the* major commission by the Roman Catholic Archdiocese of Baltimore since the original construction of the cathedral. Baldwin's seamless addition is invisible even upon close examination and matches the original design in every way.

James D. Dilts feels that the cathedral is the most important single work of architecture in Baltimore. He notes that Baldwin & Pennington's 1888–90 choir extension resulted in the longer church that Latrobe had originally sought. He also points out that Latrobe expert Charles Brownell, professor of art history at Virginia Commonwealth University, recently referred to this addition as a "miracle of sensitive adaptation." Brownell considers the Baltimore basilica to be Latrobe's masterpiece, and "one of the great buildings of Western architecture."

Plate 1. B&O Station,
Rockville, Maryland

Plate 2. B&O Station,
Sykesville, Maryland

Plate 3. B&O Station,
Gaithersburg, Maryland

Plate 4. B&O Station,
Laurel, Maryland

Plate 5. B&O Station, Oakland, Maryland

Plate 6. B&O Station, Dickerson, Maryland

Plate 7. B&O Station, Winchester, Virginia

Plate 8. Homeland Station, Lake Avenue

Plate 9. Pratt Street Power House, Baltimore

Plate 10. Grace Episcopal Church, Lexington, Virginia

Plate 11. Cathedral of
St. John the Baptist,
Savannah, Georgia

Plate 12. St. Ann's Church, Baltimore

Plate 13. Church of St. John the Evangelist, Forest Glen, Maryland

Plate 14. St. Augustine's Church, Elkridge, Maryland

Plate 15. Mount St. Mary's Chapel of the Immaculate Conception, Emmitsburg, Maryland

Plate 16. Country Building (Cloud Cap), Catonsville, Maryland

Plate 17. Gibbons Hall Annex, College of Notre Dame, Baltimore

Plate 18. McSweeney Hall, Mount St. Mary's College, Emmitsburg, Maryland

Plate 19. Mount de Sales Academy of the Visitation, Catonsville, Maryland

Plate 20. Baltimore City College, Baltimore

Plate 23. Baltimore County Court House, Towson, Maryland

Plate 24. Merchants National Bank, Baltimore

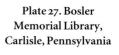

Plate 27. Bosler Memorial Library, Carlisle, Pennsylvania

Plate 28. Masonic Building, Fairmont, West Virginia

Plate 29. William
Donnell House,
Baltimore

Plate 30. Grafton Farm
Gate House, Upperville,
Virginia

❧ CHAPTER 6 ❦

Education Buildings

Baldwin & Pennington had a lot to do with shaping the form and appearance of several educational institutions in the Baltimore area in the late 1800s. In order to provide a framework for reviewing their work, I have established three categories: buildings for centers of higher education, such as colleges, universities, and seminaries; religious schools and convents for the Roman Catholic Church (a large group, reflective of Baldwin's interests and influence); and buildings for private schools and the Baltimore public school system.

Seminaries and Colleges

Nine academic institutions or facilities are presented below roughly in the order in which Baldwin became associated with them.

St. Vincent's Seminary. In April 1871, Baldwin & Price were engaged to furnish the design for a new "center building" and a church for this seminary in Germantown, Pennsylvania. Drawings for the new building, estimated to cost about $36,000, were completed in June. The church design was not accepted and work on it was delayed. In July the contract for the seminary building was awarded to James Kinear & Son for $27,000. The work was accomplished during the remainder of 1871 and into 1872. From their journals, it is clear that both Price and Baldwin made visits to Germantown every two or three months to oversee the construction of the four-story seminary building.

Construction of the chapel for the seminary did not begin until 1875. The cornerstone was laid on July 19, 1875, but the chapel was not completed until four years later, at a cost of over $51,000. It was dedicated on November 9, 1879 (fig. 55).

Over twenty years later, Baldwin & Pennington were hired by the seminary to design another building for the school. A $32,767 contract was awarded

to M. R. Dougherty in June 1900. The building was probably completed in 1901. (Blueprints in the seminary's archives are dated September 25, 1900.) Four years later the same architects were commissioned for an unspecified addition. The primary contractor was Melody & Keating; the cost of the addition was $57,921.

St. Mary's Seminary was the first seminary established (in 1791) in the United States, in the city that had become the first Catholic Diocese only two years earlier. Thus it must have been quite an honor for Baldwin to be commissioned as the architect for a complex of new buildings to be erected on North Paca Street in Baltimore in the 1870s. He submitted his plans for a four-story main building (to cost $21,700) and south wing (for $52,000) and described the proposed work in a letter, dated November 11, 1875, to Very Rev. Father Dubreul.

One issue to be resolved was the location of the buildings on the site. Baldwin noted the two possibilities: fronting on Paca Street in the rear of St. Mary's Seminary Chapel, or fronting southwest, adjoining existing buildings. Baldwin recommended the former, citing convenience of access, proximity to the cathedral, a more elevated site on a clean private street with better drainage, a better location of the kitchen and with main entrance in the main building, less disruption during construction, and unobstructed grounds once the old buildings were removed.

Baldwin's advice on location was taken, and the cornerstone of the first main section of the new seminary (fig. 56) was laid on May 31, 1876; the only laymen present at that ceremony were Baldwin and the contractors, John Stack, Mr. Hanrahan, and Mr. Simpson. The five-story seminary building was ready for occupancy in 1877, but it was not finished and dedicated until February 11, 1878. The total cost, as reported by the *Baltimore Sun*, was about $80,000.

Fig. 55. St. Vincent's
Seminary, Germantown,
Pennsylvania

In 1880, Baldwin designed the first addition to his main building, a wing extending to the north. He agreed to furnish drawings and superintendence for a 3 percent fee. This building was constructed between June 1880 and July 1881 by John Stack under a contract for $40,784. With this addition, the total frontage of the seminary on Paca Street amounted to 320 feet. A wing extending to the west from the north wing was constructed in 1891 by Edward Brady for about $40,000. The last addition, extending north from the end of the 1891 wing, was built in 1894. This so-called Philosophy Wing was built by John McKnight. Baldwin recorded repair work on the Paca Street complex by John F. Buckley, in 1900, at a cost of $1,076. Baldwin's plans in the early 1900s

for a new chapel for the seminary on Paca Street apparently were not fulfilled.

In 1975, just before its 100th birthday, the buildings of St. Mary's Seminary were torn down and the lot made into a park. Being listed on the National Register of Historic Places did not deter destruction of one of Baldwin's finer buildings. (The haste with which the demolition was undertaken made photogrammetry the only practical means of accurately recording the structure for posterity.)

Cloud Cap. St. Mary's Seminary purchased fifty acres of land in 1885 from the estate of Dr. Nathan R. Smith, called Cloud Cap, for a retreat for the students from the Paca Street complex. According to Baldwin's records, the seminary engaged him in 1886 to design a "country house," which was built by Edward Brady for $13,300. Baldwin specified a payment schedule for Brady contingent upon completion of stages of construction, which began in April 1886 and was probably finished by year's end. This stone building, also known as the Refectory, or the Science Building, became part of the Catonsville campus of St. Charles College after the facilities in Ellicott City had been destroyed by fire in 1911.

The location of this building, and more information about it, were found in the Sulpician Archives, where the seminary's records are held. These records are consistent with Baldwin's, showing a payment to him on February 5, 1887, of $465.50 for the "main building" at Cloud Cap. (This is precisely 3½ percent of $13,300.) The records also show payments to Brady for a "Farm House" ($3,800) and a "Barn" ($2,658) at Cloud Cap, but there is no indication of Baldwin's involvement in either of these structures.

Remarkably, this once-unidentified building, which is still standing, is located only a few yards from the Sulpician Archives, now housed in the former St. Charles College buildings, at 711 Maiden Choice Lane in Catonsville, Maryland (plate 16).[1]

In January 1884 Baldwin recorded proposals for work on the library of the **United States Naval Academy** in Annapolis amounting to a total of about $2,500 for woodwork, stonework, and galvanized ironwork. This is presumably in the nature of simple alterations to the "Old Governor's mansion," which served as the library from 1869 to 1907. In 1885 Baldwin handled some minor work on the academy's "Sick Quarters." He made journal entries of proposals for slate and tiles and a "stair to

1. The identification is properly credited to Rev. John W. Bowen, S.S., archivist.

the piazza" by Bartlett-Hayward & Company. In
December of 1888, Baldwin received eight bids for
work on the "Boat House;" a $24,244 contract for
this work was given to George H. Morrow. These
items have not been corroborated; the records for
this period are unavailable at the Academy, but the
academy archivist doubts the very existence of the
1888 building, noting that a boathouse had been
built in 1896.

Catholic University. In 1884 the Bishop of Richmond, John J. Keane, was given the task of overseeing the creation of a new university to be located in
the nation's capital. He set about raising the funds
and was fortunate to make contact with Miss Mary
Caldwell, an heiress to a large fortune, who contributed $300,000 for the first building of Catholic

University: the "Divinity Building," later renamed
Caldwell Hall. A design competition was announced and ten plans were submitted to a Building
Committee headed by Archbishop Williams of
Boston. (One of the competitors was George Frederick.) In a meeting with Cardinal Gibbons in Baltimore in May 1886, the top three plans were selected
and it was suggested that the first plan be awarded
$500, the next $200, and the third $100. Bishop
Keane subsequently became rector and rejected all
of the proposals. He and Mr. Black of Richmond
prepared new plans and submitted them to Archbishop Williams. In November 1886 an architect was
chosen. The *Baltimore American* of November 1,
1886, reported that "Mr. E. F. Baldwin has been
entrusted with the building of the Catholic College

in Washington. None of the various plans submitted by the architects of this and other cities were satisfactory. It was decided by the Building Committee to place the work in the hands of Mr. Baldwin who will at once prepare drawings from which a selection will be made. Ground is to be broken March 1st."

In September 1887 it was announced that the site for the university building had not yet been selected—and there was a hint of a controversy over the selection of the architect. According to the *Sun*, "the Washington *Critic* reports that Messrs. Cluss and Schulze of that city were not pleased with the action of the trustees in accepting the plans of Mr. E. F. Baldwin of Baltimore. Cluss and Schulze were awarded first prize of $500 for a plan of the proposed building. The circular said that $500 was to be paid for the best plan and 2½ percent of the cost of the building, with the $500 to be deducted from the percentage. Mr. Schulze said that $500 would not pay for making the plans." (Cluss and Schulze are perhaps best known for their 1881 design of the Arts and Industries Building of the Smithsonian Institution.)

Baldwin's selection as the architect for Caldwell Hall (fig. 57) was final. The contractor was Edward Brady; the stonework, including the unusual decorative grotesques,[2] has been attributed to Bryan Hanrahan. The cornerstone was laid on May 24,

1888, in a ceremony attended by Cardinal Gibbons, President Grover Cleveland, E. F. Baldwin, and the builder. The building was completed and dedicated in November 1889. President Benjamin Harrison attended that ceremony, and it is likely that Baldwin did also.

Soon after the Divinity Building had been completed, Baldwin was commissioned to design the second major building at Catholic University, **McMahon Hall**, which was built in the years 1892–95 (fig. 58).

Unfortunately, practically no Baldwin records exist for these two major buildings. For Caldwell Hall, there is only a page or two on proposals and the expenditures for interior furnishings and a simple calculation of the cost, based on a volume of 620,000 cubic feet at 18½ cents, which came to $300,000—precisely the sum that Mary Caldwell had contributed. What the real total was is unknown. The only mention of McMahon Hall in the available Baldwin memorabilia are entries in lists in a pocket notebook citing "work on hand" in 1893 and 1895.

Baldwin makes reference to a "professor's cottage" that was built in the latter half of 1895 by Edward Brady at a cost of $6,916, and one of his lists for the school includes a "barn" at a cost of $1,500 in 1890.

The Johns Hopkins University. The original campus of Johns Hopkins, which opened in 1876, was on a two-square-block area between North Howard and North Eutaw Streets, extending from West Centre Street beyond Monument Street. The

2. Also called gargoyles. Stone carvers often based these creations on people who had some association with the buildings they adorned.

first college buildings were located where Druid Hill Avenue now extends to Howard Street.

The earliest association of E. Francis Baldwin with John Hopkins appears to be for work done in July 1884 for the school's warehouse building at 19 South Gay Street. Baldwin earned a 5 percent commission on a $2,829 job to "strengthen" this building. Other jobs that Baldwin recorded were strengthening the floors and roof trusses of the biological laboratory building ($2,116, in December 1885), alterations and changes to the Chemical Building and Hopkins Hall Building ($4,080, May 1891), and rebuilding a warehouse at 32 West Baltimore Street ($16,407, 1893).

Baldwin was involved in the design of three major buildings built in 1885 to 1898 on the "old campus" of Johns Hopkins.

The **Physical Laboratory** building (fig. 59) was designed by Baldwin in mid-1885. Construction on the building, located on the NW corner of West Monument and Garden Streets, began in September and the cornerstone was laid on March 29, 1886. The lab was four stories high, of brick and stone, measuring 72 by 116 feet with a 95-foot tower in the SE corner supporting an observatory dome 21 feet in diameter. The contractors were William Ferguson & Brothers. The building was opened for use on April 22, 1887. According to Baldwin's records, the basic cost of the laboratory was $119,988, for which he earned a 3.5 percent commission.

Detailed descriptions for the physics building can be found in the Johns Hopkins University *Circulars* for May and July 1886. The university archives contain a letter from Baldwin to physics professor Henry A. Rowland dated April 5, 1887, noting that the Building Committee had requested that the work forces be out of the building soon and that the architects' responsibility would "shortly cease."

Baldwin & Pennington were selected in 1891 as the architects for **McCoy Hall**, a general-purpose academic building of classrooms, offices, and lecture halls (fig. 60). Preliminary plans were submitted in October 1891, with various cost estimates over $165,000, depending upon the addition of another story and other internal details. In January 1892 the architects reached an agreement to proceed with the preparation of detailed plans and specifications at a 4 percent commission. The 176-by-112-foot, four-story red sandstone building was constructed by Philip Walsh on the NW corner of Little Garden and Ross Streets. McCoy Hall had a 109-foot tower on the Monument Street side and a 125-foot clock tower on the Little Ross Street side. Baldwin recorded its completion in 1895 for a total cost of $185,283.

Construction of McCoy Hall was complicated by the necessity of relocating Levering Hall, a two-story, 44-by-80-foot brick building. This 2-million-pound load was moved some 200 feet westward by contractors Spicknall & Binyon. Daniel Gilman, the university's president, wrote to Baldwin in January 1893 after the move and asked the architect to investigate the building and "pronounce upon its condition" before it was used.

Fig. 58. McMahon Hall, Catholic University, Washington, D.C. *Laurence V. Baldwin*

Fig. 59. Physical
Laboratory,
The Johns Hopkins
University, Baltimore.
Laurence V. Baldwin

McCoy Hall was destroyed by fire on November 27, 1919. It is interesting that Professor Rowland had written to the architects, complaining about the noisy floors in McCoy and saying that the attic was a "fire trap." Rowland added, "it is useless for you to ignore science in this way as I warned you before the building was built."

In 1897, Baldwin & Pennington designed a new **athletic building** as an addition to the old 1883 gymnasium, on North Howard Street. The new two-story building, which measured approximately 103 by 130 feet, was divided into two basic parts: the gymnasium, with offices, trophy room, and quarters for boxing and fencing; and the "cage," a 65-by-130-foot enclosure suitable for indoor practice of

lacrosse and with a banked cinder track, ⅟₇ of a mile long, around the perimeter. The new gymnasium was built by J. J. Walsh at a cost reported to be about $35,000. The building was also destroyed in the fire of 1919.

College of Notre Dame of Maryland. The first building at this Roman Catholic college for women, built in 1873 at 4701 North Charles Street, was the Administration building, later called **Gibbons Hall.** It was designed by two of Baldwin's mentors, Niernsee and Neilson, and built by the contractor Samuel Adams.

It was fitting that Baldwin & Pennington were selected in 1894 to prepare the plans for an **annex** to be built on the east side of Gibbons Hall. This annex was intended to house the faculty sisters' residence and a 250-seat vaulted chapel. Twelve bids were received for the work; a contract was awarded to Edward Brady & Sons for $51,767. Construction began on March 19, 1895, and was completed in September 1896. Baldwin's records show that the final cost, exclusive of extra plumbing and the marble altars for the chapel, was $65,731; the total cost was $70,231.

The chapel in the annex (now called Theresa Hall) was restored by Murphy and Dittenhafer, architects, to its original appearance in 2002. This followed a 1968 modernization that had hidden most of the interior features (plate 17).

The small building called Caroline House, located just to the north of the annex, was formerly a gashouse and a stable. Built by Jesse Hutchinson in 1884, its architect is not known; its designer may be E. Francis Baldwin. (The next building to the east of the annex is LeClerc Hall, which was designed by Baldwin's eldest son, Francis, in 1926. It housed the gymnasium, pool, auditorium, and music room and was built by Henry Knott.)

St. Charles College. This Sulpician preparatory seminary was established in 1830, on the north side of Old Frederick Road, about four and a half miles west of Ellicott City, Maryland. The first building, designed by William E. Small and built in 1848, was expanded by additions in a westerly direction, in about 1859, 1860, 1866, and 1877, until it reached a length of 360 feet or more. One of the architects for the addition was S. Robinson Powell of Baltimore.

Baldwin & Pennington presumably had a continuing relationship with St. Charles College for minor alterations and modifications. In late 1896, Baldwin recorded work done by the builder Edward Brady on two bowling alleys for the sum of $4,614. Baldwin's records of March 1899 include a

26-foot-square laundry built by Werner brothers at a cost of $4,470.

In 1905, however, Baldwin & Pennington were commissioned to design a major new addition to the seminary building, a 50-by-105-foot, two-story granite assembly hall and recreation building. The college records report in June 1906 that "at present there is under construction in the rear of the main building a spacious hall equipped with a stage and designed for recreation and entertainments." The work was completed in 1906. Available records show no cost data or the addition's builder.

On March 16, 1911, the entire school complex was destroyed by fire. Baldwin made a half-dozen trips to the site afterward, presumably to discuss repairs or restoration. The college was not rebuilt but was relocated in Catonsville. In the late 1980s, only the granite walls of the 1906 addition still stood, and one could just barely trace out the foundations of the older structures in the underbrush. The area was developed and the ruins have been preserved.

Mount St. Mary's College. E. Francis Baldwin must have been proud when he was chosen to design new buildings that were to be constructed, in the early 1900s, at the college he and his son had both attended, in Emmitsburg, Maryland. In addition to the large 1906 chapel (cited above), Baldwin designed the gymnasium, the seminary building, and the administration building.

The gymnasium building, **Flynn Hall**, was built in 1902–3 by a builder named Hobbs, allegedly from materials that had been salvaged from an uncompleted 1857 chapel building. This is the only building for this college mentioned in the available Baldwin journals, and that information pertains only to the proposals for pool and bowling alley equipment.

The seminary building, **McSweeney Hall** (plate 18), was built in 1906–7. The cornerstone for this 52-by-176-foot T-shaped building was laid on October 8, 1906.

The administration building, **Bradley Hall**, or the Minim Building, was built last, in 1915–6. The cornerstone was laid on October 15, 1915. Frank J. Baldwin was probably the lead architect on this project, and the building was completed after his father's death.

McDowell Hall, at **St. John's College**, was a 1742 building intended as the first governor's mansion in Annapolis. It was seriously damaged by fire on February 20, 1909. Baldwin & Pennington were selected to do the restoration, which was carried out by the contractor John P. Waters of Baltimore.

Fig. 60. McCoy Hall, The Johns Hopkins University, Baltimore. *Ferdinand Hanburger Archives of the Johns Hopkins University*

Baldwin's records show that he personally traveled to Annapolis to deal with this project. The structure is still standing and has the distinction of being the third-oldest academic building in continuous use in the United States. McDowell Hall was featured on a postal card that was issued on June 1, 1996, unofficially as a commemoration of St. John's 300th year.

Religious Schools and Convents

On April 17, 1872, Baldwin & Price agreed to furnish the plans and specifications for the **Carmelite Convent**, to be erected on the SW corner of East Biddle and North Caroline Streets in Baltimore. The architects agreed to a flat fee of $250, which included an occasional visit and superintendence at the construction site. The builder, John Stack, signed a contract for $34,000 on May 4, 1872. The cornerstone of the 91-by-89-foot brick building was laid on July 21; the building was dedicated on March 23, 1873. The final cost, as reported in the *Sun*, was $45,000.

St Peter's School. In February 1872, Bishop Becker requested Baldwin or Price to visit Wilmington, Delaware, regarding plans for a school. By March, drawings had been sent and costs estimated as $8,000. The final working drawings were finished the next month and were expressed to Sister Kostka Flynn, a school superior. On April 13 she wrote back, saying that the work would have to be delayed, and asked for a bill. A $400 bill was prepared, but the architects agreed to a payment of $250, with the balance due upon commencement of construction of the building. The building at Sixth and West Street was completed, but the dates and final costs are unknown. The school building has been destroyed.

No records are available for corroboration, but Baldwin's advertisements list **St. Catherine Normal Institute,** on the NE corner of Harlem and Arlington Streets, as one of the buildings he designed. This building was dedicated on March 11, 1875.

Baldwin designed a schoolhouse for **St. Aloysius,** in Washington, D.C., which was built between May 1876 and August 1877. Located on North Capital and I Streets, the school was a 47-by-100-foot brick and stone structure, three stories high. The contractor was W. B. Downing & Brothers, and the cost was $20,110.

On July 2, 1877, Baldwin met with Brother Azarius of the Xaverian Brothers and agreed to prepare plans and specifications for a 40-by-60-foot, three-story schoolhouse for a fee of $100. The building was estimated to cost $7,100. It was a part of the Mount St. Joseph's School complex on Frederick Avenue in Irvington.

St. Mary's Industrial School, where George Herman "Babe" Ruth was once a student, was located on the SE corner of Caton and Wilkens Avenues. The main building was erected in 1867 and additions were made to it in the following years. In November 1877, Baldwin records the preparation of sketches for Father Colgan for an unidentified addition to this school which was to cost about $16,000. He also agreed in late 1877 to prepare plans for a two-story frame workshop; it was built by Edward Brady for $3,050. Brady had been the builder of the original building as well as additions in 1879 and 1886. Baldwin was one of a succession of architects who worked on this school complex over the years; others were Thomas C. Kennedy (1886), Tormey & Leach (1906), and Robert C. Ullrich (1910).

Baldwin was asked in June 1878 to prepare plans for a new academy building in Washington for the **Convent of the Holy Cross.** The drawings were sent to the superintendent on June 8; on July 1 Baldwin noted that he had by then made his fourth trip to Washington to discuss the plans and had opened the bids from the nine contractors seeking the job. The contract was awarded to the low bidder, William Harper, for $16,142. Work on the building at 1312 Massachusetts Avenue commenced on July 12. Baldwin's records on this building are meticulous, and he made a total of thirteen trips to the site before work was completed in mid-March 1879. In 1910 the academy was relocated to Maryland, and this building was subsequently demolished.

E. Francis Baldwin was the architect for a front addition to the **House of the Good Shepherd** building on the corner of Hollins and Mount Street in Baltimore in 1882. The three-story addition was 40 by 77 feet and had a mansard-style roof. The shape of the building was trapezoidal to fit the unusual lot; the builder was J. F. Adams. This building has been demolished.

The original building for **Mount de Sales Academy of the Visitation** in Catonsville was built in the years 1852–57. In 1882, Baldwin was selected as the architect for the west wing, which practically doubled the size of the facility (plate 19). In May, John Stack was selected as the builder for $51,400, the lowest of four proposals. The addition was completed in 1883. The final cost is not known, but the heating plant, provided by Bartlett-Hayward & Company, cost $8,548. The buildings are now on the National Register.

When an addition was required for the sisters' house at the **Immaculate Conception Female School** on Mosher and Druid Hill Avenue, which was near Baldwin's home, Baldwin made the plans. Four proposals were received on April 24, 1885, for the job. The low bid of $3,998, by Lewis C. McCusker, won the contract. In 1893 another addition to the sisters' house was handled by Baldwin, and its builder was Cornelius Sheehan at a cost of $9,920.

Rev. Henry Urben of the **Sacred Heart School** in Highlandtown hired Baldwin in 1888 for additions and modifications there. Five bids were received; the contract was awarded to August Degenhardt for $6,800. Eleven years later Albiens Schuck, under Baldwin's supervision, rebuilt the roof and did some work on a stairwell for $5,315.

Less than eight years after he had designed the church, Baldwin set to work on plans for **St. Leo's parochial school.** This 40-by-61-foot building, located on Stiles Street between High and Exeter, was built by Buckley & Winn and dedicated on November 18, 1888.

In 1890, Baldwin prepared the plans for an addition to the **Paulist Fathers Mansion House**, which was probably near Catholic University in Washington. It was built by Edward Brady & Sons under a contract for $9,500. The total costs, including electricity, piping, and heating, came to $10,660.

Baldwin was also the architect for the **St. Elizabeth's Church schoolhouse** and **residence hall**, on the NW corner of East Baltimore Street and Lakewood Avenue, near Patterson Park. Six contractors bid for this job, which was awarded to Cornelius Sheehan on May 23, 1895, for $17,787. The cornerstone was laid on July 7, and the building was dedicated by Cardinal Gibbons on November 19, 1895. The total cost of the work was $20,659.

Some of the buildings surrounding George Frederick's St. James Church in East Baltimore were designed by Baldwin. In 1892, Baldwin & Pennington were selected for the L-shaped addition to the **Institute of Notre Dame**, on Aisquith near Eager. The three-story, 44-by-56-foot and 45-by-105-foot structure was built by Otto Goldbach. Two years later these same architects designed a four-story brick building, measuring 27 by 54 feet, at the rear of the existing structure, as well as a four-story, 33-by-42-foot wing on the south end. Some work was also done on the front of the building. The total cost, according to an article in the *Sun*, came to about $30,000. In 1908, Goldbach built a two-story addition at 904 Somerset Street and, in 1909, a three-story brick laundry building for the institute at a cost of about $18,000.

Baldwin & Pennington were engaged for work on the **St. James Hall and School** buildings. Nine bids were received by Baldwin for the St. James Hall and Lyceum on June 20, 1896, from a high of $44,663 to George Blake's low (winning) bid of $33,400. The cornerstone was set on August 2, 1896, and the construction was completed the following February at a total cost of $37,971. The 60-by-110-foot, two-story brick building replaced one that had been destroyed by fire the year before. This was a well-equipped building: the basement had a bowling alley, billiard room, and social rooms; there were classrooms and meeting rooms, a library, and a kitchen on the first floor; the second-floor concert hall had a stage and seating for 900 persons. Baldwin's notes indicate that the total volume of the structure was 510,000 cubic feet, and his estimated cost, at a rate of 7½ cents per cubic foot, was $38,500. The St. James School building, located behind the hall on Somerset Street, is also a likely Baldwin design, though there are no records to prove this.

In a 1900 listing of work on hand, there is an entry for a **House of Industry**. Though this term was sometimes used to refer to a prison, it is believed here to refer to the St. Joseph's school building for girls at Waverly Terrace, on the SE corner of Carey and Lexington Streets. Baldwin was probably involved in alterations, since the original building had been purchased in 1868. They were sold in 1908, when the House of Industry was relocated to a building on 28th and North Charles Streets (designed by Tormey & Leach), and became what is known as the Waverly Apartments.

St. Augustine's School was built to accompany the church in Elkridge in early 1900. Baldwin received bids for this small building in February and the contract was let to Werner brothers for $4,100, work to be completed by June 15, 1900.

For the Dominican Sisters Convent on Frederick Road in Irvington, a **chapel** and **sisters' house** (actually a wing in the rear of the convent) were built by John Carey. He was awarded the $16,305 contract in October 1903, and the work was completed on January 21, 1904.

Baldwin's records show unspecified work on "**St. Paul's Girls School**" in the period 1893–95. An entry in his ledger dated February 1, 1895, shows charges of 5 percent for work that amounted to $55,667. The account was settled in full with a check for $1,500, with the difference noted as written off as a "special reduction." The nature and location of this work is unknown; the amount of money involved suggests that it was for a completely new structure or for extensive additions or modifications to an existing building. One possibility is that it was for the Catholic school for St. Paul's Church on North Caroline Street. (John Stack built a school building there that his children attended.)

Private and Public Schools

Baldwin & Pennington's work on educational facilities included a couple of minor jobs for two private schools and, more significantly, some fairly well-known buildings that they designed for the Baltimore City school system.

In September 1888, Baldwin agreed to prepare drawings and specifications for additions and alterations to the **Hannah More Academy** in Reisterstown, at a rate of 3 percent of the final cost. The nature of the work is not known. In October 1889 Baldwin was paid $150 for his services by a check from William Keyser.

The Bryn Mawr School for Girls was built on the corner of Preston and Cathedral Streets in Baltimore from funds provided by Miss Mary Elizabeth Garrett. The architect for the main building was Hornblower & Marshall. Baldwin & Pennington were engaged in December 1891 to work on the basement swimming pool in this building. They received a 5 percent fee on a total cost of $4,268 in a check from Robert Garrett in November 1892. The Bryn Mawr School was torn down in the early 1970s to make way for the Joseph Meyerhoff Symphony Hall.

Grammar School #7 (fig. 61) was the first in a series of schools for the City of Baltimore. Better known as the William Patterson school, it was located on the SE corner of Eastern Avenue and Burke Street. Baldwin was hired by the city's Inspector of Buildings on April 30, 1880, to prepare plans and specifications for the school, at what Baldwin noted was his "regular rate" of 3½ percent. The two-story brick building, measuring 58 by 104 feet, with twelve classrooms, was built by Francis T. Gallagher at a reported cost of $14,000. Dedicated in May 1881, it was destroyed in early 1981.

Baltimore City College. The building for Baltimore City College, on North Howard and Centre Streets, was one of Baldwin & Pennington's finest

and most artistic works (plate 20). Their involvement with it spanned nearly a decade, during which construction was hampered by numerous difficulties. A disaster had even originated the need for this building.

The school's existing 1875 building had been undermined by excavations beneath Howard Street for the B&O Railroad tunnel from Camden Station; it partially collapsed on August 4, 1892, and was condemned. The B&O apparently assumed responsibility for replacing the building and must have engaged Baldwin & Pennington, since this firm was already involved with all the tunnel project structures.

The architects began their preliminary work in 1893. In January they submitted a report containing estimates, rough plans of the old building, and a design for a new front. In December 1894 Pennington reported to Mayor Ferdinand Latrobe that the drawings for a new building were finished and bidding was open to contractors. The builders who submitted proposals for the project constituted a veritable who's who in the Baltimore building industry of the 1890s. Fifteen proposals, ranging from $130,000 to $212,000, were received. The bidders were George Blake, Edward Brady, J. B. Beatman, Brown & Garber, George Burnecke, P. K.

Lauter, Morrow Brothers, E. M. Noel, Probst Construction Company, J. E. & A. L. Pennock, Henry S. Rippel, H. Smith & Son, John Stack & Sons, Cornelius Sheehan, and J. J. Walsh. The low bid of Rippel's was accepted. George Walther was separately given the contract for $3,300 for gas and plumbing. Crook, Horner & Company won a $16,638 contract for heating and ventilation, and McCay-Howard did the lights and clock for $4,120.

The cornerstone was laid in a Masonic ceremony in August 1895, with Baldwin in attendance, according to an account in the *Sun*. For the next couple of years construction was plagued by problems that were partly due to foundation problems stemming from the difficult construction of the Howard Street tunnel under the building. These and other problems may not have been so unusual, but they attracted the attention of the press, which duly reported the fits and starts.

In April 1896 Baldwin met with architect Benjamin Buck Owens, the building inspector, about alleged "defects." A commission made up of Henry Brauns, E. D. Preston, and J. E. Adams was set up to examine the building. In June, Owens and the architects reached an agreement in the matter and the architects agreed to fix certain defects. According to the *Sun* account, iron lintels would be reset and cracks repaired, but a "small lean" could be ignored.

An inspection of the progress by mid-1897 revealed that some $144,497 had already been spent and that an estimated $78,075 would be required to bring the work to completion. Engineer William Rich Hutton, who was called in for consultations in 1898, certified that the necessary corrections had been made, but he made recommendations for additional changes. Work continued on and off until the building was finally completed, in June or July of 1899. The high school opened for classes on Baldwin's birthday, October 4, 1899. Baldwin's final personal accounting of the cost was $236,746.

The Baltimore City College building was gutted by fire (arson) on October 17, 1980. It was repaired and restored and became the Chesapeake Commons condominium. It is on the National Register of Historic Places.

In June 1909, Baldwin & Pennington secured the commission for the construction of buildings for the **Baltimore Polytechnic Institute,** located on the NE corner of Calvert Street and North Avenue in Baltimore. The *Sun* announced in July that the architects's plans had been completed for a building that would cost about $350,000 and would accommodate 1,200 students. Henry Adams was later selected as the builder.[3] The "Poly" school buildings were completed in 1912. They are still standing, recently refurbished and rebuilt.

Waverly Elementary (plate 21), on 34th Street near Memorial Stadium, was one of the finest public school buildings in the Baltimore system. When Baldwin & Pennington were commissioned to design it, it was simply called "Public School No. 51." Plans were begun in early 1910 for a three-story gray brick and limestone building of twenty-four rooms, measuring approximately 80 by 165 feet, at a cost of about $150,000. The cornerstone was laid on October 20, 1910, and the work was completed in time for the 1911–12 school year. This was reportedly the first school to have a well-equipped cooking and manual-training department. Waverly Elementary was demolished in 1981. Its demise was lovingly and painfully recorded in detail in a small book published the next year by a former student.

3. Henry Adams was born in Duisburg, Germany, on February 11, 1858, and came to Baltimore in 1880, working initially for the firm of Benjamin F. Bennett. He formed his own engineering firm in 1898 and was involved with the "Bromo-Seltzer" Tower, the Equitable Building, the Belvedere Hotel, the Emerson Hotel, and the Calvert Building. He died on December 9, 1929.

❧ CHAPTER 7 ❦

Health Care Facilities

Over a forty-year period beginning in the mid-1870s, E. Francis Baldwin was involved in the design of complete buildings or additions to existing structures for nearly twenty institutions involved with health care. These works include hospitals, asylums, sanatariums, and homes for the aged or infirm. Many of these were for Roman Catholic institutions, as might be expected, but there were a few buildings for the government or for private parties. Nearly all were in the Baltimore area. Excepting his possible involvement with Niernsee & Neilson's work on Mount Hope Retreat, the first of Baldwin's hospital projects was the St. Agnes Hospital in Catonsville, Maryland. Coincidentally, his last hospital building was also in Catonsville.

St. Agnes Hospital (fig. 62) was the first Catholic hospital in Baltimore, established in 1863 and located at Lanvale Lane and Greenmount. Within a decade it became necessary to expand these facilities, and plans went forward for a new building to be erected on land donated for this purpose by Lady Stafford, a grand-daughter of Charles Carroll of Carrollton. Baldwin was chosen as the architect for this new building on the SW corner of Wilkens and Caton Avenues. The builder John Stack began construction in the summer of 1874 on the 64-by-210-foot central building and a 200-foot-long wing on the north end. The cornerstone from the old Lanvale Lane facility was removed and transferred to the new site in elaborate ceremonies on May 30, 1875. The four-story brick buildings were completed in October 1876 at a reported cost of about $120,000.

The south wing—the Whiteford Memorial Wing—was added in 1891 and brought the hospital to its full cruciform configuration with a total length of 480 feet. William Ferguson was selected as the builder in March with a contract for $64,107. The new wing was dedicated on July 2; Baldwin, of course, was the architect for this wing as well as for

further additions and improvements that followed. In 1898, Edward Brady built a sanatarium and a gymnasium costing $24,431; the following year a coal vault for the boiler house was built for $2,687. In 1908 a barn and a stable were built by Edward Brady & Sons, costing $25,087. The old St. Agnes Hospital complex was demolished in 1961 and replaced by a new facility.

St. Mary's Industrial School. In 1883 Baldwin designed a small frame hospital building that was built by Edward Brady at a cost of $5,400. In 1898, Baldwin designed a second story for the hospital, which Brady built for $4,539.

Baldwin prepared plans in April 1877 for a wing to the main building of the **Little Sisters of the Poor**, a home for the aged in Washington, D.C. John Stack was the builder; the cost was $9,900. In July, a 20-by-26-foot addition was built by Herlihy & Wade for $16,000; in 1879 Stack built a 25-by-47-foot stable for the facility for $1,350.

In 1879, Baldwin prepared drawings and specifications for an addition to the **St. Joseph's Orphan Asylum**, also in Washington. This is probably the facility near Eastern Avenue and Bunker Hill Road.

The original buildings of **St. Vincent's Infant Asylum**, on the corner of Division and Lafayette Avenue, in Baltimore, was designed by the architects Long & Powell in 1860. In 1884, Baldwin designed a new wing and a laundry building measuring 30 by 60 feet. The contract was given to J. F. Adams in February for the low bid of $14,968. (This is probably the building that stands on the very corner of the block there.) In 1898 Baldwin was chosen to design a new chapel for the asylum, built by Edward Brady & Sons for $8,562, including a marble altar for $800 by J. B. Mullan Company. In April 1902, Baldwin made the plans for an additional story for the "center building," which was built by Edward Brady under a contract for $8,743. These

buildings have been used in recent times as apart-ment houses.

Baldwin & Pennington were the architects of record for an addition to the **Church Home and Infirmary**, on Broadway and Fairmont Streets in East Baltimore in the years 1887–89. This seven-story brick and stone structure, 66 by 81 feet, was on the west side of the original building. It was built by Brady & Son. In a perhaps rare example of preci-sion, the *Sun* reported that when the wing opened in January 1889 it had cost $44,674.78. Baldwin's ledgers, which show that he received a 4 percent commission, cite a cost of $49,486. And for some unknown reason, the architect notes that there was a "special reduction" of the fee by $79.45. This building has recently been demolished.

St. Mary's Female Orphan Asylum (fig. 63), on the SE corner of Cold Spring Lane and Roland Avenue in north Baltimore, was designed by Bald-win in 1887. A number of contractors bid for this job, which was awarded to John Waters, with bids ranging from $78,878 to $82,400 (depending upon the kind of stone to be used). The building was described in the *Sun* as being of granite with brown-stone trim, three stories high, measuring 96 by 169 feet, with an 84-foot tower in a Romanesque style. It was completed in the spring of 1889. In 1903, Bald-win planned a two-story addition to the infirmary

and a laundry, which was built by Edward Brady. The costs were listed as $11,342 and $13,199, respec-tively. The facility was closed in 1960; the building was razed, and an apartment house is now located on the site.

The **College of Physicians and Surgeons** build-ing, on the SE corner of Calvert and Saratoga Streets (fig. 64), was designed by Baldwin in 1888 after his firm had been selected in a design competition with two other architectural firms. His drawings were completed in April and the foundations dug in June. Cardinal Gibbons presided over the corner-stone-laying ceremony on September 30, 1888. The 110-by-114-foot brick structure was built by Henry Smith and inaugurated on Christmas Day, 1889. The total cost, as reported in the newspaper, was about $150,000. Baldwin's records on this building are incomplete; an entry in May-June 1889 shows work on the fifth story and operating rooms, with payments to Smith, Thomas J. Walsh (for tiling), and H. C. Bowman (for lavatories).

Baldwin designed the five-story **Baltimore City Hospital** on Calvert Street adjoining the College Building in 1891 and its large addition in 1911. These buildings, which later became Mercy Hospital, were demolished in 1981.

The original buildings of **Mount Hope Retreat**—better known to many Baltimoreans, perhaps, as the

Seton Institute—were designed by Long & Powell in the late 1850s. Niernsee appears to have assumed responsibility in the next decade or two, though the architect for the major additions, in 1867 and 1877, is unknown. John Stack was named as "architect and builder" for some work in the early 1880s. And it seems clear that by the mid-to-late 1880s, Baldwin and his firm were established as the responsible architects for additions and improvements on the northwest Baltimore site. That role would last almost until the time of Baldwin's death in 1916.

Baldwin designed an addition to the dining room and a "physician's residence" here in 1888–89. These were built by Cornelius Sheehan for $11,180 and $8,295, respectively. In 1890, Edward Brady constructed two "pavilions" here: a one-story building referred to as "No. 1" for $2,121, and a two-story building ("No. 2") for $2,359. In March 1891 John Stack built a bay on the main building for $3,825. A large building or an addition for a kitchen was built in 1893 by Edward Brady under a Baldwin-supervised contract for the sum of $40,847. Although there were probably many other Baldwin projects at Mount Hope Retreat during the next twenty years, the only ones cited in newspapers or in the architect's ledgers are two two-story wings on the main building and a chapel.

The brick and stone wings built in 1911 at a cost of about $90,000 were declared in an annual report to be the "third improvement" to the main building of Mount Hope Retreat since its construction thirty-five years earlier. The chapel at Mount Hope Retreat was built from April 1911 to October 1912 by John Waters under a contract for $114,384. Baldwin's fee for this building—the highest he ever recorded—was 8 percent. The facility closed in 1972. With the possible exception of the "doctor's house" and one or two "pavilions," these buildings were all razed in 1984.

The **Western Maryland Home**, referred to briefly in the Baldwin ledgers, is the original name for the Western Maryland Home & Infirmary, which was located on Baltimore Avenue in Cumberland. According to Baldwin, it was built between October 1890 and December 1892. Baldwin charged a 5 percent commission on its cost, which was estimated to be about $15,000. The building was dedicated on November 21, 1892. It later became the Western Maryland Hospital, until 1929. When it burned down in 1973, it was known as the Allegany Inn.

The **Garrett Free Hospital for Children** was founded by Mrs. H. B. Jacobs, the widow of B&O president Robert Garrett. In September 1889 it was relocated to a building at 27 North Carey Street in

Fig. 64. College of
Physicians & Surgeons,
Baltimore.
Mercy Hospital Archives

Baltimore and opened on January 1, 1890. Baldwin records work on this building in 1891, probably for minor additions or alterations, which cost only $1,475.

Baldwin also noted that he had prepared plans for the "Mount Airy Sanatarium," which was built in 1893 for the Garrett Hospital. The **Garrett Sanatarium**, in Mount Airy, Maryland, was the summer residence for the children of the Free Hospital. During June, July, and August, the Baltimore facility was closed and the children were taken by train on the B&O to Mount Airy. The sanatarium first opened in June 1894. It was located on a hill about one-quarter mile north of the B&O station that Baldwin had designed just a few years earlier. The sanatarium complex consisted of seven buildings, including two two-story wood-frame hospital buildings with porches on both levels, a kitchen, a

laundry building, and a large open-air pavilion for sleeping. The sanatarium could accommodate 100 patients. The Mount Airy buildings apparently survived serious fires in 1903 and 1914. Only the pavilion, which was reportedly converted to a dance pavilion and later a private home, still stands.

In May 1893 Baldwin prepared plans and specifications for an unidentified building for **St. Vincent's Sanatarium**, which was located near Mount Hope Retreat. Five proposals were received; Edward Brady & Sons got the contract. The final cost of the building was $28,240.

St. Elizabeth's Home. The *American Architect and Building News* of May 19, 1883, noted that a permit had been approved for a three-story brick addition to this facility at 317–319 St. Paul Street in Baltimore. In December 1894 Baldwin recorded the receipt of seven proposals for construction of a four-story building, and the contract was awarded to James F. Buckley on December 28 for $17,282. Scheduled for completion on October 1, 1895, it was finished in December at a final cost of $22,148. Baldwin calculated $20,970, for an "area" of 233,000 feet at 9 cents per cubic foot.

Maryland General Hospital and the Baltimore Medical College were clients of Baldwin & Pennington. The original building (the college), built in 1881, was located on the corner of Madison and Linden Avenues. Baldwin & Pennington designed an addition to this facility, which was built in 1894 by George Blake at a cost of about $50,000. Further additions were made later, extending the hospital to 817 North Linden Avenue. J. F. Buckley completed one addition in November 1896 at a cost of $36,276. Due to extensive rebuilding of this hospital, only the northern-most section of the Baldwin & Pennington addition is still standing.

St. Joseph's Hospital was built on Caroline Street in East Baltimore, between Oliver and Hoffman. The original architect was George Frederick; the builder was John Stack, who won the contract with his low bid of $46,000. This was a three-story brick building, about 80 by 170 feet, with a mansard roof. In 1880, a two-story addition, probably also designed by Frederick, was built at the rear of the original building for a washhouse and bakery.

Baldwin & Pennington, however, obtained the commission for the south wing of this hospital, which was built in 1896 and 1897. John Waters had the contract for $39,073, which was to include a chapel. The final cost, in January 1898, was $86,380. In early 1901 an addition to the kitchen and laundry was made by the builder Henry L. Maas at a cost of $10,388. In 1904, when Baldwin & Pennington planned the three-story annex to this hospital, Maas was awarded that contract for $42,764. Baldwin & Pennington were probably also the architects for a new laundry and powerhouse that Edward Brady built for $18,000 and for a 27-by-43-foot addition to the operating room, built by Brady in 1909 for approximately $10,000. Brady was also the builder for a two-story addition to the south wing in 1913; the architect was not identified, but it most likely was Baldwin. All of these buildings have been demolished.

St. Vincent's Hospital, Birmingham, began as a mission of the Daughters of Charity, whose parent organization was in Emmitsburg, Maryland. Four sisters were sent from Maryland to set up a public hospital in Birmingham, Alabama, in 1898. They established a temporary facility in a large residential building while plans and fund-raising were going on for a permanent hospital building. It is probably through the Emmitsburg organization that Baldwin's firm came to be chosen as the architect of this project.

On October 27, 1898, Baldwin & Pennington reached a cooperative agreement with architects Walter & Ullman of Birmingham for the hospital. The Baltimore firm would receive 2½ percent of the cost of the structure for the drawings and specifications, while the local architects would receive 1 percent for superintendence of construction. This was one of but a handful of jointly run projects that Baldwin entered into in his professional career.

In January 1899 the Mother Superior from Emmitsburg visited Birmingham, and a site, on 27th Street and Ninth Court South, was selected for the hospital. On February 25, the basic contract for construction was awarded to Cook & Laurie of Montgomery, Alabama, for $69,139. Ground was broken on March 11, 1899. The building was partly occupied on September 27, 1900, and finally dedicated on November 29, 1900. The final cost of the hospital was about $200,000. In 1972 it was demolished and replaced with a new hospital complex.

There is a cryptic entry in a 1900 list of Baldwin's work on hand for a "Casino Sheppard" and an amount of $10,000. This is doubtless a reference to the so-called **Casino Building**, which was built in 1901 on the grounds of the Sheppard & Enoch Pratt Hospital near Towson, Maryland. The Casino was a one and one-half story, 36-by-66-foot building with a 12'-6" veranda on three sides. There was a bowling alley and a billiard room in the basement, a gymnasium and recreation room on the ground floor. It was purposely set away from the main buildings of the hospital's north side so as to encourage the patients to get out of doors. It cost about $30,000. The Casino Building now serves as the student community center for University Village, a new apartment complex.

A long project was undertaken by Baldwin & Pennington in the early 1900s for a building at the United States Soldiers' Home in Washington, D.C. Called the **Mess Hall** (plate 22), this building was authorized in 1903 and construction began in 1904 or 1905. A very large building, it measured 260 by 290 feet and was four stories high. It employed steel-girder construction with white marble exterior facades and brick interior walls. It was finally completed in 1912, though it had opened for partial use two years earlier. The Mess Hall could seat 2,400, and it had a bowling alley, a gymnasium, and dormitories for about four hundred men. The total cost was well over $1 million.

The landscape architect Frederick Law Olmsted Jr. noted in an October 6, 1903, letter that Baldwin & Pennington were "entirely in ignorance of the proposals of the Park Commission affecting the problem of the location of the new building." Olmsted indicated that the Trustees of the Home were also unaware of the commission's recommendations.[1] This Renaissance Revival style building, later known as the Grant Building, is still standing at the northern-most end of the grounds of the Solders Home on North Capitol Street.

1. Olmsted noted that he had "some business to do with Baldwin & Pennington." The nature of that business is unknown; perhaps it was for work in Roland Park. This letter is the only evidence suggesting a possible joint effort of Baldwin & Pennington and the Olmsted Brothers.

In 1908 and 1909 the *Baltimore Sun* reported on the construction of two three-story wings for the **Annapolis Emergency Hospital**, in Annapolis, Maryland, and cited Baldwin & Pennington as the architects, Henry Smith as the builder.

An account in the *Sun* in 1911 referred to Baldwin & Pennington's work on buildings for the Maryland Hospital for the Insane. References were made to a three-story, 46-by-114-foot stone structure built by John Waters at a cost of $80,000. This is probably the **Female Crafts Building** of Spring Grove Hospital in Catonsville. Other sources note an appropriation in 1911 for remodeling and improvement of the hospital kitchen and a female "industrial shop," constructed of stone, with facilities for sewing, weaving, and fancy work. This building, completed in 1912, is no longer standing.

Health Care Facilities

CHAPTER 8

Government Buildings

Baldwin & Pennington were responsible for work on a few government buildings, including some public utility and public works facilities and two of the most important commissions from the State of Maryland. (Buildings for the government at the U.S. Naval Academy and the Soldiers Home are discussed in other chapters.)

The first instance of work in this category is a small job for a county courthouse in West Virginia. E. Francis Baldwin recorded on June 11, 1878, that he had "sent to J. C. Holmes drawings and specifications for the improvement of the acoustics and appearance of the Jefferson County Court Room, as ordered by Judge Baylor." We can only presume that the directions Baldwin referred to were followed and that the courthouse is the one in Charles Town, West Virginia—site of the famous John Brown treason trial in 1859. The building, which still stands, is on the National Register of Historic Places.

There are no other works of this type by Baldwin or his firm until after 1900, when Baldwin & Pennington were commissioned by the State of Maryland for a prestigious series of buildings in Annapolis.

Court of Appeals (fig. 65). In 1900, the state authorized funds for the acquisition of land and the construction of a "Public Building" that would provide courtrooms and offices for the Maryland Court of Appeals, a portion of the state library, offices for the comptroller, and offices for the treasurer. The site selected was on Bladen Street, across from the governor's residence and the State House. Baldwin & Pennington were selected as architects; Henry Smith & Sons as builder. The Court of Appeals Building was constructed during the period 1901–3.

It is a legend in the Baldwin family that this building was one of E. Francis Baldwin's favorite works, though Josias Pennington seems likely to have had the major responsibility for the project.

The location and exterior design of the Court of Appeals building were not particularly compatible with the nearby State House and other Maryland buildings, but its interior was deemed to be a magnificent and elegant work.

The Court of Appeals Building was demolished in 1973 and its ornate fittings and materials sold to dealers and collectors. (At least one observer considers its demise to be one of "the most shameful acts the legislature ever did, architecturally.") The state attempted to preserve the courtroom interior, but not the dome of the original, which was designed by Pennington and fabricated by the Tiffany Glass Works of New York.

Josias Pennington was the primary architect for the **annex** to the **Maryland State House** and a new heating plant for the state's buildings in Annapolis. These were built in the period 1902–5. Pennington was listed as the architect member of the State House Building Commission at the time. Henry Smith was the contractor-builder. The annex was completed on December 21, 1905, at a cost of approximately $800,000. It housed new chambers for the Senate and House of Delegates.

Annapolis Waterworks. In 1907, the City of Annapolis commissioned Baldwin & Pennington for the design and construction of one of the city's waterworks buildings, located on the north side of Route 450, a few miles west of the town. A cornerstone in this brick building identifies the architects and names Edward D. Skipper as the builder. The stone refers to this as the "Annapolis Water Company."

One of Baldwin's lists of buildings in progress includes an unidentified item and a cost of $267,000. One possibility, unconfirmed, is that this refers to an addition of a wing to the Maryland State **House of Correction** (fig. 66) at Jessup, Maryland. A large wing on the south side of the main building

Fig. 65. Maryland Court of Appeals, Annapolis, Maryland. *Postcard*

was indeed constructed here circa 1905. The original buildings of this prison complex were designed by George Frederick in the mid-late 1870s.

Baldwin & Pennington were the architects for the **First Modern State Armory** in Annapolis, which was built in 1913. The builder was David M. Andrew Company. The appearance of the armory was reminiscent of the street-railway carhouses that Baldwin & Pennington were designing at about the same time in Baltimore for the UR&E. The armory building was razed in 1939, when the new State Office Building was erected on its site.

Fig. 66. House of Correction, Jessup, Maryland

Baltimore County Court House (plate 23). Discussions with the Building Commission for the proposed additions to the original courthouse by Thomas Dixon in Towson began with Baldwin & Pennington in mid-1908. By December, plans for two wings, on the north and south sides of the original 1855 structure, were completed. These wings were to be approximately 50 by 56 feet and to cost about $60,000. In January 1909 bids were in hand from thirteen contractors, for two versions (plan "B" and a less expensive plan "A"), ranging from $80,000 to $180,000.

Among the bidders for the courthouse work were some familiar names: John Waters, Henry S. Rippel, J. J. Walsh & Son, Henry Smith, and George D. Blake. After an unexplained delay, the contract was awarded to the low-bid, plan "B" option from David M. Andrew Company, for $120,300. With additional subcontracts for heating, plumbing, and electricity, the total cost was $127,326. The work was completed in 1910. In 1925, an addition was made to the west side by Pennington & Pennington. And, with the addition in 1958, the courthouse became one of the few H-shaped buildings in the state, according to the National Register citation.

❖ CHAPTER 9 ❖

Commercial, Industrial, and Cultural Buildings

Banks and Financial Institutions

Except for churches, the banks and financial buildings designed by Baldwin constitute the most populous, distinctive, and durable class of examples of his work. Baldwin's hand was felt strongly in Baltimore's banking and financial district, around Charles, Baltimore, and South Streets. Outside of Baltimore, a mere handful of bank buildings are scattered in the expected (and some not-so-expected) places, such as Catonsville, Cumberland, Elkins, and Rockville.

The beginning was modest—only two commissions for some modifications to existing buildings, the only two "bank jobs" done while Baldwin and Price were in partnership. On June 29, 1869, Baldwin recorded a fee of $25 for "alterations on the counters" in the Chesapeake Bank, for which H. W. Jenkins did work amounting to $460. John S. Gittings was the president of this bank, which was located on the SE corner of North (now Guilford Avenue) and Fayette Streets. (Baldwin's work must have been satisfactory, for Gittings became a client for other work in years following.) In June 1871, the young architects worked out "improvements" for the Burwell Bank, on the SW corner of Richmond Street and Plover Alley. Philip Walsh was the successful bidder for this $2,250 job.

Safe Deposit & Trust Company (fig. 67). The design of this bank in 1876 earned Baldwin a reputation and marked a milestone in his professional career and the real beginning of his string of bank buildings in Baltimore. From Baldwin's personal records, newspaper accounts, and drawings we are able to unravel and follow this interesting building's development and alterations over the years.

E. Francis Baldwin was the winner in an invited design competition for the Safe Deposit & Trust

Company building in 1875. He was awarded a 5 percent commission, while the two losing competitors were paid $250 for their efforts. The building was a 47-by-101-foot brick structure, with Cheat River stone cornices and facings. Baldwin's original design included a random mix of black bricks in the walls, but this was rejected by the Building Committee. By October 1875 the foundations were completed by the builder, J. E. Marshall. The bank opened in November 1876.

In May 1902, the *Baltimore Sun* reported that Baldwin & Pennington had made plans for an addition on the north side of the original building. The original doorway would be removed and a new one put in the center of the new combined structure, where the buildings adjoined. The new doorway was described as being flanked by a pair of columns. The addition, estimated to cost some $220,000, was barely complete when the disastrous fire swept the district in February 1904. The Safe Deposit bank, however, was supposedly the only building in the banking district to emerge from the fire nearly unscathed—it was able to open its doors for business the day after the fire had been extinguished, although it did require about $15,000 in work to repair the fire damage. Some two dozen other bank buildings were severely damaged or totally destroyed in that fire.

Baldwin & Pennington prepared plans in 1908 for a third component of the Safe Deposit building: a 45-by-94-foot addition along Commerce Street at the back of the original building. J. E. Marshall was again the builder for this addition, which cost about $150,000 and matched the design of the original building. The fourth and final section of the bank building was an addition along the south side, designed by Laurence Hall Fowler in 1929.

The Safe Deposit & Trust Company building was demolished in 1986. Portions of the facade were

Fig. 67. Safe Deposit &
Trust Company,
Baltimore.
Laurence V. Baldwin

received a 3½ percent commission on the cost of the building, which was $10,500, plus his expenses of $20 for each of the four trips he made to Cumberland during the construction. The building was replaced in 1912 by the building that now stands on the site. (There is a hint that the store adjoining the 1886 bank was also worked on by Baldwin; no details are given, but he received a fee of $100 in 1889 for his work there.)

In 1887, the **Farmers & Merchants National Bank** of Baltimore purchased the lot on the NW corner of South and Lombard Streets for a new building. Baldwin & Pennington were given the commission to design the building, and it was reported that the architects were soon traveling to other cities to examine banks for ideas. In December 1888, an agreement was made with the contractor, William Ferguson, and the five-story Romanesque structure—very much in the Richardsonian style—was begun. The final cost for the 58-by-85-foot building, which opened on September 24, 1889, was $114,603 (fig. 68).

This F&M building has an added significance in that the firm of Baldwin & Pennington moved its own offices to its top floor in 1889. This was the first move for Baldwin, who had spent almost twenty years in the office at Charles and Lexington. One can imagine the architects in the lofty location at 44 South Street, with a commanding view of the harbor area (which was not nearly as pristine and elegant, however, as it is today). This building was destroyed by the 1904 fire and replaced by another building designed by the same architects.

Drawings were prepared by Baldwin & Pennington from May to July 1889 for alterations and additions of an unspecified nature to the **Easton National Bank** in Easton, Maryland. The architects were paid a fee of $75. The building was destroyed and replaced in 1903.

In 1890, Baldwin was commissioned by Henry G. Davis for the design of the **Elkins National Bank**, which was completed in mid-1892 at a cost of $15,671. Baldwin charged Davis 3½ percent plus $25 and expenses for the sole trip he made to Elkins, West Virginia, to oversee its construction. It opened on March 5, 1892. This was Baldwin's only known bank outside of Maryland. The building was razed after a fire on April 26, 1967.

The **Hopkins Place Savings Bank** was perhaps the nicest and most unusual bank that Baldwin & Pennington designed (fig. 69). A sketch, description, and plan of this building was published in the April 22, 1893, issue of *American Architect and Build-*

carefully dismantled, stored, and reassembled in 1991 on the south side of the Commerce Place office tower, which was built on the South Street site.

Drovers & Mechanics Bank. In March 1880 Baldwin made an agreement with Jacob Ellinger, the president of this bank, to furnish drawings and superintendence of work here at a 5 percent commission plus $10 for taking measurements. The work may have been for alterations to an existing building or for a new building. The present building at the site on Eutaw and Fayette Streets was built in 1894.

The **First National Bank** in Cumberland, Maryland, was designed and built under Baldwin's superintendence in 1886. His records show that he *ing News.* Granite was used, very much in the Richardsonian style, but the footprint was oddly shaped to accommodate the available lot: a quadrilateral, with no two sides equal or parallel. The publication mentioned that the cost would be about $60,000 exclusive of vaults. The building was completed and opened on November 24, 1893. The architect's records give a cost of only $39,140—obviously an incomplete figure.

The Hopkins Place bank was gutted in the 1904 fire. It was rebuilt, using the remaining stone walls, but the front facade was altered slightly from the original. In June 1904 Henry Smith & Sons were engaged for the reconstruction job under a contract for $40,840, to be completed by December 1. The building was extended to the rear at this time. The cost of the rebuilding came to $70,731. Redevelopment of the area finally did what the great fire had failed to do, and the bank was razed in the 1960s.

Merchant's National Bank (plate 24). In March 1892, Baldwin & Pennington agreed to design and superintend construction of this bank building, on the SE corner of South and Water Streets, a block away from their offices. In July, plans for the seven-story structure were completed. The building itself was completed in 1894 at a cost of $428,199, for which the architects earned a 4 percent commission.

Merchant's National Bank was heavily damaged in the 1904 fire, but the two bottom floors were saved and the structure was refurbished by Wells Brothers, with architects Parker and Thomas supervising the work. (Douglas H. Thomas Jr. [1872–1915] was the son of the bank's president.) In the latest developments in the past ten years, only the outer walls of the old facade survive, beneath a multistory modern office building.

The **Fidelity & Deposit Company** building, on the NW corner of Charles and Lexington, was the tallest—if not the largest—building that Baldwin & Pennington designed (fig. 70). On December 8, 1890, the architects were engaged at a 3 percent commission. A week later they traveled with the Building Committee to a number of large cities to view existing buildings and gather design ideas. In November 1891 Baldwin wrote that the plans had to be altered because the available lot size had been changed owing to some action on the city's part. But construction was soon under way and the eight-story granite building was completed in 1893 or 1894. The cost was $431,212 for the main building and $94,454 for the interior work; the architects only charged a 2 percent commission for their interior work.

In February 1908 Baldwin & Pennington began discussions about a possible addition to the building. The options included a three-story addition and an expansion onto adjacent sites, but in 1909 a vertical option, seven added stories, was chosen. While the original building had load-bearing granite walls, the addition used a steel framework with a terra cotta sheath that simulated the granite below.

In October 1909 the contracts on what the *Sun* reported as "the most important building operation in the city this winter" were awarded. Morrow Brothers were selected. Construction was carried out over the years 1910–12. At one point it was reported that Edwin Warfield, a member of the

Fig. 68. Farmers & Merchants National Bank, Baltimore. *Laurence V. Baldwin*

Board of Directors, had Pennington demonstrate some hydraulic pumps for the building. The cost of the addition was reportedly $1–1.5 million.

The records are incomplete, but it appears that Baldwin & Pennington were the architects for the **Farmers & Planters National Bank**, on the NW corner of South and German (Redwood) Streets. Entries in the ledgers for 1894 and 1897 refer to plans for an elevator, added stories, and a new entrance. A cost, dated 1899, is recorded in the sum of $115,500. The work may have been for major improvements, because it was reported that the banking services were temporarily located in the Merchant's National Bank building while the work was going on. The Farmers & Planters Bank was destroyed in the 1904 fire.

In 1898, Baldwin & Pennington designed the original building for the **Commonwealth Bank**, on the SE corner of Howard and Madison Avenue. John F. Buckley was awarded the contract for $21,682, exclusive of vaults and internal furnishings. Baldwin illustrated his rule of thumb for estimating costs on this building by assuming 20 cents per cubic foot (though he called it "area") and 113,000 cubic feet, for a total of $22,600, which was close to Buckley's bid. The additions to the Commonwealth Bank in 1902 and 1912 were also designed by Baldwin & Pennington and built by John Buckley. The first addition (which included a clock) cost $13,742, and the second (a 21-by-73-foot building) cost $23,496.

Maryland Trust Company (fig. 71). In 1898 plans were begun to erect this new ten-story building, also known as the Guardian Building, on the NW corner of German and Calvert Streets, the site of Rennert's Restaurant. Baldwin & Pennington secured the commission and in September 1899 received bids for the granite structure. This was another instance in which the list of bidders was a veritable who's who of the trade. Eighteen bids were submitted; George A. Fuller won the $314,077 contract. The building was completed in 1901, with a final cost in Baldwin's ledger of $444,505. The Guardian Building was heavily damaged in the 1904 fire, but it was restored by Baldwin & Pennington— a task made easier because the original drawings had not been destroyed in the fire. The architects maintained an ongoing relationship with this bank, as there is a reference to interior remodeling work by them in 1911, as noted in an item in the *Sun*. The building is now called 16 Calvert South.

The **German Savings Bank**, on the SW corner of West Baltimore and Eutaw Streets, engaged Baldwin & Pennington for their 50-by-65-foot, one-story stone building in 1900. Henry S. Rippel was chosen as contractor over four other bidders and built it at a cost of $49,642.

The **First National Bank** (fig. 72), at Frederick and Ingleside Avenues in Catonsville, was designed by Baldwin & Pennington in 1901. Eight firms— including John Stack, George Blake, William Flagg, and H. S. Rippel—competed in July for the contract. Werner Brothers of Ellicott City was awarded the final contract for $12,130, with work to be completed by December 15, 1901. This two-story, 26-by-60-foot building was constructed of stone from the Wilkens Avenue Quarry, with Indiana limestone trim. The iron grillwork and railings were provided by Krug & Sons; interior work was by Joseph Thomas and National Market & Tile. Published accounts indicate the total cost was about $25,000.

Baldwin's pocket notebooks contain references to work for the Baltimore banking firm Hambleton & Company; the tabulations of "work on hand" for the years 1902, 1904, and 1905 show an entry for this firm. No other information has been found on this possible work, and its nature remains unknown. The entry is probably for work on the building at 8–10 South Calvert Street, near the Guardian Building.

The **Montgomery County National Bank** in Rockville, Maryland, was designed by Baldwin & Pennington (fig. 73). The contract for the one-story red brick and limestone building on Montgomery

Avenue and Perry Street was awarded to William E. Speir, of Washington, in October 1904, with the expectation that work would be completed by June 1, 1905. The basic contract was for $23,314. The final cost recorded by the architect was $30,374. According to the *Baltimore Sun*, the building was not completed until January 1906, at a cost of about $35,000. This fine building has been destroyed, a victim of the 1970s redevelopment in downtown Rockville.

The August 1907 issue of the *Architectural Record* has an article, "The Bank Buildings of Baltimore," which contains descriptions, plan views, and photographs of five buildings designed by Baldwin & Pennington:

—**National Union Bank of Maryland**, 3–5 E. Fayette St. Twelve contractors bid for the job in August 1899. The winner is unknown; the highest bid was from Henry S. Rippel and the lowest from D. H. Thomas (for $83,750). The final cost in 1901 was $109,116.

—**National Bank of Commerce**, 26 South St. (fig. 74). Bids were received in August 1901; work was probably completed in 1902 or later. This 57-by-106-foot bank replaced an 1881 structure. This building still stands.

—**German Bank of Baltimore**, NW corner of Holliday and E. Baltimore Sts. A contract for $54,779 was awarded to George Burnecke in April 1905, with the building to be completed by November 15. A final cost was given as $72,212. This building has been destroyed.

—**Farmers & Merchants National Bank**, NW corner of South and Lombard Sts. (plate 25). Seven bids were received on January 20, 1905. A contract was given to Wells Brothers for $70,836, with a completion date of August 1. This bank is 53 by 82 feet, in a modern French Renaissance style. Its final cost, probably exclusive of interior furnishings, was $87,102.

—**National Bank of Baltimore**, NE corner of St. Paul and Baltimore Sts. Nine bids were received; the contract was awarded to Henry Smith & Sons for $89,400, work to be completed by September 1, 1905. Costs of vaults, plumbing, wiring, and furnishings came to $30,500. The bank was built of Nova Scotia pink granite and was 36'-6" by 103'-2". In 1911, Baldwin & Pennington were engaged for plans for alterations and remodeling of this bank, but the work apparently went to Sperry in 1913, with Edward Brady its builder. This building was razed in 1988.

Fig. 70. Fidelity & Deposit Company, Baltimore. *Laurence V. Baldwin*

Baldwin & Pennington designed the west addition to the **Eutaw Savings Bank,** on the SW corner of Eutaw and Fayette. The original building was designed in 1887 by Charles I. Carson, who had won the job in a competition with five other architectural firms. The 50-by-65-foot addition was to cost over $100,000. Built by J. Henry Miller, the addition was completed in early 1911.

The last-known bank project by Baldwin & Pennington is gleaned from an item in the *Sun* in 1915 which mentions that Daniel M. Andrew had been awarded a $20,000 contract for work on the **Farmer's National Bank,** a small bank at 5 Church Circle in Annapolis, Maryland. Baldwin & Pennington were the architects for an addition.

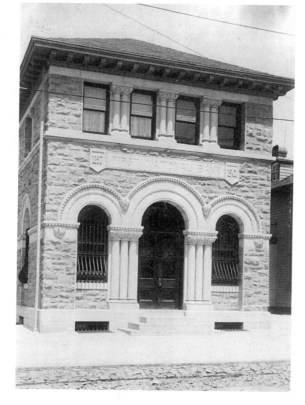

Stores, Offices, and Warehouses

This catch-all category is meant to encompass the miscellaneous work that was done by Baldwin & Pennington and interspersed through the years of their association. Included are stores, office buildings, warehouses, factories, and buildings in the Baltimore harbor area for commercial maritime businesses. Keep in mind that taking Baldwin's references to "warehouses" literally could be misleading: these buildings were not always used just for the storage of goods and commodities but were often facilities that might well be called stores or office buildings today.

With less than a half-dozen exceptions, the nearly 60 items in this category of work are in Baltimore. The buildings run the gamut from very large structures for prestigious and well-known businesses to mundane and now-forgotten structures for little-known entrepreneurs, tucked away in the alleys and byways of an industrial, late-nineteenth-century seaport. In the aggregate, however, these Baldwin-designed buildings were part and parcel of the tableau that made up this busy and thriving Maryland city.

In 1877, E. Francis Baldwin was engaged by Mr. C. O'Donnell to plan improvements for his business building at 107 North Charles Street. Three bids for about $4,000 were received, from John Stack, Henry Smith, and Philip Walsh. None was accepted; the work was postponed and probably never done, as there is no further mention of it.

In May 1878, Baldwin prepared plans for a warehouse for the **Keyser Brothers** which had been requested the previous month. Six bidders responded for the work on the four-story building to be built at 23 South Calvert. The contract was awarded to E. W. Robinson for $6,234. In 1883–84, Baldwin was the architect for improvements and alterations for the same client. That work reportedly cost about $25,000 for a 43-by-80-foot stone and terra cotta building on German (Redwood) Street, between South and Calvert Streets.

Thomas M. Lanahan approached Baldwin in early 1878 requesting plans and specifications for a warehouse, intended for the candy manufacturing firm of Cole & Gilpin, on the SW corner of Lombard and Light Streets. Baldwin agreed, for a 3 percent commission, and the plans were completed by June. Nine builders bid for the work, which was awarded to J. P. Towson. The four-story, 20-by-90-foot brick structure with Cheat River stone trim was completed in 1879 at a cost of $12,988.

Fig. 73. Montgomery
County National Bank,
Rockville, Maryland.
*Charles Brewer
Collection, Courtesy
Peerless Rockville*

Baldwin recorded the expenditure of $721 to Bartlett, Robbins & Company in August 1880 for columns. It has been suggested that this work, for Henry M. Jenkins, was for his building at 66 North Charles, which was built at about this same time. Baldwin's role in Jenkins' building is unknown.

Baldwin was hired by **John King** for a fairly large complex of warehouses on Sharp Street, between Lombard and Pratt Streets. These were four- or five-story brick buildings with stone trim and iron fronts. In 1880 Baldwin apparently designed four buildings that measured approximately 215 feet in length and were 30–60 feet wide. William T. Markland was the builder. The costs are estimated to be over $100,000. These buildings were all destroyed by a fire in 1888, and Baldwin designed replacement structures, which were built by William Ferguson in 1889 at a cost of $165,524.

The five-story brick building at **10-12 North Howard Street** (fig. 75) has more history than is apparent to a casual observer today. The land itself was part of the estate of John Eager Howard, for whom the street is named. Arunah S. Abell, of the *Baltimore Sun*, acquired the land and demolished the buildings that were there to build a warehouse, which was designed by Baldwin. (At this time, before the Baltimore street renumbering process, the warehouses were designated 7-9 North Howard.) That building was built in 1885, but the contractor and the

Fig. 74. National Bank of
Commerce, Baltimore

costs were not recorded by Baldwin. The building was shown in the October 1889 issue of *Inland Architect and News Record*, with the ground-floor stores being occupied by the Cohen Adler Shoe Company and the Meyer Reinhard Company (later to become the Meyer and Thalheimer Printing Company). In 1915, this 50-by-110-foot building was further altered and modified under the direction of architect Louis Levi. This building, a so-called double warehouse, is now called the Business Block.

The **Austin Jenkins** warehouse, at 180 West Baltimore Street, was designed by Baldwin and built by John Stack in mid-1886. Stack submitted the lowest of four bids and won the contract for $11,510.

7 North Calvert Street, built for the National Mechanics Bank, was designed by Baldwin & Pennington for use as a store and office building. The *Sun* described it as a three-story brick and stone structure measuring 25 by 75 feet. John Stack was the builder. The upper floors were occupied by a chiropodist, Dr. Goldberg, and the lower floors by the clothiers Bach, Koss & Fortune. The cost of the building was $13,919. (Baldwin noted that his 5 percent fee of $41.50 for the clothing store's interior furnishing was credited to his account at the store for clothing he had made.)

In 1887–88, Baldwin was engaged by **Francis White** for work on his warehouses on South Howard Street and on Sharp Street near Lombard. These warehouses were built by William Ferguson. They adjoined the King warehouse complex and were the same type of five-story brick building that Baldwin had designed for King.

Hutzler's Palace Building. It must have piqued George Frederick in 1887 to learn that Baldwin had been chosen as the winner in the competition for a design of a new building for the Hutzler Brothers department store and that the buildings that Frederick had designed for Hutzler's less than ten years earlier were to be demolished to make way for the new "Palace" building.

The original design of the Palace Building, at 210-218 North Howard, was five stories high, three bays wide, and measured about 80 by 120 feet. Its facade, of limestone and pressed copper, was a "Romanesque eclectic" design. It was also set off with a tower and turret in the NE corner (which was removed when the store was expanded northward along Howard Street). The Palace Building was built in 1888 by S. H. & J. F. Adams at a cost reported by the *Sun* to be about $100,000 (fig. 76).

The south bay of Hutzler's, at #210, was added in the 1901–4 period. Baldwin & Pennington were the architects for this "Annex," which was built by George A. Fuller under a contract for $94,064, won in a field of nine bidders. Illustrative of the costs required to finish a building of this type, the interior fittings, elevators, and utilities amounted to $92,431—nearly equal to the cost of the basic building itself.

Baldwin & Pennington maintained a continuing association with Hutzler's during the early 1900s. In 1913, they were responsible for another addition, at 226 North Howard, which was built by West Construction Company under a $72,916 contract. That addition was a 28-foot-wide, five-story structure. Further additions and modifications were made to

Fig. 75. 10–12 North Howard Street, Baltimore.
Laurence V. Baldwin

the complex in the ensuing years. The building still exists as part of a modernized store complex, which is now occupied by state offices.

The **A. S. Abell** business organization hired Baldwin again for work on stores and warehouses in the 1880s. One small job was to handle improvements to a store at 325 West Baltimore Street; this building was destroyed in the fire of 1904. A more significant assignment was the design of a warehouse at 318–320 West Baltimore Street (fig. 77). In October 1888 a contract was made with the builder Thomas B. Marshall for $52,800. This six-story brick building, which has a faint similarity to the Hutzler building because of the bay windows, is still standing.

Richard Cromwell, who had employed Baldwin for work on his home, engaged the architect for work on his factory buildings on Pratt and Fremont Avenue. Baldwin earned a 2½ percent commission on this 1888–89 project, which cost a total of $53,000.

Robert Garrett & Sons engaged Baldwin for alterations to buildings for the **Maryland Sugar Refining Company:** $2,700 in 1890 and an additional $4,000 in 1896. The location, nature, and extent of this work are unknown. Also in 1890, Baldwin handled alterations to stores for **James Thompson** (Light and Baltimore Streets; $2,000) and **Julian LeRoy White** (303 West Baltimore Street; $3,036). A new building for the firm of **Vaile & Young,** on Calvert Street, was designed and built in 1890–91 by Baldwin & Pennington. This is very likely the rather simple, unadorned brick building still standing at 216 North Calvert.

Baldwin received an out-of-state commission (unusual for him) for work in 1890 and 1891 with the **Tradesman Grain Elevator & Storage Company** of Philadelphia. He listed the buildings here as a corn mill, a hay shed, a changing warehouse, and an elevator, for a total cost of $40,306 at a 3 percent commission. The *Philadelphia Real Estate Record and Building Guide* has an entry for August 20, 1890, for this company, at 2300 St. David Street. It would be interesting to know more about this company and how the Baltimore architects got involved.

The Old Bay Line. The Baltimore Steam Packet Company (also popularly referred to as "The Old Bay Line") was a Chesapeake Bay steamship company that had a terminal in Baltimore's Inner Harbor. In the 1880s and 1890s this terminal was located at Union Dock, at the foot of Concord Street. Baldwin might have worked on the office that was built here in 1882. It is known that he was hired to develop plans and specifications for piers and a new office in 1892 or 1893. John Hiltz was the contractor. Baldwin

Fig. 76. Hutzler Palace Building, North Howard Street, Baltimore. *Laurence V. Baldwin*

charged a 2½ percent commission on the piers, which cost $23,900, and a full 4 percent on the office building, which cost $15,475. The Union Dock facilities of the Old Bay Line were destroyed by a fire on May 17, 1898.

The Old Bay Line acquired property along Light Street to build its new terminal and docks. Baldwin & Pennington designed the twelve-bay, 274-foot brick structure, with a central ornamental tower, in 1899. It was built by E. M. Noel. Baldwin's records noted work for the "Bay Ridge Pier and Wharf at 10 Light Street," at a cost of $4,405 with a 3 percent fee. When this facility was damaged in the 1904 fire, and again by another fire in 1911, it is likely that Baldwin & Pennington handled the reconstruction. After the fire in 1911, the tall tower was equipped with four clock faces instead of the original open-columned arrangement.

Fig. 77. 318–320 West Baltimore Street, Baltimore

In 1892 Baldwin & Pennington arranged for alterations and reinforcements of a warehouse for the **Ulman Goldsborough & Company**, at 41 North Gay Street. The architects received a 5 percent commission on the work, which cost $5,358.

In July 1893 the *Sun* described the remodeling and reconstruction work that was going on in the **Builder's Exchange Building**, on the NE corner of Charles and Lexington. The contractors were S. H. & J. F. Adams. According to the paper, the marble walls of the original building were to be retained, but the interior would be entirely rebuilt. The architect's fees were a bit different in this case: a percentage of the work ($76,722) plus twenty shares of stock.

William E. Walsh, a prominent businessman in Cumberland, hired Baldwin & Pennington in 1893 to design a large store and office building. The **Walsh Building**, on Main Street, was built in 1893

and 1894 at a cost of "something over $30,000," for which Baldwin charged a straight commission of 5 percent, but no separate charges for his expenses or visits to the construction site.

In 1895 or 1896, Baldwin & Pennington were hired to design a warehouse for **William P. Harvey** on Hanover Street, at a cost of $33,552. At about the same time, these architects also designed a small warehouse on Davis Street for **Patrick Rodgers,** built by J. H. Carstens for $4,424.

According to a February 1897 article in the *Sun,* a contract was awarded to John Hiltz for the construction of a warehouse for **Deford & Company,** tanners, adjoining the existing warehouse on the NW corner of Calvert and Lombard. The 25-by-100-foot structure was to be six stories high. Baldwin & Pennington were named as the architects.

O'Neill's Department Store, on the SW corner of Charles and Lexington, was a landmark and a popular business dating to the 1880s, when Baldwin had his own office on this same corner—Baldwin was probably well-acquainted with the owner, Thomas O'Neill. The first known instance of Baldwin being hired by O'Neill, however, is in 1889, for a new addition to a building at 108-110 North Charles. In May, eight bids were received for the job, and John Hiltz, after some negotiating, signed the final contract for $65,664. Work proceeded on the six-story brick structure over the next two years, until its completion in 1901. The complete costs of the building, including internal fitting and utilities, are unknown but must have exceeded $100,000. Baldwin & Pennington may have overseen additions and alterations to the O'Neill building for some time afterward. There is, for example, a reference to a "covered bridge" over Crooked Lane in the back of the store, which was built in 1911 by John Waters for $1,351.

Baldwin's work on O'Neill's in the 1890s seems to mark a beginning of a great flurry of work on stores and business buildings in the central corridor of Baltimore. Over a dozen projects were undertaken in the next fifteen years along Charles Street or within a block or two of it.

A store and office building on North Charles Street was designed for **A. Leo Knott.** The $15,000 construction contract was won by George Blake in 1902. This was a three-story building with a one-story back building. Baldwin estimated the cost as $15,600, based on 104,000 cubic feet at 15 cents per cubic foot.

The oddly shaped building on the corner of Lombard and Howard Streets, where Liberty ends, was designed by Baldwin & Pennington for the dry-goods company of **Lloyd L. Jackson.** This seven-story brick and stone building was built in 1902. It fronted 120 feet on Lombard and 134 feet on Liberty. Later known as the Sutton Building, it survived the 1904 fire, which started directly across the street to the north. Baldwin recorded a cost of $240,000 for Jackson's building.

The **Marburg Building**, at 213–215 East Fayette Street, may have been designed by Baldwin & Pennington. This five-story brick building, 36 by 105 feet, was used as a store and warehouse. Henry Smith was the builder. A list on one of Baldwin's notebooks shows an entry for this building, but no cost data. It was built in 1903.

Baldwin & Pennington were hired in 1903 by the Emerson Laboratories of Maywood, New Jersey, to design a building there for a citric acid plant and a laboratory for Dr. Isaac E. Emerson. The architects must have traveled to the site to assess the job, because they made a preliminary cost estimate of $17,500. In June, the $16,262 contract was awarded to W. H. Whyte of Hackensack, New Jersey.

There is a brief reference in Baldwin's records to a job at **117 West Baltimore Street** in 1904 for Summerfield Baldwin (no relation), of the mercantile company Norris & Baldwin. Mr. J. E. Marshall was the contractor for the work.

Baldwin & Pennington designed the **Baltimore Evening News Building** on Calvert and Fayette Streets. Construction began in April 1904 and was completed by October 1905. Baldwin's only record on this work is for a cost of $164,637.

The **Baltimore Sun Building**. A far more impressive endeavor began in 1904 for a competitor newspaper, the *Baltimore Sun*. Baldwin & Pennington was selected as the winner in a design competition involving four architectural firms for a new building to be built on the SW corner of Baltimore and Charles Streets. Baldwin & Pennington's original design was a 53-by-115-foot structure, 86 feet high; the final design was much larger (fig. 78).

The Sun building was in the French Renaissance style. Four stories high, it had a 53-foot front on Baltimore Street and 202 feet on Charles. The roof, floors, and interior partitions were supported by a steel framework; the outside walls, with twenty-four Ionic columns, 32 feet high and 3'-8" in diameter, were self-supporting. The base was of Maryland granite, the upper levels of Bedford Indiana limestone.

Edward Brady & Sons were the general contractors under a contract for $289,206. The street struc-

tural work was by the American Bridge Company of Pittsburgh; Walther & Company supplied the plumbing and electrical fixtures, Bartlett-Hayward & Co. the elevators. The ends of the building had prominent pavilions with large clocks supplied by Howard & Company of Boston. The electric-light fixtures were designed by the architects. The counting room had nine suspended cut-glass globes and five ornamental bronze torches. The Sun building had its own steam and generating plants in the basement. The cornerstone was laid on December 11, 1905; the building was completed and in operation on November 17, 1906. The final costs, including land and equipment, were well over $500,000.

Fig. 78. Baltimore Sun Building, Baltimore. *Sun Almanac*

The Sun building was not without its problems. The ventilating system was said to be inadequate, there was no hot water for the editorial staff, and there was no passenger elevator. Workers also had to endure the glaring reflection of the afternoon sun from the white marble facade of the new Savings Bank of Baltimore across the street, and there was no way to install protective awnings! The newspaper moved to a new facility in December 1950; the Sun Building was demolished in 1963 or 1964. The site is now occupied by the Morris A. Mechanic Theater.

Two buildings were designed by Baldwin & Pennington and built for the **A. S. Abell** estate, with the Safe Deposit & Trust Company bank acting as the agent. A store at 115-117 West Baltimore Street was built under a contract of $16,683 by E. D. Preston and completed in late 1904. The following year, the 53-by-116-foot, three-story building located at 210-214 East Baltimore Street was built by Edward Brady & Son for $43,892.

Another Baldwin & Pennington project in the "burnt district" of Baltimore was the commercial building at 119 East Baltimore Street, built in late 1904 by John Waters. This 34-by-97-foot structure was originally two stories high; a third story was added later. It is now occupied by Rite-Aid Pharmacies.

The **Professional Building** (plate 26), at 330 North Charles Street, was another building that Baldwin & Pennington designed for Thomas O'Neill. Nine builders bid on this project in July 1905 and the contract was awarded to George A. Fuller for $125,600, with the expectation that the building would be finished by the first of February the next year. This six-story brick and stone building was not completed until April, at a final cost of $140,841. Baldwin received a 5 percent commission for the work and promptly relocated his own offices to a suite on the sixth floor.

Another O'Neill building designed by Baldwin & Pennington was erected on the NE corner of Charles and Franklin Streets in 1910. The Athenaeum Club building was demolished to make way for this four-story gray stone building, built by Edward Watters, who won the $78,671 contract over nine other bidders. The building was completed in 1911.

In 1907, Baldwin & Pennington were involved with the plans for two stores at 143 North Calvert for Mendes Cohen. Nine bids were received in July 1907, ranging from $13,000 to $18,000. This project may not have gone any further.

It would be interesting to know more about the circumstances that resulted in a Baldwin & Pennington entry in a 1905 design competition for a large office building and department store in Roanoke, Virginia. The architects were successful. The contractor for the **Watt, Rettew & Clay Building** (on the corner of Campbell and Kirk Avenues) was E. Tatterson, who was given a $165,748 contract in September. The six-story, 100-by-200-foot building had walls of brick and stone over a cast-iron framework built by the Camden Iron Works of Salem, Virginia (fig. 79). The main supports of this building were large hollow iron columns bolted together end to end. The building was completed in 1906 and demolished in 1956.

Baldwin & Pennington were the architects for the following buildings built in downtown Baltimore from 1906 to 1908:

—the **Lycett Building**, 317 N. Charles, built in 1906 by Edward Brady
—the **Miles White Building**, 339–341 N. Charles, a 34-by-137-foot structure built in 1907 by the Engineering Construction Company
—**The Johns Hopkins Hospital Trustees Building**, on the NW corner of South and Water Sts.; a 64-by-109-foot brick and reinforced concrete building costing about $70,000
—the **J. McGill Walker** jewelry store, 334 N. Charles; built in 1909 by J. Henry Miller for Thomas O'Neill.

The **State Tobacco Warehouse**, on Conway, Light, and South Charles Streets, was designed by Baldwin & Pennington in 1909. This huge, six-story building was completed in 1910 by the builder John Waters. It was razed in the course of the Inner Harbor redevelopment in Baltimore.

In 1908 the *Baltimore News* was acquired by Frank A. Munsey, and the next year he acquired the adjoining property on the site of the old Mechanics Bank building. The News building was torn down to allow construction of a new and larger building on the combined lots. Baldwin & Pennington were teamed with the firm of McKim, Mead & White of New York to design the **Munsey Building** (fig. 80). This was another rare instance of the Baltimore firm working on a joint project. Work was begun in March 1910. Completed in April 1911, the 138-by-102-foot, fourteen-story building overlooked the Courthouse, the Equitable, and the Post Office buildings on Calvert

Fig. 79. Watt, Rettew &
Clay Building,
Roanoke, Virginia.
Roanoke Times

and Fayette Streets. The Munsey building was converted to apartments in 2002.

The **Grindall Building**, on the SE corner of Charles and Franklin, was built by Edward Watters from the plans of Baldwin & Pennington. This building was redecorated and altered in 1911, with a new front and interior work, in a contract for $13,000.

The **Manufacturer's Record Building**, on Water and Commerce Streets, was designed by

Baldwin & Pennington in 1912. This reinforced concrete building, measuring 75 by 87 feet and three stories high, was built by the West Construction Company at a cost of about $90,000. It occupied the site of Niernsee's old Rialto Building.

From 1913 to 1915, Baldwin & Pennington were the architects for three adjoining buildings on North Charles Street, just north of the Fidelity Building. Each of these was four stories high with

approximately 25-foot fronts and extended more than 100 feet back from the street:

—Schoen & Company, at #214, built by the Morrow Brothers at a cost of about $30,000
—Jenkins & Jenkins silversmiths, at #216, also built by Morrow Brothers
—F. Bucher & Sons jewelers, at #218, built by Henry Smith & Sons.

The store and office building at 315 North Charles was designed by Baldwin & Pennington in 1914 for Morton C. Stout and built in 1915. The three-story, 25-by-87-foot brick and marble building reportedly cost about $45,000.

The **C. D. Kenney Company Building** on South Eutaw Street, across from the B&O's Camden warehouse, was designed by Baldwin & Pennington in 1914. This large structure was originally intended to be five stories high but was increased to six when built by Edward Brady.

The **Atkinson Building** was a small office building at 37 South Street designed and built for M. S. Atkinson in mid-1914. A two-story brick building, measuring approximately 20 by 54 feet, it was built by the Consolidated Engineering Company for about $5,000. This building was torn down in the 1980s as part of the redevelopment of the Inner Harbor area.

Hotels

Baldwin and his partners, whose work on the B&O resort hotels and the stockyard hotel have already been mentioned, were the architects for a few additional hotels built for private individuals. That Baldwin was the architect of the fondly remembered Rennert may be known at least to some older Baltimoreans. Less well known, perhaps, is that Baldwin and Price were the architects for the Albion Hotel. And fewer still are likely to be aware of Baldwin's work on the Penmar or Baldwin & Pennington's work on hotels in West Virginia. Baldwin's journals also have cryptic references to some hotels that may never have been built. Perhaps more will eventually come to light.

Drawings were listed in Chapter One for John Gittings, Richmond and Cathedral Streets. What in 1870 was Richmond Street is now Read Street, so the building in question is, in fact, the **Albion Hotel**. On March 20, 1869, Baldwin and Bruce Price made an agreement with Gittings, who was then president of the Chesapeake Bank, to prepare drawings and specifications for $700 for a "dual-purpose" structure. Considering the date, this is one of the earliest commissions secured by the fledgling firm of Baldwin & Price.

The architects were challenged to design a building—actually five "English basement houses"—that could either be used as separate residences or combined into a hotel. Each unit was to have a parlor, dining room, kitchen, and nine to twelve sleeping chambers. Doorways were provided to link the units to form a family hotel if desired. The building was to be on a triangular lot, four stories in height, with fronts of 148 and 119 feet. Each unit was to have a bay window balcony on the second floor.

John P. Towson was the general superintendent for construction, which took place during 1869 and

1870. Other subcontractors were John Coburn (masonry), John P. Mullan (marble), James Healy (plumbing), Carvel Reynolds & Company (brick), Smith & King (windows and frames), Andrew Hamilton (stairs), Robinson & Cunningham (ironwork), and R. E. Kirk (bell hanging). The total construction costs are not known (fig. 81).

J. Appleton Wilson was responsible for alterations to the Albion in 1887; a 1912 addition was designed by Archer & Allen and built by John Cowan. The Albion Hotel still stands, appearing externally much as it did when it was built more than 125 years ago; the bay windows over the first story have been removed. It is presently the Cathedral Court Apartments.

The **Rennert Hotel** was Baldwin's most impressive hostelry. This seven-story brick structure was located on the intersection of Saratoga and Liberty Streets in Baltimore (fig. 82). Baldwin was proud of this work—he mentioned it in his advertisements, the B&O Railroad featured it in their promotional literature, and a photograph of it hung in a prominent place on a wall of Baldwin's office.

Baldwin signed an agreement for the Rennert on February 13, 1883, for a commission based on the cost of the building: 5 percent on the first $50,000, and 4 percent on the balance. He began making the drawings and on May 8 invited proposals from builders, asking for their bids both by percentage of the cost and by the day. Six responded; Henry Smith

Fig. 81. Albion Hotel, Baltimore.
The Maryland Historical Society, Baltimore, Maryland

Fig. 82. Rennert Hotel, Baltimore.
Laurence V. Baldwin

Humbird supervised its construction, which reportedly was accomplished in only seventy days. The hotel, also called the Blue Mountain House, opened on July 12, 1883. It was destroyed by a catastrophic fire on August 5, 1913. Baldwin & Pennington prepared plans for the rebuilding of the hotel, but they were never carried out.

Hints that the Penmar Hotel may have been planned for some time, as well as Baldwin's possible involvement in other hotel projects, are contained in some of Baldwin's journal entries. He noted in August 1878 that he had "loaned to Mr. J. C. Holmes a plan and elevation and photograph of Penmar Hotel, plan of Deer Park Hotel, plan of Belpré Hotel and sketch for hotel at Harpers Ferry to take to Capon Springs. Besides these he has some plans and sketches for small country houses that are to be returned." On the same page, Baldwin notes that he had agreed to make plans and specifications for a hotel for Mr. John Dailey for $80. In November 1877 Holmes had requested sketches for a hotel for a George Green of Harpers Ferry. Baldwin thought that Green's hotel would cost $10,000–$12,000. Then, in February 1879, Baldwin sent Mr. Robert Wilson of Woodstock, Virginia, a bill for $30 for drawings of a proposed hotel at Mount Jackson (a town in the Shenandoah Valley near Woodstock). Whatever became of these unidentified hotels is unknown.

Julius C. Holmes was a builder or possibly an architect in Charles Town, West Virginia.[1] He was involved in the work on the Jefferson County courthouse and the B&O's Oakland Hotel. On November 2, 1877, in Winchester, Virginia, Baldwin met with Holmes and the Superintendent of Public Schools, to whom Baldwin had sent a plan for a schoolhouse.

Hotel Powhatan (fig. 83). The Charles Town Mining, Manufacturing & Improvement Company engaged the services of Baldwin & Pennington in 1890 for drawings and specifications of a hotel. The architects agreed to a commission of 3½ percent of the total cost, plus $25 and expenses for each trip that was needed to the site in Charles Town, West Virginia. Three such trips were made during the construction, which was completed by 1893. The cost was $28,575 plus $4,200 for plumbing and heating. The hotel, known locally as the Hotel Powhatan, was

& Son, with a 2 percent bid, was selected. Construction commenced and the 130-room building was completed in 1885 at a cost of about $305,000. The Rennert officially opened on October 5. Baldwin also designed the annex to this hotel, which was constructed by Smith in 1894 or 1895. The hotel was closed in December 1939, demolished in 1941, and replaced in 1950 with a particularly ugly parking garage. The site was cleared in the late 1990s.

Penmar Hotel. In early 1883 the Blue Ridge Hotel Company was formed to develop a resort hotel in the Catoctin Mountains near Pen Mar, Maryland. One of the directors of this company was Theodore Hooper of Baltimore. Baldwin was selected to be the architect for this large, three-story wood building, about 500 feet long, with 300 rooms. James S.

1. It was reported that T. C. Holmes, of Charles Town, W.Va., was the architect and contractor for the Queen Anne style depot built by the Norfolk & Western Railroad in Norfolk in 1882. This is probably another example of a simple typographical error: it undoubtedly is J. C. Holmes.

Fig. 83. Hotel Powhatan,
Charles Town,
West Virginia

eventually taken over by St. Hilda's Girls' School. The building has since been demolished.

Robert Garrett enlisted Baldwin & Pennington to make additions and improvements to his hotel, the **Eutaw House**, on the NW corner of Baltimore and Eutaw Streets, during the period 1887–93. At least one job was to add a billiard room; the others are unknown. Baldwin earned 5 percent on the work, which cost a total of $70,560.

Hotel Randolph. Henry G. Davis of Elkins, West Virginia, employed Baldwin & Pennington to design a hotel in Elkins, as well as a bank and his personal mansion, Graceland. The Elkins Hotel was located on the NW corner of Fourth Street and Railroad Avenue and cost $15,886. The architect made three trips to Elkins to oversee construction between 1890 and 1893. Extensively enlarged in 1904 and 1905, this three-story structure had nearly a hundred rooms and a fifty-four-seat restaurant. In the 1940s it was the Memorial General Hospital.

Baldwin's records also show work on a hotel in Camden-on-Gauley, West Virginia, under the heading "W Va & P RR." Such a building has not been identified, but this railroad line did indeed run to this small and remote mountain town, and it is likely that Davis had a railroad-owned hotel or station-hotel built there.

Cultural and Social Buildings

Baldwin's oeuvre includes but very few buildings that can be said to serve cultural or entertainment purposes. Outside of additions or modifications to existing buildings and a minor job for the Maryland Historical Society, there is an exposition building, a library, and a small theater.

In 1871, Baldwin & Price were hired to oversee some alterations to the Maryland Academy of Arts building. This work, on a "gallery," contracted out to Philip Walsh for $1,750, commenced in May and was completed by the end of June. In the period 1893–95, plans were prepared by the architects for the fireproofing of the "record room" of the Maryland Historical Society. Baldwin received a fee of $100 for this work, which was probably in the Athenaeum Building, on the NE corner of St. Paul and Saratoga Streets.

In the early 1890s, Baldwin & Pennington were engaged to oversee plumbing and drainage work on the Academy of Arts Building on North Howard Street. They were also involved in the preparation of plans and supervision of work on a "brick proscenium arch," which was constructed by Harris, Britton & Dean in 1896. (The Academy Building had originally been built in the period 1873–75 by Benjamin F. Bennett.)

The **Maryland Building**, designed for the Chicago Exposition of 1893, deserves some discussion, not so much for its architecture—it was, after all, only a temporary building—as for the insight its creation offers into the machinations associated with its funding and the selection of Baldwin & Pennington as the architects.

In 1891, a commission was formed to oversee the construction of a building and exhibits for the State of Maryland in the World's Columbian Exposition of 1893, to be held in Chicago. A Building Committee was formed and began soliciting proposals for the design of the Maryland Building. Baldwin & Pennington were among the architects who responded to the notice. In early January 1892 they agreed to do the necessary work for the committee for 5 percent of the cost of the building, with an understanding that, if selected, they would make a contribution upon completion of the building.

On May 4, 1892, the Building Committee met with the only architectural firms that had responded: Baldwin & Pennington, George A. Frederick, and John Laing. The committee wanted the architects to submit their sketches of the front elevation and the ground floor plan of their proposed buildings. The architects refused without an assurance that the one who had prepared the winning design would be employed to do the work, and they suggested that it would be better simply to select the winning firm. The committee agreed, with an understanding that the plans would be ready by May 10. Time was of the essence, since groundbreaking was set for the May 31. The cost of the building was to be limited to $30,000—and there were already problems getting the necessary funding for the building.

The next day the committee announced the selection of Baldwin & Pennington. The architects had agreed on an initial fee of $500 plus expenses incurred outside the office. By May 7, after Pennington's return from a trip to Chicago to meet with Daniel Burnham, the "Chief of Construction" of the Exposition, preliminary drawings were completed.

On May 11, the Building Committee voted to adopt the plans submitted by Baldwin & Pennington. Feeling the pinch of money, the committee had by then scaled down to a limit of $20,000 for the building. It was also asking for the loan of furniture and mantels to use in the exhibition building.

There was, of course, some unhappiness over the process of selection of the architect. A writer to the *Sun* in late May complained that the architects had already been selected by the committee when the notices were issued for the architects to meet at City Hall for the May 4 meeting. But the work went on.

In mid-June, the contract for the construction of the building was awarded to F. Merten & Son, of Cumberland, Maryland. An earlier round of contractor proposals apparently had to be redone because the builders had failed to understand that the materials for the building would be provided, presumably from separate donations.

Colors to be used by the exhibitors at the Exposition were a big issue. In fact, the first "Director of Color," who favored variegated coloration, resigned because Burnham insisted on a more uniform white or off-white for the buildings (hence the nickname for the Exposition as Chicago's "White City"). In late August, Maryland received its instructions: the body of the building was to be buff with white cornices, columns, windows, and door trim; the metal roof would be red-brown, the canvas portions of the roof olive green, and the steps and parapets would be drab.

Other problems came and went during the construction. Burnham wrote to complain of faulty wiring and stopped work, causing Pennington to go to Chicago in September to investigate. A member of the Building Committee, Frank Hoen, also went there and reported that electricity would be too expensive for lighting, and gas would be used instead.

The building continued into the winter months. finally, in March 1893, the Building Committee went to Chicago and made final acceptance of the building. Interior finishing began and the building was ready in May. (The fair had been officially dedicated, however, the previous October.) In the final accounting, the budget had been exceeded: the contractor cost $19,622, and the painting by Emmart & Quartley cost $984. The architect's fee was $699, and the superintending architect in Chicago, Peter Bonnet Wight (1838–1925), received $600.

A pictorial history of the exposition described the Maryland Building as being 142 feet long and 78 feet wide. The central section was a reception area; the right wing an exhibition area for women's work, and the left wing a general exhibit area. In sum, it was an "elegant club house."

The Chicago fair closed officially on October 30, 1893. Many of the buildings remained on a permanent basis. The state buildings were mostly built of staff (plaster and fibrous material) and not intended to remain. There was some discussion in Baltimore about dismantling the Maryland Building and having it rebuilt in one of the city parks, but that did not happen. When and how the Maryland State building was demolished is unknown.

The **Bosler Memorial Library**. In early May 1898, the estate of the late Herman Bosler of Carlisle, Pennsylvania, commissioned Baldwin & Pennington to design and erect a memorial library. Specifications for the building were set and signed on May 28. On July 14, 1898, the building contract was signed with A. M. Brindle of Carlisle.

How Baldwin & Pennington came to obtain this commission in Pennsylvania is probably answered by the list of members of the Board of Directors of the Fidelity Trust Company in the 1890s. Herman E. Bosler was a member, and he had undoubtedly become acquainted with the architects when they designed the Fidelity Building just a few years earlier. Bosler died on November 18, 1897.

The Bosler Library was dedicated on January 30, 1900, and has been in use as a public facility ever since. The building measures 59 feet across the front and is 88 feet deep. The front facade is white marble; the remainder of the building is brick. The roof was covered with slate. Baldwin's records show a cost of $20,671, which seems low, considering the nature of the building and the quality of the interior finishings involved (plate 27).

The **Great Wizard Picture Show**. According to the *Sun*, Baldwin & Pennington completed plans in December 1908 for a movie theater for the Great Wizard Company, at 30–34 West Lexington Street. The theater was to have a capacity of 500 seats. A later newspaper account indicated that the building would be 48 by 112 feet and that the contractors were John Waters, J. J. Walsh, and Edward Brady. In June 1909 the theater was described as a five-story building, for Thomas O'Neill (who disclaimed having anything to do with the moving-picture enterprise, which was to be housed on the ground floor). The building in its final configuration appears to have been only two stories high. Costs are not known, a figure of $30,000 was mentioned in one newspaper account.

The first of a small number of occasional commissions for work for private clubs was a small, unspecified job in 1880 for the "Carroll's Island Ducking Club," which may have been for a hunting club located on Middle River Neck in Baltimore County. Philip Walsh & Sons were the contractors; the total cost was $2,000.

The next club commission is probably one of the best-known of Baldwin & Pennington works: the **Maryland Club** (fig. 84), on the SE corner of Charles and Eager Streets in Baltimore. This corner property was owned by Robert Garrett, who for many years had planned to erect a hotel on the site, but never did.

Fig. 84. Maryland Club, Baltimore.
Laurence V. Baldwin

Baldwin & Pennington were set to the task of preparing plans for the club in 1889, Pennington probably had the primary responsibility for this project. The *Sun* reported that he had traveled to New York, Boston, and Chicago to examine buildings in the course of designing the Maryland Club building. The gray stone Richardsonian Romanesque building was completed in 1891 by the builder, Henry Smith. The firm was engaged for additions to this building in 1902 and again in 1910. The 19-by-33-foot addition in the rear was built in 1910 at a cost of about $10,000. Baldwin recorded that the original building cost $134,773, for which a 5 percent commission was earned. The Maryland Club building was severely damaged in a fire on August 19, 1995, but it was repaired and the building restored to service the next year.

The **Iroquois Club** began planning in November 1891 for a clubhouse on an unimproved lot on the corner of McCulloh and Mosher Streets. Baldwin & Pennington were engaged to prepare the plans in March 1892. The building was to be brick with a 55-foot front, with facilities to seat 500 persons. The basement was to have a 75-foot bowling alley and a barber shop. The cost was reported to be about $9,000.

When the **Catholic Club** moved to the building at 409 North Charles Street in 1892, Baldwin was responsible for the remodeling. A competitive contract was awarded to George Blake, at a cost of $11,100. Additional costs, for plumbing, heating, electricity, gas, and the bowling alley, came to $3,500. The Catholic Club opened on April 6, 1893.

Baldwin & Pennington were responsible for remodeling the old Ellicott house, on the NE corner of Park Avenue and Franklin Street, for the **Baltimore YWCA** in 1892. The contractor was Cornelius Sheehan, at a cost of $21,689, but the architects agreed to make a compensating donation if the work exceeded $20,000. So instead of a 5 percent fee, the architects charged only $600 for this work.

Additions and alterations to the **Baltimore Club** on North Charles Street in 1895 were done under the direction of Baldwin & Pennington. The contractor was H. Smith & Son; the cost of the work was $7,160.

In early 1898, Baldwin & Pennington arranged for work on the **Germania Mannerchor Club**, which may have been located on North Howard Street. Henry S. Rippel was the successful bidder, with a low bid (of the five submitted) of $6,500. The nature of this work is unknown, but it likely involved alterations or improvements to an existing building.

Josias Pennington was the principal architect for work at the **Elkridge Hunt Club**, in Woodbrook on North Charles, in the 1900s. The minutes of the club's meetings in 1903 recount Pennington's negotiations for additions and alterations to the clubhouse, which was built upon an old tenant house on an estate the club had purchased. Pennington also did the architectural work for an addition here in 1908, consisting of sixteen game rooms and a porch, and in 1910 for kennels that were built by W. E. Harn & Company, for $3,500.

Two projects were undertaken by Baldwin & Pennington in the years 1905–8 in Fairmont, West Virginia. Both were built by the Brady Construction & Engineering Company, the low bidder. The contract for the **Masonic Building** (plate 28) was awarded in September, 1905. This 55-by-109-foot, five-story building, which housed a post office on the ground floor, was completed in early 1907 at a cost of $91,928. The **Fairmont YMCA** contract was let in February 1907 for work to be completed in 1908. This 65-by-115-foot building, with a basement and four upper floors, was to cost $66,820. Construction difficulties on these buildings necessitated a trip to Fairmont by Baldwin in April 1907; his $20 travel expense was divided equally between these two accounts.

Finally, although nothing is known about the outcome—if any—there was a design competition for the Baltimore Elks Clubhouse in 1913 that involved six local firms: Parker, Thomas & Rice, T. W. Pietsch, Otto Simonson, John Kelly Stack, Wyatt & Nolting, and Baldwin & Pennington.

❧ CHAPTER 10 ❧

Private Residences and Estates

Some private homes and cottages that Baldwin designed have already been mentioned or alluded to. In addition to these and the rectories for the churches, Baldwin's practice included a large number of private dwellings, from simple row houses to mansions on large estates. Nearly all of these are in and around Baltimore, although there are some important works some distance away. The clientele for these works ranged from common citizens to some of the richest and most influential families of the day. Work on private residences and estates spanned most of Baldwin's active career, from the late 1860s to the early 1900s.

Baldwin & Price (1869–1873)

A series of residential works was executed during the five years when Baldwin and Price were partners. The first-known project of this type was the **John Street houses,** with James C. Neilson and J. C. Keighler. On April 1, 1869, an agreement was made with the builders William Wells and A. I. Arnold to construct two houses on John Street, near North Avenue. The contract price was $3,650 for each house. Construction was completed in December at a final cost of $7,652.

From 1870 to 1872, Baldwin apparently designed and had built a group of four row houses on Druid Hill Avenue. James Forbes is the probable builder of these three-story Italianate houses, which cost a total of $23,314. The houses may have been built for Baldwin as an investment or for sale. (One of the houses, at #359, became Baldwin's residence in 1881.)

In July 1871 work stopped on a "country residence" that had been begun the previous year for Prudencio de Murguiondo, a diplomatic officer from Uruguay, reportedly because of "money matters." Philip Walsh was the builder in the $12,850

contract. Where this house was located, or if it was ever completed, is unknown.

In mid-1871, Baldwin & Price arranged for the construction of a laundry and fuel shed for William Kennedy. The work was done by James F. Darling for $2,660. At about the same time, the architects prepared plans and drawings for the builder James Forbes for three houses to be built on the corner of Eutaw and Hoffman Streets. Forbes himself may have lived in one of these, 1030 North Eutaw Street.

In 1871–72, Bruce Price took the lead in making arrangements with clients in his hometown of Cumberland. In August of 1871, Ferdinand Williams left an order for the architect to proceed with developing plans and specifications for a house that was to cost less than $3,000. Within the month the drawings were sent to Cumberland. The house is probably the one located at 535 Washington Street, which was built in 1872. Price also prepared drawings for a house for his father, William M. Price, at 41 Harrison Street. That house reportedly cost about $6,500; it has been demolished. In 1872, Price sent sketches to Lloyd Lowndes in Cumberland for an addition of a nursery and a bathroom to the house of this future governor of Maryland. The neoclassical Lowndes House, 27 Washington Street, designed by architect John Notman in 1842, was demolished in 1964 for a parking lot for courthouse employees. It was the birthplace of Bruce Price.

The **Chase Street houses**. Baldwin & Price have been credited—erroneously—with the design of four adjoining houses on the north side of East Chase Street in Baltimore, next to Christ Episcopal Church. The records indicate that Price alone was responsible, and only for the three identical three-and-a-half story marble and stone houses at nos. 12, 14, and 16; he was not involved with the house at 10 Chase Street. The entries in the Baldwin & Price journal on the matter are all in Price's handwriting, and only three houses, or items in multiples of three, are ever mentioned. These houses appear under the heading "Bruce Price Chase St. Houses." He seems to have kept one of these houses (the center one, #14) and sold the two adjoining ones for profit.

A contract for the houses was signed on March 26, 1871, with Philip Walsh as general contractor for $26,000. On the first of April, a contract was signed with Peter Snyder for $6,000 for stonework and marblework. Construction began on the foundations on April 12. The Chase Street houses were probably completed in early 1872, and Price and his wife moved into one soon thereafter. These three houses are on the National Register of Historic Places.

Baldwin & Pennington (1874–1916)

The first house that is of interest in this period is one that was actually started while Baldwin and Price were partners but was dropped. In 1871, Philip Walsh had a contract with Mrs. Clementina Grace for a country house near Ilchester for $1,500. The work was abandoned and Walsh was paid $68.50 for his efforts; Baldwin & Price received $31.50 for theirs. The work was resumed in 1874 with Baldwin as the architect, and the house was completed by the builder John Kelly under a contract for $1,850. Baldwin's notes also mention a back building and improvements for Mrs. Emily Hillen in 1874.

The **William Donnell House** (plate 29), on the SW corner of St. Paul and Biddle Streets, was the first house of real significance that can be attributed solely to Baldwin. Baldwin sometimes referred to this as the "McDonnell" house in his notebooks. In July 1874 Baldwin received builders' proposals for this three-story brick house, and he engaged John Stack to build it under a $38,000 contract. Construction was completed a little over fifteen months later with the final cost amounting to $45,583; the house at 1120 St. Paul Street still stands.[1]

Grafton Farm. It would be interesting to know how E. Francis Baldwin came to be involved with the Dulany family in northern Virginia. In May 1877 Baldwin recorded that Mr. H. G. Dulany Jr., P.O. Upperville, Fauquier County, informed him that he had decided to adopt Baldwin's design for his country residence. George Frederick was one of the losing competitors for this job; his design was published in the *American Architect and Building News* for May 15, 1884.

Baldwin visited Upperville in late May, along with I. H. Curtis, a landscape gardener, to discuss the location and plans for Dulany's mansion and associated buildings. Baldwin returned from this two-day trip with instructions to prepare plans for a gardener's house, a dairy and an icehouse, a gate lodge (the dairyman's residence), one stable for thirty riding horses and a second for ten farm horses. Within a week, drawings and specifications had been prepared for the gardener's house and sent to Dulany. The architect's estimates for the buildings was listed as follows:

stable @ .6 cts. [per cubic foot]	$9,700
gardener's house @ .10	$2,200
dairyman's house @ .10	$1,200
mansion @ .15	$44,000

The buildings were apparently completed within the next year or so. The estate is well known as the old Grafton Farm, located in Upperville near Route 50. The mansion was destroyed by a fire in 1900; the gate lodge (plate 30), and perhaps some of the other buildings, is still standing.

Henry Grafton Dulany's farm and its mansion, Grafton Hall, were passed on to the son, Col. Richard Henry Dulany, who rebuilt it after the fire. This son may be the person Baldwin referred to in an October 1878 journal entry as "R. Hunter Dulany," or it could be another relative. That entry refers to another house, unidentified, but is interesting because it is another example of the fiscal competition between architects of this time. Baldwin wrote that he had "agreed to make plans for a country house for $100 according to a sketch approved by (Dulany). Should have been $200 but someone else (Dixon & Carson) had agreed to do it for that amount. So it goes."

Some of Baldwin's houses for the next few years are less pretentious and more mundane, but they were probably profitable nevertheless:

—a "country house" or "cottage" for **John S. Gittings** at Ashburton, Baltimore County. The contract for this 42-by-32-foot house with a back building was let in April 1879 with builder J. P. Towson for the sum of $3,660. It was to be completed by July.

Private Residences and Estates

1. This house has been erroneously attributed to George A. Frederick, who designed the pair of houses next door, 1118 being his own; 1120 appeared in some scenes in the 1988 movie *The Accidental Tourist*.

—a "country house" for **J. Harry Lee** at Melvale, in Baltimore County. A December 1882 contract was negotiated for $5,783, for which Baldwin earned a 5 percent commission.

—a similar house for **Columbus O'D. Lee**, also at Melvale; for $4,780 in January 1883. (Melvale is located near where Cross Keys is today.)

—a townhouse for **Mrs. Arabella Russell**. This is the three-story brick structure at 1708 Park Ave. (fig. 85). It was described as being 20 feet wide and 60 feet deep. Its cost, in October 1883, was about $7,000.

—a house for **John A. Carey** at 1607 W. Fayette St. It was to be completed by October 15 at a cost of $7,000 according to a contract signed in April 1883.

—a country house for **William Keyser**, Brentwood, for a cost of $9,928 in 1886. Baldwin personally handled this job; in 1883 he had also been involved in a stable for Keyser on Maryland Ave.

—a three-story brick house for **A. Gottschalk** on the SW corner of Oliver St. and Hudson Alley. A $6,050 contract with builder John H. Carstens was signed in September 1886.

A separate ledger detailing Baldwin's investments and personal business transactions contains abundant information on the construction costs, sale, and rental of lots and dwellings with which the architect was involved. He seems to have been something of an entrepreneur, as there are purchases and sales of individual properties that he had nothing to do with as an architect. But there are two cases in which he apparently designed the buildings and had them built for himself:

—four three-story brick buildings (row houses) on the east side of Carey St. between Lanvale and Townsend Sts. in 1882. These dwellings, at #257–263, were built for Baldwin at a total cost of $10,600 for investment purposes. In October 1883 he sold #261 for a profit of $880; the other three were kept for rental until he sold them, between 1905 and 1909.

—a string of twelve three-story brick row houses, at 1201–1221 Mosher St., between Carey and Carrollton Ave. These houses must have been nearly identical, with 13-foot fronts; they were built for Baldwin in 1883 by the contractors Buck & Jackson, for about

Fig. 85. Arabella Russell House, Baltimore

$1,600 each for investment and sale. Six were sold almost immediately, the others were evidently rented for ten to twenty years or more before being sold at a profit.

A Baldwin family collection of photographs provided clues to the existence of works of E. Francis Baldwin that do not appear in the architect's ledgers and were not found in newspapers or other published material. The photos, numbering nearly fifty in all, had been gathered in a scrapbook and, with the exception of about half a dozen, are all well-known buildings that Baldwin designed.[2] It seems reasonable, therefore, to conclude that the unknown buildings were also Baldwin-designed. Two of these were large, palatial houses that have now been identified as homes for the Abell and Garrett families of Baltimore.

The Abell mansion, **The Ridge** (fig. 86), is located on West Joppa Road, west of Towson, near Riderwood. It is believed to have been the private

2. The collection of photos also includes two still-unidentified commercial buildings. One remains a total mystery at this writing; the other appears to be one of the now-demolished warehouses and lofts on Hopkins Place (the photo is of the Gans Brothers umbrella store at 115 Hopkins Place).

Fig. 86. The Ridge,
Towson, Maryland.
Laurence V. Baldwin

home of Jennie Abell (Mrs. Francis T. Homer), a daughter of Arunah S. Abell. The building still stands and, from the outside, appears nearly the same as it did in the Baldwin photograph. No information has been found on the particulars of its origins: its date of construction, builder, or costs. It is today, after serving as the Ridge School for many years, again a private residence.

In the early 1850s, Ann and William Frick were given an estate on Old Frederick Road in Catonsville by her father. They named it **Uplands,** and a mansion, attributed to the architect William H. Reasin,

Fig. 87. Uplands,
Catonsville, Maryland.
Laurence V. Baldwin

was built there in 1853. The Frick's daughter Mary Elizabeth married Robert Garrett and, in 1885, inherited Uplands. About this time, a new building was built here, adding to or replacing the 1853 house, to be used as a summer retreat house for the Garretts.

The Uplands mansion (fig. 87) still stands at 4501 Old Frederick Road. Even the most casual examination of it reveals strong resemblances in design and detail to many known Baldwin works. There is one entry on this Garrett house in the available Baldwin ledgers: an 1886 reference to improvements by John Stack for $4,813. Considering these facts and Baldwin's long association with the Garrett family and the B&O Railroad, there is little doubt that Baldwin was the architect of Uplands.

Graceland. Baldwin & Pennington's high-water mark in grand houses is undoubtedly the mansion Graceland, which was designed for Senator Henry Gassaway Davis in Elkins, West Virginia (fig. 88). Both architects were involved in this effort, but Baldwin may have taken a leading role in overseeing this special project for an old friend. The commission was secured on May 20, 1890, by an agreement to provide drawings, specifications, and superintendence of construction at Elkins for 3½ percent of the cost of the work plus $25 and expenses for each trip to the site. The contractor was W. E. Porter, a civil engineer and a former construction superintendent on Davis's railroads in West Virginia.

The Davis house was built in 1892–93, during which time the architects Baldwin, Pennington, and Tormey made at total of at least nine trips to Elkins. The reason for at least one trip to Elkins may have been to solve problems that were encountered during the construction of one of the towers, which Senator Davis wanted to be built entirely of stone. Correspondence between Baldwin and Davis in the summer of 1892 indicates that Davis wanted to change one of the towers, which had originally been designed as a frame structure. Baldwin noted that there was an insufficient inner foundation for a "full octagon tower above the roof lines" of the house. Baldwin sent Davis a sketch of what he described as "a very low and dumpy tower," but noted that this was the best that could be done in stone without adding very costly foundations and a framework of iron beams and posts necessary to support a larger tower. He suggested that the tower be built according to the original design, with wood sides, but possibly with a roof of a different shape.

Graceland mansion was located on a 360-acre estate on a hill overlooking the town of Elkins. The

Fig. 88. Graceland, Elkins, West Virginia

house was palatial—what a Cumberland paper described as a "grand and stately pile." It had thirty-eight rooms, including thirteen master bedrooms and twelve bathrooms; the dining room could seat twenty-two people. It was equipped with gaslights, electricity, telephones, steam heat, electric call bells, speaking tubes, and a burglar alarm system. Baldwin's records show a payment of $1,750 to the firm, or 3½ percent of an estimated total cost of $50,000. This is probably an incomplete or partial cost; the contract for some of the interior wood paneling, mantels, and doors alone came to over $10,000.

The Davis family moved into their new home on July 3, 1893. The Davis estate and Graceland mansion (which was named after the youngest Davis

123

daughter) was sold in 1939, and in 1941 it became part of the campus of Davis and Elkins College. It is listed on the National Register of Historic Places. Until about 1970 the mansion was used as a residence hall. It was closed in 1971 and, unused, was falling into ruin until the 1990s, when efforts were made to stabilize or restore it in a joint project by the West Virginia Division of Culture and History and the National Park Service.

The building has now been restored and refurbished as the Graceland Inn and Conference Center. It has guestrooms and conference rooms as well as a restaurant (the Mingo Room, named after the original name of the mansion: Mingo Moor or Mingo Hall).

Private Residences and Estates

In Baltimore, the firm was involved in the early 1890s with work for William P. Harvey. There is a record of alterations or additions to the porch of a country house for this client in 1888, and drawings for a house on Calvert Street in 1890 that was never built. Then, in 1892, Baldwin & Pennington designed a dwelling for Harvey at a location near Charles and Eager Streets at a cost of about $14,000. A country house at Deer Park was designed for J. Swan Frick and built there in 1893–94. A "country residence" was built in the years 1892 to 1894 for

Henry A. Parr at Riderwood, in Baltimore County, at a cost of $17,506. The architects gave Parr what was noted as a "special deduction" for this job: a 3½ percent commission, instead of the usual 5 percent typical of such work at this time. And from 1893 to 1896, Baldwin & Pennington recorded work for Douglas H. Thomas at 1010 St. Paul Street at an estimated cost of $20,000.

Around the turn of the century, the firm's records list homes for which very little information was given other than some dates and cost figures. These include a residence at Ruxton for Martha Smith in 1897 costing $19,909; a house for James J. Ryan on Lafayette Avenue, which was built by Cornelius Sheehan for $7,395; and a country house for Charles E. Parr in Pikesville in 1899, built by C. E. Thomas for his bid of $6,556. The final total cost for the house and stable was given as $8,234.

In 1902, Baldwin & Pennington designed homes for Charles M. Lanahan, at 1209 St. Paul Street ($39,000) (fig. 89); Elizabeth Oliver, at Cathedral and Biddle Streets ($16,246); Allen McLane, at 1035 North Calvert ($19,402); and N. Winslow Williams, at 2 East Biddle ($16,682).

In 1906, when they were working on the YMCA and the Masonic Building in Fairmont, West Virginia, the architects also designed five houses on Gaston Street for Mr. J. O. Watson, who was also the secretary of the YMCA Building Committee. Two of these houses cost $6,885; the other three cost $10,329. The locations and current status of these houses are unknown.

The *Sun* reported in August 1910 that E. F. Baldwin had purchased a three-story dwelling on the north side of 24th Street, near Oak Street. Whether this was a simple investment or otherwise is unknown.

Residential Additions and Alterations

Baldwin also had projects on private homes and residences that consisted of the design or supervision of additions or alterations to existing older structures. Some involved work on important houses designed originally by other architects, but most of these projects are less significant than are those listed in Appendix E. In many cases, little is known about the nature of these projects, which were not described in detail in the Baldwin records.

In retrospect, Baldwin's work on private residences or estates for individuals was but a small fraction of his total body of work, amounting to

Fig. 89. Charles Lanahan House, Baltimore

barely one-eighth of all known projects, and of these only about a dozen houses are really significant and enduring examples of his craft in this category. Clearly, Baldwin placed emphasis on work for corporate clients and the Catholic Church. Of his 500-plus projects, nearly one-third were for the Baltimore & Ohio Railroad; nearly the same number were for ecclesiastical, educational, and governmental clients, and about one-fifth were for a commercial clientele. An expanded tally of Baldwin projects is displayed in Appendix B.

For the Baldwin enthusiast interested in seeing this architect's works firsthand, Appendix A tabulates his extant works as best I know as of this writing. The buildings listed were designed, either wholly or in part, by Baldwin himself or by his firms (Baldwin & Price, 1869–73; Baldwin & Pennington, 1874–1916). At the rate these buildings disappeared, there is no doubt that the list is already obsolete; the threat to old buildings from urban renewal, development, neglect, and arson is real and ever-present. We should treasure and protect the large number—and rich legacy—of Baldwin's buildings that still remain standing.

The Extant Works of E. Francis Baldwin

The buildings are listed in approximate chronological order. An alphabetic list seemed dull—though logical—and an arrangement by location would be unbalanced and less informative, since most of the buildings are in Baltimore or other parts of Maryland. Where addresses seem important in locating the building, they have been included wherever possible. Unless otherwise indicated, the listed building is in Baltimore. Cities, unless otherwise noted, are in Maryland.

Dates given here (as almost everywhere else) are not always precise. A building can be given more than one characteristic date, for example, when construction began, when construction was completed, when the building opened for use, etc. The text should be consulted for such details, if available. The dates here serve primarily to give the reader a rough idea of the timing of the building and correlations between building type, location, style, and so on.

The buildings listed below were designed, either wholly or in significant part, by Baldwin himself or by his firms: Baldwin & Price (1869–1873) and Baldwin & Pennington (1874–1916). As another means of underscoring the recognized significance of some of these buildings, those that are now included in the National Park Service's National Register of Historic Places are shown in boldface.

1869	Row Houses, 1520–1526 Druid Hill Ave.
1869	Christ Episcopal Church, NW cor. St. Paul and Chase Sts.
1869	Albion Hotel, cor. Richmond and Cathedral Sts.
1870	Cathedral of St. John the Baptist, Savannah, Ga.
1871–80	Grace Episcopal Church, Lexington, Va.
1871	**St. Paul's Church** (addition), cor. Charles and Saratoga Sts.
1871	Ferdinand Williams House, Cumberland
1872	St. Vincent's Seminary Building, Germantown, Pa.
1873	**B&O Railroad Station**, Rockville
1873	St. Ann's Church, cor. Greenmount and 22nd St.
1874	William Donnell House, 1120 St. Paul St.
1875	Christ Church (addition), 111 S. Harrison, Easton
1875	St. Aloysius Church (addition), Washington, D.C.
1875	**B&O Railroad Station**, Point of Rocks
1875	B&O Railroad Station, Keyser, W.Va.
1876–82	B&O Railroad Station, Mt. Airy
1876	B&O Railroad Station, Brosius, W.Va.
1876	**B&O Railroad Station**, Martinsburg, W.Va.
1878	**Jefferson County Court House** (alteration), Charles Town, W.Va.
1878	Gate Lodge, H. G. Dulany Estate, Upperville, Va.
1878	**Charles Carroll Estate** (addition), Howard County
1878	**Garrett Estate** (Evergreen), stable
1879	Chapel, St. Vincent's Seminary, Germantown, Pa.
1879	Woodville Church, Aquasco
1879	**Baltimore Cathedral** (additions), 401 N. Cathedral St.
1879	St. Teresa of Avila Church, 13th and V Sts. SE, Washington, D.C.
1881	**St. Leo's Church**, 227 S. Exeter St.
1882	B&O Railroad Station, Paw Paw, W.Va.
1882	**St. John's Church** (addition), cor. Valley and Eager St.
1882	**Mt. de Sales Academy** (addition), Catonsville
1882	Huntington Ave. Car House, 25th and Howard Sts.

1883	Arabella Russell House, 1708 Park Ave.
1883	Pastoral House and Sisters' House, St. Ann's
1883–85	Deer Park Cottages, Deer Park
1883	B&O Railroad Station, Lexington, Va.
1884	St. Vincent's Infant Asylum (wing)
1884	**B&O Passenger Car Shop**, Mt. Clare Station
1884	**B&O Railroad Station**, Sykesville
1884	**B&O Railroad Station**, Laurel
1884	B&O Railroad Station, Morgantown, W.Va.
1884	**B&O Railroad Station and Freight House**, Gaithersburg
1884	B&O Railroad Station, Mountain Lake Park
1885	**B&O Railroad Station**, Oakland
1885	St. Gregory's Church, 1542 N. Gilmore St.
1885	**B&O Freight House**, Ellicott City
1885	Robert Garrett Estate (Uplands), Catonsville
1885–86	Abell Warehouse, 7–9 N. Howard St.
1886	Seminary Retreat (Cloud Cap), Catonsville
1886	J. G. Pangborn House (addition), 2008 Madison St.
1887	T. Deford Residence (addition), 8 W. Mt. Vernon Pl.
1887	St. Ann's Parochial School, Greenmount Ave.
1888	St. Leo's Parochial School, Stiles and Exeter Sts.
1888	**Hutzler's Palace Building**, 218 N. Howard St.
1888	Homeland Station, 607 W. Lake Ave.
1888–89	Abell Warehouses, 318–320 W. Baltimore St.
1889	C. F. Mayer House (addition), 303 W. Monument St.
1889–90	Our Lady of Good Counsel Church, Fort Ave.
1889	St. Michael's Church (addition), cor. Lombard and Wolfe Sts.
1889	Cape Charles Church, Cape Charles, Va.
1889	Episcopal Residence, 222 E. Harris St., Savannah, Ga.
1889	Caldwell Hall, Catholic University, Washington, D.C.
1890–95	McMahon Hall, Catholic University, Washington, D.C.
1890	St. Mary's Church, 727 Fifth St. NW, Washington, D.C.
1890	Vaile & Young Store, 216 N. Calvert St.

1890	The Maryland Club, SE cor. Charles and Eager Sts.
1891	**St. Joseph's Academy Chapel** (addition), Emmitsburg
1891	St. Ann's Church, 2013 Gilpin, Wilmington, Del.
1891	C&P Railroad Station, Frostburg
1891	B&O Railroad Station, Kensington
1891	B&O Railroad Station, Dickerson
1892	B&O Railroad Station, Brunswick
1892	B&O Railroad Station, Washington, Pa.
1892	B&O Railroad Station, Weston, W.Va.
1892	Western Maryland Railroad Station, New Oxford, Pa.
1892	Institute of Notre Dame, Aisquith St.
1892	Merchants National Bank, SE cor. South and Water Sts.
1892–93	**H. G. Davis Mansion** (Graceland), Elkins, W.Va.
1892?	Abell Mansion (The Ridge), Riderwood
1892	B&O Railroad Station (addition), Frederick
1892	B&O Railroad Station, Quicksburg, Va.
1893	B&O Railroad Station, West Newton, Pa.
1893	St. John the Evangelist Church, Forest Glen
1893	William Walsh Store, Baltimore St., Cumberland
1893	E. Stanley Gary House (addition), 857 Park Ave.
1893	Albert Marburg House (addition), 1111 St. Paul St.
1894	**Brown Estate** (Brooklandwood) (addition), Baltimore County
1894	Maryland General Hospital (addition), N. Linden Ave.
1894	George Small Residence (addition), 16 W. Mt. Vernon Pl.
1894	St. Mary's Church (front), Alexandria, Va.
1894	Fidelity Building, 210 N. Charles St.
1894	**Baltimore City College**, 530 N. Howard St.
1894	St. Mary's Church, 300 Mill St., Cambridge
1895	St. Elizabeth's School and Residence, Lakewood St.
1896	St. Mary's Church Rectory, Cambridge
1896	St. Gregory's Church Rectory, N. Gilmore St.
1896	St. Martin's Church Rectory, N. Fulton St.
1896	B&O Railroad Station, Harpers Ferry, W.Va.
1896	Gibbons Hall Annex, College of Notre

	Dame
1896	B&O Tobacco Warehouse, Henderson's Wharf
1896	**Mount Royal Railroad Station**, 1400 Cathedral St.
1896	T. Marburg Residence (addition), 14 W. Mt. Vernon Pl.
1896	Ridgely Church, Ridgely
1896	Chapel, Alberton
1897	David Hutzler House (addition), 1801 Eutaw Pl.
1897	St. Patrick's Church, NE cor. Broadway and Bank St.
1897	St. James Hall and School, Aisquith St.
1898	Commonwealth Bank, SE cor. Howard and Madison Sts.
1898–1905	**B&O Warehouse**, Camden Station, S. Eutaw St.
1898	Bosler Library, 158 W. High St., Carlisle, Pa.
1899	St. Thomas Church Rectory, Hampden, Roland Ave. and 37th St.
1899	Carroll Park UR&E Shops, Washington Blvd.
1900	**UR&E Power House**, 601 E. Pratt St.
1900	Casino, Sheppard-Pratt Hospital, Towson
1900	German Savings Bank, SW cor. W. Baltimore and Eutaw Sts.
1901	St. Augustine's Church, Elkridge
1901	First National Bank, 640 Main St., Catonsville
1901	Guardian Building, NW cor. German and Calvert Sts.
1902	National Bank of Commerce, 26 South St.
1902	Charles Lanahan House, 1209 St. Paul St.
1902	Allan McLane House, 1035 N. Calvert St.
1902	Flynn Hall Gymnasium, Mt. St. Mary's College
1902	St. Katherine's Church, Preston and Luzerne Sts.
1902–5	**Maryland State House Annex**, Annapolis
1902	St. John's Church Rectory, Frederick
1903	St. Wenceslaus Convent Building, Ashland St.
1904	Farmers & Merchants Bank, NW cor. South and Lombard Sts.
1904	Store, 210–214 E. Baltimore St.
1904	Commercial Building, 119 E. Baltimore St.
1904	Elkridge Hunt Club (addition), N. Charles St.
1905	German Bank of Baltimore, Holliday and

	Baltimore Sts.
1905	Professional Building, 330 N. Charles St.
1906	Lycett Building, 317 N. Charles St.
1906	McGovern (Grotto) Chapel, Emmitsburg
1906	McSweeney Hall, Mt. St. Mary's College
1906	Masonic Building, Fairmont, W.Va.
1906	YMCA Building, Fairmont, W.Va.
1906	York Road Car House, York Road
1907	Edmondson Avenue Car House
1907	House of Correction (wing), Jessup
1907	Annapolis Water Co. Building, Rt. 450, Annapolis
1907	Miles White Building, 339-341 N. Charles St.
1908	The Johns Hopkins Building, NW cor. South and Water Sts.
1908	Chapel, Mt. St. Mary's College, Emmitsburg
1909	**Baltimore County Court House** (addition), Towson
1909	UR&E Park Terminal Car House, Druid Hill and Fulton Aves.
1909	Eutaw Savings Bank (addition), SW cor. Eutaw and Fayette Sts.
1909	I. McGill Walker Store, 334 N. Charles St.
1909	McDowell Hall (restoration), St. John's College, Annapolis
1910	Immaculate Conception (basement), Germantown, Pa.
1910	O'Neill Building, NE cor. Charles and Franklin Sts.
1911	Grindall Building, SE cor. Charles and Franklin Sts.
1912	Baltimore Polytechnic (additions), Calvert St. and North Ave.
1912	Mess Hall (Grant Building), USSH, Washington, D.C.
1912	Munsey Building, SE cor. Calvert and Fayette Sts.
1912	Church of the Blessed Sacrament, York Rd. and 42nd St.
1914	Stout Building, 315 N. Charles St.
1914	St. Katherine's Rectory, Preston St.
1915	St. Wenceslaus Church and Rectory, Ashland St.
1915	Bradley Hall, Mt. St. Mary's College, Emmitsburg
1915	Farmer's National Bank (addition), Annapolis
1916	Sacred Heart Church, Mt. Washington

The Extant Works of E. Francis Baldwin

The Works of E. Francis Baldwin
Project Tally

	Maryland		Out of State	
	Extant	Destroyed	Extant	Destroyed
B&O Railroad structures				
Stations	15	39	16	33
Station-hotels, resorts		6		1
Freight stations	3	4		4
Elevators, warehouses	2	8		3
Shop, yard, right-of-way	2	20		8
Ma&Pa/C&P/WMRR stations	2	7	1	1
Street-railway buildings	4	9		
Churches/rectories	36	10	12	5
Seminaries/college buildings	7	11	5	1
Religious schools/convents	8	15		3
Public/private schools	2	4		
Health care facilities	3	17	1	3
Government/public works	4	3	1	
Business/industrial buildings	14	40		3
Banks/financial buildings	8	16		1
Hotels	1	4		3
Cultural buildings		4	1	1
Clubs	2	6	2	
Residences/estates	19	48	2	2
Totals	132	271	41	72
	403		113	
Grand Total		516		

❧ APPENDIX C ❧

Baldwin's Work-in-Hand Lists, 1889–1907

These lists transcribed from Baldwin's pocket note-books illustrate the scale of business being done by the firm of Baldwin & Pennington at selected points in time near the peak of Baldwin's productivity. The costs are, in come cases, only partial payments on work in progress. These lists also include a few entries that have not been fully identified, for example, the Sloan, Small, and Waters projects, the Stewart and Ould warehouse, and the not inconsequential $90,000 project for Col. Alex Shaw.

Buildings and Costs (1889)

Francis White Warehouse	20,000
Naval Academy Boat House	30,000
Catholic University	250,000
Bishop's House, Savannah	25,000
Abell Estate—Store	60,000
B&O RR Depot, Washington	15,000
Cathedral—Additions	
St. Lawrence Church	26,000
St. Paul's Orphanage	
J. McDonald	1,500
Mt. Hope Additions	12,000
Maryland Club	80,000
Wm. Keyser	
John King Jr. Warehouses	150,000
Fr. & Mer. Bank	90,000
St. Mary's Ch., Washington	
City Hospital	80,000
R. Cromwell Factory	18,000
Ch. Cape Charles	12,000
St. Michael's Ch. Tower &c	40,000
C. F. Mayer's House	78,000
Hannah More Academy	5,000
W. P. Harvey	25,000
St. Aug. Ch., Washington	
Mt. Hope Doctor's House	8,000
John K. Cowen	

On-Hand List (1890)

Abell Estate 325 Balto St.	
R. Cromwell Factory	16,000
St. Michael's Church	46,000
Mt. Hope Retreat	6,000
Maryland Club	100,000
College of P & S	28,000
Paulist House	10,500
Im. Conception	6,500
R. Garrett	2,500
Elkins Hotel	15,000
Seminary	33,000
Eutaw House	20,000
E. F. Abell Lexington St.	16,000
Cathedral Additions	36,000
Fr. Hagan's Ch.	26,000
St. Aug. Ch., Washington	9,000
St. Mary's Church, Wash	70,000
J. LeR. White	3,000
Cath. University—Barn &c	1,500
St. Catherine's	15,000
Elkins Bank	15,000
H. G. Davis	30,000
Asylum, Cumberland	15,000

Work in Hand (1893)

McMahon Hall	
Fidelity Bldg.	
Merchants Bank	
Mt. Hope Retreat	
Jas. Sloan	
G. W. Abell	
E. S. Gary	
Mrs. Geo Brown's	
German Savings Bk.	
McCoy Hall	
Builders Exchange	
Notre Dame	

St. Vincent's Sem.
14 Holy Martyrs
Mrs. Small's
J. S. Frick
Bon Secours
B&O RR Co.

Heating Plant Md.	25,000
Maryland Club	50,000
A. Leo Knott	15,000
Infant Asylum	8,000
Hambleton Bank	50,000
Fr. Kane, Frederick	

Work in Hand (1895)
McMahon Hall
City College
Belt RR Power House
St. Elizabeth's Home
Merchants Bank
Notre Dame of Md.
St. Mary's Church, Alexandria

Work in Hand (Jan. 1, 1900)

O'Neill & Co.	80,000
N. Union Bank	107,000
Carroll Park Plant	250,000
B&O Warehouse	276,000
St. V. Hospital	60,000
Col. Alex Shaw	90,000
H. Waters	10,000
Seminary Chapel	
House of Industry	
German S. Bank	50,000
Guardian Bldg	437,000
U. Ry. Power House	270,000
Sav. Cathedral	50,000
St. V. Seminary	30,000
Casino Sheppard Asy.	10,000
C. Lanahan	10,000
St. Jos. Hospital	

Work in Hand (Oct. 1902)

State Building	250,000
H. of Corrections	100,000
L. L. Jackson	240,000
St. Catherine's Ch.	25,000
Commonwealth Bank	15,000
Safe Deposit Co.	150,000
Fr. Nagengast	
Mt. St. Mary's College	
State House	250,000

Work in Hand (1904)
Evening News
State House
House of Corrections
Soldiers Home
N. Union Bank
N. Bank of Commerce
Hopkins P. Sav. Bank
Bank of Balto.
Hambleton & Co.
Md. Trust Co.
Theo. Marburg
Steward & Ould
Hutzler Bros.
St. Jos. Hospital
115 W. Balto St.
117 W. Balto St.
210–214 E. Balto St.
St. Wenceslaus Ch.

Work in Hand (1907)

Md. State Building	311,000
J. LeR. White Store	51,789
Stewart's Warehouses	27,000
House of Corrections	267,000
Montgy. Co. Nat. Bank	30,374
Hambleton & Co.	30,000
Md. Trust Bldg.	
Th. Marburg	
State House Annex	820,000
N. Bank of Commerce	50,812
Hopkins Place Savings Bank	70,731
Balto. News Bldg.	164,637
German Bank	72,212
Farmers & M. N. Bank	87,102
Bank of Baltimore	
Mrs. Perin	

❋ APPENDIX D ❋

Church Additions and Alterations

The remaining church additions and alterations by Baldwin and his firms are tabulated below, giving the church, the dates, the nature of the work, and the cost and the contractor, if known.

1871   St. Paul's Episcopal Church, Charles and Saratoga Sts.
        Cloister, transept, entrance stairs; $5,244, P. Walsh

1871   Immaculate Conception Church, Mosher and Division Sts.
        Altar, communion rail, steps; $10,000, Hugh Sisson & Son

1871   St. Joseph's Church, Howard and Barré Sts.
        Belfry and steeple; $1,800

1875   St. Aloysius Church, N. Capitol St., Washington, D.C.
        Pulpit; $395

1874–75 Christ Church—St. Peter's Parish, Easton, Md.
        Chancel, choir, vestry (22' × 20') and roof; A. H. Reynolds

1879   Chapel, Widows and Infants Asylum, Buffalo, N.Y.
        Altar; $600, Hugh Sisson & Son

1880   St. Patrick's Church, Roxbury Station, Boston, Mass.
        Altar; $3,700, Hugh Sisson & Son

1887   St. Vincent's Church, Front and Fayette Sts.
        Skylight; $1,400

1888   St. Peter Claver Church, Fremont St. and Pennsylvania Ave.
        Additions; $7,100, Philip Walsh

1891   St. Joseph's Academy Chapel, Emmitsburg, Md.
        Addition; $3,083

1893   Church of the Fourteen Holy Martyrs, Lombard and Mount Sts.
        Addition/alteration: $21,442, Joseph Thuman

1894   St. Mary's Church, Duke St., Alexandria, Va.
        New front and a 135-foot spire; $18,000, John Stack

1896   J. A. Gary Memorial Chapel, Alberton, Md.
        Alterations; $350

1897   Chapel, Little Sisters of the Poor, John and Valley Sts.
        Alterations, additions; $18,287, Edward Brady
        Altar; $525, Otto Duker

1902   St. Mary Star of the Sea, 1419 Riverside Ave.
        Rebuilding tower and steeple; $13,585, Rullman & Sheehan

Residential Additions and Alterations

1875	E. Austin Jenkins, 125 Park Ave.
	Improvements; $8,696 (John Stack)
1877–78	Charles Carroll, Howard County[1]
	"Country house completion," $3,910
1877–78	Richard Cromwell, York Rd. near North Ave.
	Alterations, addition, and icehouse; $4,400 (John Stack)
1878	J. Goldsmith, Charles Town, W.Va.
	Second story and mansard roof (J. C. Holmes)
1878	John Garrett Estate (Evergreen)[2]
	Stable; $6,022 (S. H. & J. F. Adams)
1878	Thomas M. Lanahan
	Stable; $1,764 (August Degenhardt)

1883	Robert Rennert
	Conservatory; $4,015 (Edward Brady)
1886	J. G. Pangborn, 2008 Madison St.
	Stairs, interior refinishing
1886	Lambert Gittings, 247 Linden Ave.
	Repairs, $200
1887–88	Thomas Deford, 8 W. Mt. Vernon Pl.
	Alterations and improvements; $7,300
1888	J. A. Knecht
	"Front building," $4,141 (John Stack)
1888	Jesse Hilles, 12 Read St.
	Stable; $4,372
1889	Charles F. Mayer, 303 W. Monument St.
	Alterations and additions; $18,000
1889	John B. McDonald, 1011–1013 N. Charles St.
	Stable, $3,806; repairs, $1,260
1890	J. Swan Frick
	Bookcase, $155 (J. S. Gosnell & Co.)
1891	Mendes Cohen, 825 N. Charles St.
	Alterations; $800
1892–93	Albert Marburg, 1111 St. Paul St.
	Three-story "back building" $16,000
1892–94	George Small, 16 W. Mt. Vernon Pl.
	Alterations; $16,644
1892–96	George Brown (Brooklynwood), Baltimore County[3]
	Alterations, additions; $34,748

1. In May 1877 Baldwin received proposals from three contractors for work for Charles Carroll. On August 31, a contract for $3,300 was signed with Gerhard Marischen, representing Walsh & Marischen. The work was completed on April 1, 1878, at a final cost of $3,910. This work is probably not for the Carroll mansion, Doughoregan Manor. (The owner of the estate cannot identify any addition to the building that corresponds with work in 1877–78.) It may be for the Homewood estate.

2. This stable for the Garrett estate was described by Baldwin in May 1878 as being of brick with twelve stalls and a carriage house. The Adams brothers received the contract over three other bidders. The final cost of the stable, completed in May 1878, was $6,004.32. In addition, there was an expenditure of $300 to E. S. Heath & Son for a "horse power pump." In 1889, Baldwin records additional work amounting to $1,818 for alterations to the stable which, by this time, was owned by T. Harrison Garrett. (Baldwin also notes a visit to Princeton to "examine a residence" for Mrs. Garrett, for which he was paid a fee of $25. Mrs. Garrett did indeed live in New Jersey while her sons attended Princeton University, but the nature of the residence there is unknown.)

3. *Brooklynwood* was the term Baldwin used in his own records for this estate, properly known now as Brooklandwood, built by Charles Carroll of Carrollton. This home in the Green Spring Valley was owned by Alexander D. Brown, who passed it on to George Brown in 1892. The extensive alterations to this house in the 1890s were requested by Mrs. Brown; Josias Pennington may have taken the lead on this project. The home, later owned by Isaac E. Emerson, was acquired in 1952 by the St. Paul's School for Boys. It is listed on the National Register of Historic Places.

1893   Leigh Bonsal, Roland Park
          Alterations to cottage; $2,000
1893   E. Stanley Gary, 857 Park Ave.
          Alterations; $8,000
1893–94   John C. Rose (Paradise), Baltimore
          County
          Addition to country residence;
          $2,000
1895–96   Theodore Marburg, 14 W. Mt. Vernon
          Pl.
          Alterations; $20,000
1896   Nelson Perin, 1030 N. Charles St.
          Alterations; $31,800

1897   David Hutzler, 1801 Eutaw Place[4]
          Alterations and improvements;
          $27,446
1901–2   Houses, 200–202 E. 22nd St.
          Repairs; $1,665

4. David Hutzler's house, on the NE corner of Eutaw Pl. and Laurens St., was built not very long before these extensive modifications; the structure, referred to as the Hawley-Hutzler house, was originally designed by the architect Thomas C. Kennedy in about 1890. Kennedy (1854–1914) also did work on St. Mary's Industrial School, Notre Dame College, Mt. St. Agnes Academy, and St. Joseph's Church and Schools in Washington, D.C., and he designed the rectory for Sacred Heart Church in Mt. Washington.

Bibliography

American Institute of Architects. *A Guide to the Architecture of Washington, D.C.* Washington: AIA, 1965, 1974.

American Institute of Architects. *The First 125 Years.* Washington: AIA, 1988.

Anon. *City of Baltimore: Leading Manufacturers and Merchants.* New York: International Publishing Co., 1886–87.

Avery, Carlos. "The Stations on the Metropolitan Branch, B&O RR." *Bulletin of the Railroad Station Historical Society,* Sept.–Oct. 1982.

Avery, Carlos. "Baldwin & Pennington: Architects for the B&O Railroad," In *Three Centuries of Maryland Architecture.* Crownsville, MD: Maryland Historical Trust, 1982.

Avery, Carlos. "Derwood, Maryland B&O RR Station." *Mainline Modeler,* Aug. 1983.

Avery, Carlos. "E. Francis Baldwin, Railroad Station Architect." *Bulletin of the Railroad Station Historical Society,* May–June 1996.

Barnes, Raymon P. "A History of the City of Roanoke." N.p., n.d.

Beck, Herman. "The Mt. Airy and B&O Story." Ad-Pro, 1995.

Bentzel, Anne. "What's So Grotesque?" *CUA Magazine,* Summer 1995.

Berg, Walter C. *Buildings and Structures of American Railroads.* New York: Wiley, 1893.

Black, Catherine F. "The Life and Works of James Crawford Neilson (1816–1900)." Manuscript.

Bohl, Charles, and John Christensen. *McDowell Hall at St. John's College in Annapolis, 1742–1989.* Annapolis: St. John's College, 1989.

Brown, Alexander C. *The Old Bay Line, 1840–1940.* New York: Bonanza Books, 1940.

Burg, David F. *Chicago's White City of 1893.* Lexington: Univ. Press of Kentucky, 1976.

Burns, John A., ed. *Recording Historic Structures.* Washington: AIA, 1989.

Burton, Fr. Jeff, S.J. *John Stack, the Builder: His Family and Descendants.* Westminster, MD: Willow Bend Books, 1999.

Chalfant, Randolph W. "Building List: Niernsee and Neilson, Architects of Baltimore." Manuscript, 1990.

Cox, Dorothy G., et al. *Schools in and around Baltimore,* Baltimore: Consolidated Engineering Co., 1955.

Dilts, James D. "Forgotten Sentries of the Rail Age." *Maryland Magazine,* Summer 1982.

Dilts, James D., and Catherine F. Black, eds. *Baltimore's Cast-Iron Buildings and Architectural Ironwork.* Centreville, MD: Tidewater Publishers, 1991.

Dorsey, John, and James D. Dilts. *A Guide to Baltimore Architecture.* Centreville, MD: Tidewater Publishers, 1980, 1997.

Eckels, Claire W. "Baltimore's Earliest Architects, 1785–1820." Ph.D. diss., The Johns Hopkins University, 1950.

Engelmeyer, Sr. Bridget Marie. "A Maryland First." *Maryland Historical Magazine,* Fall 1983.

Englehardt, George W. *Baltimore City Maryland: The Book of Its Board of Trade.* N.p., 1895.

Farrell, Michael R. *Who Made All Our Streetcars Go?* Baltimore: NRHS Publications, 1973.

Feldstein, Albert L. *Coal Mining and Railroads of Allegany County, Maryland.* Cumberland, MD: Commercial Press Printing Co., 1999.

Forbush, Bliss. "The History of Sheppard and Enoch Pratt Hospital." N.p., n.d.

Fulton, Dennis. "Maps of Mt. Clare." Baltimore: B&O Railroad Museum, 1999.

Gilbert, John F. *Crossties to the Depot,* vol. 1, *Virginia Railroad Stations.* Raleigh, NC: Crossties Press, 1982.

Giza, Joanne, and Catharine Black. *Great Baltimore Houses.* Baltimore: Maclay & Associates, 1982.

Goode, James M. *Capital Losses: A Cultural History of Washington's Destroyed Buildings.* Washington: Smithsonian Institution Press, 1979.

Graybill, Samuel H. "Bruce Price, American Architect, 1845–1903." Ph.D. diss., Yale University, 1957.

Grow, L. *Waiting for the 5:05: Terminal, Station, and Depot in America.* Clinton, NJ: Main Street Press, 1977.

Harwood, Herbert H., Jr. *Impossible Challenge: The Baltimore and Ohio Railroad in Maryland.* Baltimore: Barnard, Roberts & Co., 1979.

Harwood, Herbert H., Jr. *Impossible Challenge II.* Baltimore: Barnard Roberts & Co., 1994.

Harwood, Herbert H., Jr. *Baltimore and Its Streetcars.* New York: Quadrant Press, 1984.

Harwood, Herbert H., Jr. *Royal Blue Line.* Sykesville, MD: Greenberg Publishing Co., 1990. Reprint, Baltimore: John Hopkins Univ. Press, 2002.

Hilton, George W. *The Ma & Pa: A History of the Maryland & Pennsylvania Railroad,* Berkeley, CA: Howell-North, 1963. Second ed., rev., Baltimore: Johns Hopkins Univ. Press, 2000.

Hoagland, Alison K. "Deer Park Hotel." *Maryland Historical Magazine,* Dec. 1978.

Horwitz, Elinor Lander. *How to Wreck a Building.* New York: Pantheon Books, 1982.

Howland, Richard H., and Eleanor P. Spencer. *Architecture of Baltimore: A Pictorial History.* Baltimore: Johns Hopkins Press, 1953.

Hunter, W. H., and C. H. Elam. *A Century of Baltimore Architecture.* Baltimore: Peale Museum, 1957.

Jandl, H. Ward, et al. *Historic Railroad Stations: A Selected Inventory.* Washington: National Park Service, National Register of Historic Places, 1974.

Jones, Carleton. *Lost Baltimore Landmarks.* Baltimore: Maclay & Associates, 1982.

Keith, Robert C. *Baltimore Harbor: A Picture History.* Baltimore: Johns Hopkins Univ. Press, 1991.

Kelly, Jacques. *Bygone Baltimore.* Norfolk, VA: Donning Press, 1982.

Leonhart, James C. *One Hundred Years of the Baltimore City College.* Baltimore: H. G. Roebuck & Son, 1939.

Lewis, Arnold. *American Country Houses of the Gilded Age.* New York: Dover Publications, 1982.

Lewis, A., and K. Morgan. *American Victorian Architecture.* New York: Dover Publications, 1975.

Lewis, Robert Erskine. "Brooklandwood, Baltimore County." *Maryland Historical Magazine,* Dec. 1948.

Library of Congress. *Historic America: Buildings, Structures, and Sites.* Washington: GPO, 1983.

Love, Richard. "Brunswick's Blessed Curse: Surviving an Industrial Legacy." *Maryland Historical Magazine,* Summer 1993.

Maddex, Dianne. *Built in the USA: American Buildings from Airports to Zoos.* Washington: National Trust for Historic Preservation, 1985.

Markwood, Louis N. *The Forest Glen Trolley and the Early Development of Silver Spring.* Arlington, VA: National Capital Historical Museum of Transportation, 1975.

Maryland Historical Society. *Baltimore: A Picture History.* New York: Hastings House, 1957.

McAlester, Virginia, and [McAlester] Lee. *A Field Guide to American Houses.* Mount Vernon, NY: Consumers Union, 1984.

Meeks, Carroll L. V. *The Railroad Station.* New Haven: Yale Univ. Press, 1956.

Mellander, Deane E. *Cumberland & Pennsylvania Railroad.* Newton, NJ: Carstens, 1981.

Mellander, Deane E. *Rails to the Big Vein.* Potomac, MD: National Railway Historical Society, 1981.

Moffson, Steven H. "Richardsonian Romanesque Bank Buildings in Baltimore, 1884–1894." M.A. thesis, University of Delaware, May 1992.

Mycoff, David. "An Architectural History of R. E. Lee Memorial Episcopal Church." Manuscript, May 25, 1974.

National Park Service. *The National Register of Historic Places.* Vols. 1 and 2. Washington: GPO, 1976 and 1978.

National Park Service. National Register of Historic Places. *Federal Register* 44, no. 26 (Feb. 6, 1979).

Newell, Dianne. *The Failure to Preserve the Queen City Hotel, Cumberland, Maryland.* Washington: Preservation Press, 1975.

Newell, Dianne. "The Short-Lived Phenomenon of Railroad Station–Hotels." *Historic Preservation,* July–Sept. 1974.

O'Gorman, James F. *The Architecture of Frank Furness.* Philadelphia: Philadelphia Museum of Art, Falcon Press, 1973.

Papenfuse, Edward C., and Joseph M. Coale III. *The Hammond-Harwood Atlas of Historical Maps of Maryland, 1608–1908.* Baltimore: Johns Hopkins Univ. Press, 1982.

Pierson, W. H. *American Buildings and Their Architects.* New York: Doubleday, 1978.

Potter, Janet G. *Great American Railroad Stations.* New York: Wiley, 1996.

Radoff, Morris L. *Buildings of the State of Maryland at Annapolis.* Annapolis: Hall of Records Commission, State of Maryland, 1954.

Richardson, Rev. H. Maunsell. *The Church on the Fort.* Cumberland, MD: Commercial Press Printing Co., 1976.

Ross, Thomas Richard. *Henry Gassaway Davis: An Old-Fashioned Biography.* Parsons, WV: McClain Printing Co., 1994.

Sagle, Lawrence W. "America's Oldest Railroad Shops—Mt. Clare." Railway and Locomotive Historical Society. *Railroad History Bulletin,* no. 127, 1972.

Scharf, John Thomas. *History of Baltimore City & County.* Baltimore: Regional Publishing Co., 1881.

Schlotterbeck, Judith A. *The Pen Mar Story.* Funkstown, MD: Tri-State, 1977.

Scott, Pamela, and Antoinette Lee. *Buildings of the District of Columbia.* New York: Oxford Univ. Press, 1993.

Soderberg, Susan C. *The Met: A History of the Metropolitan Branch of the B&O Railroad, Its Stations and Towns.* Philadelphia: Germantown Historical Society, 1998.

Stanton, Phoebe. *The Gothic Revival and American Church Architecture*. Baltimore: Johns Hopkins Press, 1968.

Tatman, S. L., and R. W. Moss. *Biographical Dictionary of Philadelphia Architects: 1700–1930*. Boston: G. K. Hall, 1985.

Thayer, Preston. "The Railroad Designs of Frank Furness: Architecture and Corporate Imagery in the Late Nineteenth Century." Ph.D. diss., University of Pennsylvania, 1993.

Traser, D. R. *A Virginia Depot Sampler*. Crete, Neb.: RRSHS, 1994.

Traser, D. R. *Virginia Railway Depots*. Richmond: National Railway Historical Society, 1998.

Van Rensselaer, Mariana G. *Henry Hobson Richardson and His Works*. New York: Dover Publications, 1969.

Vogel, Robert M. "The Engineering Contributions of Wendel Bollman." *United States Museum Bulletin*, no. 240. Washington: Smithsonian Institution, 1964.

Vogel, Robert M. *Some Industrial Archeology of the Monumental City and Environs: A Guide for SIA Tourists*. Washington: Society for Industrial Archeology, April 1975.

Ware, Donna M. *Green Glades and Sooty Gob Piles*. Crownsville, MD: Maryland Historical Trust, 1991.

Warren, Marion E., and Mame Warren. *Baltimore: When She Was What She Used to Be*. Baltimore: Johns Hopkins Univ. Press, 1983.

Weaver, Joseph H., et al. *Architecture in Allegany County: A History*. Cumberland, MD: Commercial Press Printing Co., 1989.

Whetsell, Robert C. *Elkins, West Virginia: The Metropolis Revisited*. Parsons, WV: McClain Publishing Co., 1994.

White, John H. "Baltimore & Ohio Transportation Museum." *Technology and Culture*, Jan. 1970.

Williams, Harold A. *Baltimore Afire*. Baltimore: Schneidereth, 1991.

Williams, T. J. C. *History of Frederick County, Maryland*. N.p., 1910.

Williamson, Roxanne Kuter. *American Architects and the Mechanics of Fame*. Austin: Univ. of Texas Press, 1991.

Wilson, C. B. *Mt Clare: The Birthplace of American Railroading*. Baltimore: B&O Railroad Museum, 1999.

Withey, H. F., and E. R. Withey. *Biographical Dictionary of American Architects, Deceased*. Los Angeles: New Age Publishing Co., 1956.

Wodehouse, L. *American Architects from the Civil War to WWII*. Detroit: Gale Research Co., 1976.

Wrenn, Tony P., and Elizabeth D. Mulloy. *America's Forgotten Architecture*. New York: Pantheon Books, 1976.

General Index

General Index

Name Index

The ABC's: Architects and Architectural Firms, Builders and Contractors, Clients (individuals), and Clergy

Builders and Contractors

Walsh, J. J., 42, 55, 56, 63, 89, 91, 98
Walsh, Philip, 45, 47, 58, 62, 71, 73, 83, 84, 99, 104, 115, 117, 118, 119, 120, 133
Walsh & Marischen, 134
Walter, J. B., 17
Walther, George, 71, 75, 89, 109
Waters, John P., 64, 85, 91, 92, 94, 95, 98, 108, 110, 117
Watters, Edward, 111
W. B. Downing & Sons, 86
Wells, William, 75, 103, 119
Wells Brothers, 101, 103
Werner Brothers, 75, 85, 102
West, Edward, 74
West Construction Co., 11, 65, 106, 111
Whyte, W. H., 109
Wood, William, 74

Young, Jacob, 31

Clients (individuals)

Abell, Arunah S., 12, 105, 107, 122
Abell, G. W., 131
Abell, Jennie, 122
Atkinson, M. S., 112

Baldwin, Summerfeld, 12, 17
Bogne, M. H., 16
Bonsal, Leigh, 135
Bosler, Herman E., 117
Brown, George, 12, 131, 134

Carey, John A., 121
Carroll, Charles, 90, 134
Cohen, Mendes, 11, 110, 134
Cowen, John K., 11, 131
Cromwell, Richard, 107, 131, 134

Dailey, John, 114
Davis, Henry Gassaway, 7, 11, 36, 49, 51, 53, 100, 115, 123, 131
Deford, Thomas, 12, 108, 128, 134
Donnell, William, 120
Dulany, H. G., Jr., 120, 127
Dulany, Richard Henry, 120
Dulin, A. F., 18

Ellinger, Jacob, 100
Emerson Laboratories, 109

Forbes, James, 17
Frick, J. Swan, 12, 53, 124, 132, 134
Frick, William, 122

Garrett, John W., xi, 11, 31, 49, 51, 53, 134
Garrett, Mary Elizabeth, 88
Garrett, Robert, 11, 88, 92, 107, 115, 117, 123, 131

Garrett, T. Harrison, 12, 134
Gary, E. Stanley, 128, 131, 135
Gary, James A., 12
Gill, John, 12, 17
Gittings, John S., 99, 112, 120
Gittings, Lambert, 134
Goldsmith, J., 134
Gottschalk, A., 121
Grace, Clementina, 120
Green, George, 114

Hambleton, T. Edward, 12
Harvey, William P., 108, 124
Hillen, S., Mrs., 16
Hillen, Emily, 120
Hilles, Jesse, 134
Hooper, Theodore, 114
House, William, 18
Hutzler, David, 12, 129, 135

Jackson, Lloyd L., 109, 132
Jenkins, E. Austin, 106, 134
Jenkins, Henry, 12, 105

Kennedy, William, 17, 119
Keyser, William, 12, 17, 26, 104, 121
King, John, 105, 131
Knecht, J. A., 134
Knott, A. Leo, 12, 108, 132

Lanahan, Charles, 124, 129, 132
Lanahan, Thomas, 104, 134
Lee, Columbus O'D., 121
Lee, J. Harry, 121
Lowndes, Lloyd. 12, 119

Marburg, Albert, 12, 128, 134
Marburg, Theodore, 7, 12, 132, 135
Mayer, Charles F., 128, 131, 134
McDonald, John B., 131, 134
McLane, Allan, 124, 129
Munsey, Frank, 110
Murguiondo, Prudencio de, 16, 119

Oliver, Elizabeth, 124
O'Neill, Thomas, 12, 16, 108, 110, 117

Pangborn, Joseph G., 11, 128, 134
Parr, Charles E., 124
Parr, Henry A., 124
Perin, Nelson, xiii, 12, 63, 132, 135
Price, William, 17, 119

Rennert, Robert, 12, 134
Rodgers, Patrick, 108
Rose, John C., 135
Ryan, James J., 124
Russell, Arabella, 121

Shaw, Alex, 132
Small, George, 8, 128, 132, 134

Smith, Martha B., 124
Stout, Morton C., 112

Thomas, Douglas H., 12, 101
Tyson, Henry, 17
Tyson, James, 17

Walsh, William E., 108
Warfield, Edwin, 101–2
Watson, J. O., 124
White, A. A., 17
White, Julian LeRoy, 107, 131
Williams, Ferdinand, 119, 127
Williams, N. Winslow, 124

Clergy

Azarius, Brother, 86

Becker, Bishop, 86
Bradford, Rev. George, 72
Broydrick, Father, 75

Colgan, Father, 86
Cunningham, Father, 75
Curtis, Rev. A. A., 11, 74, 76

Dubreul, Father, 77, 79

Elder, Bp. William H., 3, 20

Flynn, Sister Kostka, 86

Gibbons, James Cardinal, 11, 19, 41, 73, 74, 75, 76, 81, 82, 87, 91
Glaab, Rev. George, 74
Gross, Bp. W. H., 71

Hagan, Fr. John, 73, 131
Horning, Rev. E. J., 16

Kane, Fr. William, 76, 132
Keane, Bishop, 81

Luizelle, Reverend, 72

Nagengast, Fr. Henry S., 76, 132

Persico, Rev. Ignatius, 70, 71

Rolando, Father, 20
Rosensteel, Rev. Charles O., 74

Starr, Rev. W. E., 73

Urben, Rev. Henry, 86

Volz, Rev. Henry, 73

Walter, Rev. J. A., 72
Williams, Archbishop, 81

Carlos P. Avery received his B.S., M.S., and Ph.D. degrees in physics and mathematics from the University of Minnesota. He has been employed as an analyst with the U.S. government since 1967. His research on Baldwin began in 1977, when he moved to Rockville, Maryland, and made measured drawings of its historic B&O Railroad station and freight house. Avery is a founding member and participant in the Historic Architects' Roundtable (aka Dead Architects' Society), a research group sponsored by the Baltimore Architecture Foundation. His interests extend to architects Bruce Price, Josias Pennington, Frank Davis, and the Hutton brothers.

Herbert H. Harwood, Jr., spent thirty years in the marketing and sales departments of the Chesapeake & Ohio Railway, the Baltimore & Ohio Railroad, and their successor, CSX Transportation. He is the author of twelve books on various railroad subjects, including *Impossible Challenge: The Baltimore and Ohio Railroad in Maryland* (Baltimore: Barnard, Roberts, 1979, 1994); *Royal Blue Line* (1990; Baltimore: Johns Hopkins Univ. Press, 2002); and *Invisible Giants: The Empires of Cleveland's Van Sweringen Brothers* (Bloomington: Indiana Univ. Press, 2002).

Michael J. Lewis is Associate Professor of Art at Massachusetts' Williams College. A regular contributor to *The New Criterion* and *Commentary*, he is the author most recently of *Frank Furness: Architecture and the Violent Mind* (New York: Norton, 2001) and *The Gothic Revival* (London: Thames & Hudson, 2002).